FOCUS 2

SECOND EDITION

A2+/B1

STUDENT'S BOOK

1
Lives people live

Life is really simple, but we insist on making it complicated.

Confucius

STUDENT ACCOMMODATION

▶1 Watch the BBC video.
For the worksheet, go to page 116.

1.1 VOCABULARY

Personality • *un-, in-, im-, ir-, dis-*
• questions with *like*

I can describe people's personality and emotions.

SHOW WHAT YOU KNOW

1 Match adjectives 1–6 with their opposites a–f.

1 funny	(e)	a	boring
2 interesting	( )	b	stressed
3 loud	( )	c	negative
4 positive	( )	d	unsociable
5 relaxed	( )	e	serious
6 sociable	( )	f	quiet

2 SPEAKING Use the adjectives in Exercise 1 to describe people you know.

GENERATION GAP?
YOUNG PEOPLE SAY ...

You do charity work because you're kind and **generous**, right? Well, that's a bit <u>dishonest</u>. In fact, I really enjoy spending time with older people.

Thanks to my visits, I hope she feels less lonely than before. Mitzi helped me a lot when I had some work problems.

She's a good listener. I talk to her about my worries and she gives me advice. She's <u>wise</u>, <u>sensitive</u> and has a lot of experience. I'm talkative, and they like that.

My grandparents are very quiet and <u>polite</u>, but older people are not all like that. John's really loud and funny. We laugh a lot together.

3 🔊 **1.2** SPEAKING **Look at the photos and discuss the questions. Then listen and check your ideas.**

1 What is the purpose of the charity organising these activities?
2 What can young people do to help older people?
3 What can older people do to help young people?

4 **Read the comments in the text. Who benefits most: the young or the older people? Why?**

OLDER PEOPLE SAY ...

He's <u>adventurous</u> – he travels to exciting places. I love hearing about his adventures.

I can look after myself – I like to be <u>independent</u> but I look forward to the weekly visits.

She's **outgoing** and always **cheerful** – she makes me feel young again.

I like being with young people. I am more confident when I use the Internet now.

You read so many bad things about young people in the press – that they're selfish or <u>irresponsible</u>, but he's **caring**, **sensible** and **hard-working**.

He's got tattoos and long hair. He looks like a hippy, but he's lovely and very <u>popular</u> with the ladies!

WORD STORE 1A | Personality

5 🔊 **1.3** **Complete WORD STORE 1A with the adjectives in red from the text. Then listen, check and repeat.**

6 **Replace the phrases in brackets with appropriate adjectives from WORD STORE 1A.**

1 Charity workers are _____ (not selfish). They are kind and helpful.
2 Teenagers are _____ (not cheerful). They are always in a bad mood.
3 Young professionals are _____ (not lazy). They want to be successful.
4 Many billionaires are _____ (not mean). They give lots of money to charities.
5 Most children are _____ (not outgoing). They're not confident with strangers.
6 Young people are often _____ (not sensible). They make stupid decisions.

7 SPEAKING **Discuss whether you think the statements in Exercise 6 are true.**

WORD STORE 1B | un-, in-, im-, ir-, dis-

8 🔊 **1.4** **Complete WORD STORE 1B with the underlined adjectives in the text. Then listen, check and repeat.**

9 **Complete the sentences with adjectives from WORD STORE 1B.**

1 Gary is an _____ guy. He never tells lies.
2 Emma is very _____ . She knows everything.
3 Paul's only eighteen, but he has a job and lives on his own. He's very _____ .
4 Dan is very _____ . He always says 'please' and 'thank you'.
5 Lucy is _____ . She doesn't like travelling or trying new experiences.
6 Martha is very _____ . She is always the centre of attention.

10 SPEAKING **Change three of the names in Exercise 9 to describe people you know. Then tell your partner.**

WORD STORE 1C | Questions with *like*

11 🔊 **1.5** **Answer the questions in WORD STORE 1C with the highlighted sentences in the text. Then listen, check and repeat.**

12 **Rewrite the sentences with *like* if necessary. Then tick the sentences that are true for you.**

1 I look my dad. *I look like my dad.* ☐
2 My neighbours are kind and friendly. _____ ☐
3 My mum looks her mum. _____ ☐
4 My parents always look cheerful. _____ ☐
5 My grandmother looks Queen Elizabeth. _____ ☐
6 I chocolate. _____ ☐

13 SPEAKING **Complete these questions for the sentences in Exercise 12 with *you* or *your*. Then ask your partner.**

1 Do ...? 2 What ...? 3 Does ...? 4 Do ...?
5 Does ...? 6 Do ...?

1 Do you look like your dad?

5

GRAMMAR

1.2

Present tenses – question forms

I can ask questions in a variety of present tenses.

1 SPEAKING **Who are your role models? Think about famous people or people you know and tell your partner.**

2 🔊 1.6 **Match questions 1–6 with answers a–f. Then listen and check.**

1 Who inspires you?   d
2 Why do you admire him?
3 Does he give money to environmental charities?
4 Have you ever met him?
5 What is he doing now?
6 Are you following him on Twitter?

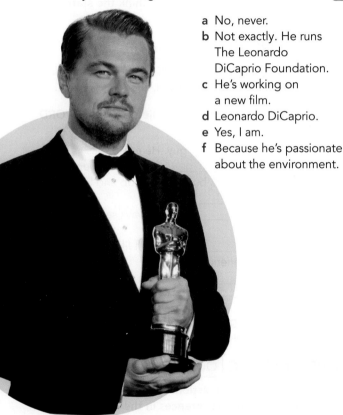

a No, never.
b Not exactly. He runs The Leonardo DiCaprio Foundation.
c He's working on a new film.
d Leonardo DiCaprio.
e Yes, I am.
f Because he's passionate about the environment.

3 **Read the GRAMMAR FOCUS. Complete the examples using the questions in blue in Exercise 2.**

GRAMMAR FOCUS

Present tenses – question forms

• To make questions, you put an auxiliary verb (*do, be, have*) before the subject of the main verb.

Present Simple → Why ¹_____ you admire him?
Present Continuous → What ²_____ he doing now?
Present Perfect → ³_____ you ever met him?

• When you ask about the subject, you don't use the Present Simple auxiliary *do/does*.

Who ⁴_____ you? NOT ~~Who does inspire you?~~

4 🔊 1.7 **Complete the questions for the interview about Michelle Obama. Then listen and check.**

1 'Who *inspires you*?'
  'The person who inspires me is Michelle Obama.'
2 'Who _____ ?'
  'She's the ex-first lady of the United States.'
3 'Why _____ ?'
  'I admire her because she does a lot of good work with young people.'
4 'What _____ ?'
  'She's trying to teach children about exercise and health.'
5 'Have _____ ?'
  'No, I haven't seen her in person, but I've watched her online.'
6 'What _____ ?'
  'She is still working with young people.'

5 **Complete the questions about the subject (a) and about the object (b) of each statement.**

1 ᵃEmily and Peter like watching ᵇscience-fiction films.
  a Who *likes watching science-fiction films*?
  b What *do Emily and Peter like watching*?
2 ᵃNeil has joined ᵇAmnesty International.
  a Who _____ ?
  b Which organisation _____ ?
3 ᵃRosie can speak ᵇthree languages.
  a Who _____ ?
  b How many languages _____ ?
4 ᵃDave has visited ᵇLondon.
  a Who _____ ?
  b Which capital city _____ ?
5 ᵃTom is reading ᵇBarack Obama's biography.
  a Who _____ ?
  b What _____ ?
6 ᵃViv admires ᵇEmma Watson.
  a Who _____ ?
  b Who _____ ?

6 **Complete the sentences to make them true for you.**

1 I'm reading _____ at the moment.
2 It takes me _____ minutes to get to school.
3 I go shopping for clothes _____ a month.
4 I've been to _____ foreign countries.
5 _____ inspires me.

7 SPEAKING **Ask and answer the questions about the information in Exercise 6. Use different question words, e.g. *what, how long* or *how often*.**

A: *What are you reading at the moment?*
B: *A book about Steve Jobs.*

FOCUS VLOG **About happiness**

▶ 3 **Watch the Focus Vlog. For the worksheet, go to page 117.**

Grammar page 132

LISTENING

1.3

Note completion

I can identify key details in a simple recorded interview.

1 **◀)) 1.8** Do you know the places in the box where people do voluntary work? If necessary use a dictionary. Then listen and repeat.

> in a developing country   in a nursery
> in a hospital   in a library   on a farm
> in an old people's home   in a prison
> in a soup kitchen for homeless people

2 **SPEAKING** Discuss whether you would like to volunteer there. Explain why or why not.

3 **◀)) 1.9** Listen to two volunteers, Karen and Martin. Where do they do their voluntary work?

4 Read questions 1–8 in Exercise 5. Match the underlined words and phrases with the words and phrases in the box.

> confident ⑦   people without a home ⬚
> two or three ⬚   impresses people ⬚
> Saturday or Sunday ⬚   chickens ⬚
> more likely to do something ⬚   in a team ⬚

5 **◀)) 1.9** Listen to Karen and Martin again and answer the questions. Write K (Karen) or M (Martin).

Who ...

1 helps <u>homeless</u> people in the local area? ⬚
2 works with <u>farm animals</u>? ⬚
3 volunteers <u>a few</u> hours a week? ⬚
4 does voluntary work every <u>weekend</u>? ⬚
5 thinks that volunteers are <u>more active</u> than other people? ⬚
6 enjoys working <u>with other people</u>? ⬚
7 thinks that voluntary work makes you <u>more sure of yourself</u>? ⬚
8 thinks that doing voluntary work <u>makes a good impression</u>? ⬚

6 **◀)) 1.10** Listen to Tim giving Becky some advice about international volunteering. Answer the questions.

1 Where does Becky want to do voluntary work?
2 Does Tim think she has the right personal qualities?
3 Is Becky inspired by the conversation?

7 **SPEAKING** Imagine you could volunteer anywhere in the world. Which country would you choose? Why? Tell your partner.

EXAM FOCUS   Note completion

8 **◀)) 1.10** Listen to Tim and Becky again and complete each gap with one or two words from the dialogue.

5 Key Questions before you volunteer for work overseas

1 **Are you fit and healthy?**
You often work in difficult conditions, and you sometimes need to work ¹_____ .

2 **Can you adapt to new situations?**
You need to adapt to ²_____ , the food, the accommodation and a new ³_____ .

3 **Are you a good team player?**
All volunteers work in teams so you need to have good ⁴_____ skills. You need to be outgoing and above all ⁵_____ .

4 **Are you sensitive to other cultures?**
You need to be open to people and remember that your ⁶_____ life is not the only way there is.

5 **Do you want to learn from the experience?**
Volunteering can change your life and you as a person. It's an excellent opportunity to help people, learn ⁷_____ and make new friends for life.

9 **SPEAKING** Discuss whether you are good candidates for international voluntary work. Ask and answer the questions in Exercise 8 and decide.

PRONUNCIATION FOCUS

10 **◀)) 1.11** Listen and put the adjectives into groups A, B, C or D depending on the stress.

> adventurous   ~~ambitious~~ fantastic   optimistic
> passionate   pessimistic   responsible   voluntary

A ■▪▪	B ▪■▪▪	C ▪■▪▪	D ■▪▪▪
	ambitious		

11 **◀)) 1.12** Listen, check and repeat.

WORD STORE 1D | *-ive, -ative, -able, -ing*

12 **◀)) 1.13** Complete WORD STORE 1D. Make personality adjectives from the verbs in the box by adding *-ive, -ative, -able* or *-ing*. Then listen, check and repeat.

READING

1.4

Matching

I can identify specific information in an article.

1 **SPEAKING Complete the table with three names of people you know. Then talk about each person and discuss the questions.**

X (Age 40–59)	
Y (Age 20–39)	
Z (Age 15–19)	

1 What are they like?
2 What do they like?
3 How often do they use technology?

2 **Read the text. Compare your ideas in Exercise 1 with the information in the article.**

EXAM FOCUS Matching

3 **Read the text again. Match generations with the statements. Write X, Y or Z in the boxes.**

Which generation …
1 enjoy new experiences? ☐
2 often don't earn as much as they'd like to? ☐
3 can do more than one activity at the same time? ☐
4 are independent? ☐
5 often appear self-centred? ☐
6 are tolerant and believe in equality? ☐
7 enjoy using social media? ☐☐

4 **SPEAKING Are you typical of Generation Z? Discuss with a partner.**

WORD STORE 1E | Verb + preposition

5 **🔊 1.15 Complete WORD STORE 1E with the verbs in blue in the text. Then listen, check and repeat.**

6 **Complete the sentences with the correct preposition. Check the verb + preposition structures in WORD STORE 1E.**

1 Amy is a cheerful kind of person. She always focuses _on_ positive things.
2 Billy believes _____ working hard and playing hard.
3 Carol never looks at a map. She depends _____ her phone for directions.
4 David thinks _____ his health too much. He always thinks he's ill.
5 Emily has younger brothers and sisters. She has to deal _____ a lot of noise at home.
6 Fred doesn't care _____ the environment. He never recycles anything.
7 Gabrielle worries _____ her grandparents because they're old.
8 Helen prefers to connect _____ her friends face to face.
9 George always sings along when he listens _____ music. It's so annoying!

7 **SPEAKING Change the names in Exercise 6 to make some true sentences about people you know. Tell your partner about them.**

8 **Complete the questions with the correct preposition.**

1 At the moment, what sort of music are you listening _____ ?
2 At school, which subject is hardest to focus _____ ?
3 What is the worst situation you have ever had to deal _____ ?
4 In your family, who's the person you can most depend _____ ?
5 Which global problems do you most worry _____ ?
6 Before you fall asleep, what do you think _____ ?

9 **SPEAKING Ask and answer the questions in Exercise 8.**

10 **🔊 1.16 Complete the table with the underlined adjectives in the text. Mark the stress. The listen, check and repeat.**

Noun	Adjective
1 adventure	*adventurous*
2 ambition	_____
3 impatience	_____
4 independence	_____
5 loneliness	_____
6 passion	_____
7 popularity	_____

A BRIEF GUIDE TO THE **GENERATIONS**

🔊 1.14

GENERATION X
Born between 1965 and 1980, now in their forties and fifties.

▶ Generation X created the Internet. When they were teenagers, mobile phones were enormous, and not many people had computers at home. They had to deal with big changes in technology. But this generation is adventurous and adaptable – they are not afraid of change. Now they use wearable technology to stay fit and healthy. Generation X believe in looking after themselves and staying young. 5

▶ Generation X grew up with both parents at work during the day. This is one of the reasons they are independent.

▶ Generation X are very sociable, but also hard-working. Even when they go out until late, they still get up for work. 10

▶ They're passionate about music. They invented punk, grunge and techno. When they were teenagers, they listened to music on cassette and CD players.

GENERATION Y / MILLENNIALS
Born between 1980 and 2000, now in their twenties and thirties.

▶ Generation Y, or Millennials, are the selfie generation, also known as Generation Me Me Me. Some people say they focus on themselves too much. 15

▶ They grew up with technology and they depend on their smartphones. They download and listen to music on their phones all the time.

▶ Generation Y have FOMO or 'fear of missing out'. They like to share experiences on social media, and they worry about being popular and having a good time. Fifty-three percent prefer to spend money on an experience than a possession. 20

▶ Lots of Generation Ys went to university, but because of unemployment they find it hard to get jobs that make them happy. 25

▶ Many of them live at home and depend on their parents. They get married later than Generation X — the average age for women is twenty-seven and for men it's twenty-nine. They would like to be more independent, but they can't afford to be.

GENERATION Z
Born between 1995 and now.

▶ Generation Z are good at multi-tasking. They can use several screens at the same time and this is why they're called Screenagers. They're fast thinkers, and when something doesn't happen quickly, they get impatient. 30

▶ Generation Z are the 'we' generation. They don't think about themselves too much. Instead they focus on global problems like terrorism and global warming.

▶ They're sociable and they enjoy connecting with friends on social media, but they can also feel very lonely. Generation Z love going to gigs or amusement parks. Eighty percent prefer to spend time with their friends in person than on the phone or online. 35

▶ Generation Z believe in getting a good education, but they worry about university fees. This generation is ambitious and want to start their own businesses. 40

▶ Generation Z don't care about where you're from or the colour of your skin.

▶ Music is an essential part of their day.

1.5

verb + *-ing* or verb + *to* + infinitive

I can use verbs taking to + infinitive and -ing forms.

WHAT IS YOUR ATTITUDE TO CLOTHES?

1 (**SPEND**)

A I spend a lot of money on clothes.

B I can't afford [1]*to spend* much money on clothes.

C I prefer [2]_____ my money on going out.

2 (**GO**)

A I enjoy [3]_____ shopping for clothes.

B I don't mind [4]_____ shopping for clothes.

C I refuse [5]_____ shopping for clothes.

3 (**BUY**)

A I love [6]_____ new clothes every season.

B I only buy clothes when I need them.

C I avoid [7]_____ new clothes for as long as possible.

4 (**WEAR**)

A I refuse [8]_____ sweatpants.

B I love [9]_____ sweatpants at home for comfort.

C I wear sweatpants all the time.

5 (**GET**)

A I hope [10]_____ a job where I can wear all my favourite clothes.

B I want [11]_____ a job where I can wear practical, comfortable clothes.

C I'd like [12]_____ a job where I can wear a uniform or a suit.

6 (**THINK**)

A In the morning, I spend a lot of time [13]_____ about my clothes.

B In the morning, I don't spend much time [14]_____ about my clothes.

C I wear the same clothes every day.

WHAT DOES IT MEAN?

Mainly As I LOVE THEM

You enjoy [15]_____ (think) about clothes (perhaps a bit too much), and the way you look is important for your personal identity.

Mainly Bs I NEED THEM

You don't mind [16]_____ (think) about clothes, but they are not your priority. You prefer casual clothes because you need [17]_____ (be) comfortable.

Mainly Cs I HATE THEM

You hate [18]_____ (think) about clothes! You choose [19]_____ (spend) your time and money on other things. But don't forget, clothes can be fun.

1 SPEAKING **Match the words in the box with the clothes in the pictures. Which of the clothes do you have? Tell your partner.**

hoodie ☐ jacket ☐ suit ☐ sweatpants ☐
tie ☐ uniform ☐

2 **Tick the sentence that best describes your opinion about clothes.**

1 I want to look good at all times. ☐
2 I enjoy wearing comfortable things. ☐
3 I'm not interested in clothes. ☐

3 **Read the GRAMMAR FOCUS. Complete the examples using the verb patterns in blue in Exercise 2.**

GRAMMAR FOCUS

Verb + *-ing* or verb + *to* + infinitive

- After some verbs and verb phrases you usually use the *to* + infinitive.

  Examples: *agree, can't afford, choose, decide, hope, manage, need, pretend, refuse, want, 'd like, 'd prefer*

  I want [1]_____ *good at all times.*

- After some verbs and verb phrases you usually use the *-ing* form of a verb.

  Examples: *avoid, can't stand, consider, don't mind, enjoy, hate, like, love, miss, prefer, spend time*

  I enjoy [2]_____ *comfortable things.*

4 **Complete the questionnaire with the correct form of the verbs in brackets.**

5 SPEAKING **Do the questionnaire. What is your attitude to clothes? Tell your partner.**

6 **Complete the sentences with *to wear* or *wearing*. Which sentences are true for you?**

1 I can't stand *wearing* formal clothes like suits.
2 I don't mind _____ second-hand clothes.
3 I refuse _____ skinny jeans. They're too uncomfortable.
4 I hate _____ heavy winter coats.
5 I can't afford _____ designer clothes. They're too expensive.
6 I avoid _____ anything yellow or pink.

7 **Complete the sentences with information about yourself. Write five true sentences and one false.**

1 I love …
2 I need …
3 I've decided …
4 I spend a lot of time …
5 I sometimes pretend …
6 I hope …

8 **Read your sentences in Exercise 7 to your partner for him/her to guess which sentence is false.**

Grammar page 133

USE OF ENGLISH

1.6

so and such

I can use so and such correctly.

1 SPEAKING Read the introduction. Then discuss the questions.

1 Do you, or would you like to, live with three generations of your family?

2 What advantages can you think of?

3 What disadvantages can you think of?

One home, three generations

Around the world, many families live with several generations in the same house. This is because young people can't afford to move away from home. Also the older generation live longer now, and they want to be useful. These homes are crowded, but the generations help and support each other. So what's it like to have grandparents, parents and children living together? We asked members of three generations of the same family.

2 ◀)) 1.17 Listen to the father's views. Which of your ideas in Exercise 1 does he mention?

3 ◀)) 1.17 Listen again and choose the correct option.

1 We have three generations in this house: it's *so / such* crowded!

2 New Zealand is *so / such* a long way from the UK.

3 Childcare is *so / such* expensive in London.

4 We were *so / such* poor that we couldn't go on holiday.

5 The house is very small for *so / such* a big family.

4 ◀)) 1.18 Read the LANGUAGE FOCUS. Complete the text below with the daughter's views. Use *so* or *such*. Then listen and check.

LANGUAGE FOCUS

so and such

- You use **so** to emphasise adjectives.
  so + adjective → *It's so crowded!*
- You use **such** to emphasise nouns.
  such + noun phrase → *It's such a long way.*
  We're such close friends. They give such good advice.

I don't mind living with my grandparents, they're ¹ *so* lovely. I like talking to them – they're very experienced and give ² _____ good advice. Mum and Dad are ³ _____ busy. They don't have time to listen to our problems. My parents are ⁴ _____ lucky because grandma and granddad are very helpful in the house. Grandma is ⁵ _____ a good cook that she does most of the cooking, while granddad looks after the garden.

5 ◀)) 1.19 USE OF ENGLISH Complete the text with the grandmother's views. Choose the correct option, A, B or C. Then listen and check.

We thought about it for a long time because we're ¹*such* independent people. Some elderly people are lonely, but not us – we've got ² ___ friends that we never feel lonely. But we wanted to help with the children. We try to be useful and it's ³ ___ fun to spend time with my grandchildren. People say that teenagers are selfish and rude, but I must say my granddaughter's ⁴ ___ polite young lady and she's very kind. I worry about her little brother though. He's ⁵ ___ lazy!

1 A so	B such	C such an
2 A so many	B such many	C such a
3 A such	B such a	C so
4 A such	B so	C such a
5 A so	B such	C such a

6 SPEAKING Which generation do you think benefits most from living in 'one home'? Discuss with a partner.

Use of English page 134

WRITING

1.7

A personal email/letter

I can write a short personal email to introduce myself.

1 SPEAKING **Choose five qualities to describe the ideal exchange student. Discuss with a partner.**

confident and independent   friendly and outgoing
generous   good-looking   good at sport   honest
interested in computers   into the same music as me
keen on the same hobbies as me   sensible

2 **Read the email from an exchange student. Tick the topics in the box that the student writes about.**

family ☐   food ☐   hobbies ☐   music ☐
school ☐   sport ☐

3 SPEAKING **Does the person in the email sound like your ideal exchange student? What details would you change? Tell your partner.**

4 **Put the sentences summarising the email in the correct order (1–5).**

a basic information about yourself ☐

b a greeting and information about why you are writing ☐

c say you're looking forward to seeing him/her ☐

d finish with a friendly goodbye ☐

e information about your likes/dislikes/hobbies etc. ☐

5 **Read the WRITING FOCUS. Complete the examples with the phrases in purple in the email.**

WRITING FOCUS

A personal email/letter

- Start the letter/email with a friendly greeting: *Dear Nick,/¹ Hi Jo,*
- Don't use full forms. Use contractions: *you're* (not *you are*)/² _____
- Use emoticons (☺) or abbreviations (but don't overuse them): *Bye for now = Bye 4 now.*
- Ask questions to show you want a reply: *What do you enjoy doing at weekends?/ What ³ _____ ?*
- Finish the letter/email with a friendly goodbye, e.g. *All the best/⁴ _____ .*

To: Jo
Subject: C U soon!

Hi Jo,

How are you doing? I'm really excited about coming to stay with you. I'm writing to tell you a bit more about myself.

As you know, I'm sixteen and I live in Venice. My brother and I go to the same school. I'm not crazy about studying but it's OK – my favourite subject is Art. What about you? What subjects are you good at?

In my free time, I'm keen on sports and I'm not bad at volleyball. I'm also passionate about music, especially British bands. At the moment I'm listening to Little Mix all the time. What kind of music are you interested in?

At weekends, my friends and I love going to the cinema. What do you enjoy doing at weekends?

I can't wait to see you next month! I'm sure we'll have fun.

OK, time to finish. Write soon ☺

Bye 4 now.

Carlo

Carlo

6 Mark these phrases as F – usually used in the first paragraph, or L – usually used in the last paragraph.

1 How are you? ☐
2 I'd better stop now. ☐
3 Looking forward to hearing from you/ seeing you. ☐
4 Give my love to …/Say hello to … ☐
5 It was good to hear from you. ☐
6 Cheers, ☐
7 Dear … ☐
8 I'm writing to tell you about …/say sorry about …/thank you for … ☐
9 C U (see you) soon/next week/in a few months. ☐

7 Replace the underlined phrases in the email with suitable phrases in Exercise 6.

8 SPEAKING Which of these statements illustrate good (G) or not good (NG) exchange students? Why? Discuss with a partner.

1 I'm obsessed with hiphop.
2 I'm mad about shopping. I spend lots of money on clothes.
3 I watch a lot of DVDs, especially horror films.
4 I'm serious about politics.
5 I love acting – I'm involved in a local theatre club.
6 I'm afraid of animals, especially dogs.
7 I'm ambitious – I'm always disappointed with low marks at school.
8 I'm useless at sport and I'm very unfit.

9 Read the LANGUAGE FOCUS. Complete the examples with the correct prepositions. Use the examples in the email in Exercise 2 and in Exercise 8.

LANGUAGE FOCUS

Adjective + preposition

- Use an adjective + preposition to give information about yourself.
  I'm crazy/excited/mad/passionate/serious/worried ¹*about*
  I'm bad/good/useless ² _____
  I'm involved ³ _____
  I'm afraid ⁴ _____
  I'm keen ⁵ _____
  I'm disappointed/obsessed ⁶ _____

Note: It's okay for questions to end in a preposition:
What subjects are you good at?

10 SPEAKING Complete the questions with the correct preposition. Then ask and answer the questions.

1 What sort of things are you interested _____ ?
2 What after-school activities are you involved _____ ?
3 What bands and singers are you keen _____ ?
4 What sports or games are you good _____ ?
5 What sort of things are you serious _____ ?
6 What are you most passionate _____ ?

SHOW WHAT YOU'VE LEARNT

11 Read the email from your English-speaking friend Jenny and the notes you have made.

It's me. Jenny.

I'm happy too!

From: Jenny
Subject: Hello!

It's great to hear that you're going to come and stay with me and my family for two weeks.

Please tell me something about yourself.

What subjects do you like at school?
What music and films do you like?
What do you do in your free time?
I'd like to plan some cool activities for us ☺

Let me know if you have any questions for me.

See you soon,

Jenny

Answer Jenny's questions

Ask Jenny about her interests

Write your email to Jenny using all the notes.

To: Jenny
Re: Hello!

Hi Jenny,

Thanks for the email.

_____

_____

_____

13

SPEAKING

Showing interest

I can show interest in a conversation and express similarity or difference.

1 SPEAKING **Look at the activities in the box. Discuss the questions.**

> eating and drinking   travelling   doing sport
> listening to music   shopping
> socialising with friends   meeting new people
> watching films   being online

1 How much of your free time do you spend on each activity?
2 What other things do you do in your free time?
3 How similar or different are you to your partner?

2 🔊 1.20 **Listen to two dialogues and answer the questions.**

1 What do Ed and Nick have in common?
2 What do Rachel and Kate have in common?

3 🔊 1.20 **Listen again and complete the SPEAKING FOCUS with responses a–e.**

a Do you? Right …
b Really? That's cool!
c Is she?
d Really? I love it.
e Me too.

SPEAKING FOCUS

Statement	Showing interest
A: I've got loads of friends and they want to meet you.	B: ¹*Really? That's cool*!
A: I've just got one sister. She's a model.	B: ² _____
A: She's training to be a pilot.	B: Wow, that's interesting.

Statement	Saying you are similar
A: I love travelling and meeting new people.	B: ³ _____
A: I don't really like rock or heavy metal.	B: Me neither.

Statement	Saying you are different
A: I'm not very keen on tea.	B: ⁴ _____
A: I don't like travelling.	B: Don't you? Oh, I do!
A: I play the violin.	B: ⁵ _____

4 🔊 1.21 **Cross out the response that is NOT possible in each case. Then listen, check and repeat.**

1 A: I've got thousands of songs on my phone.
   B: *Have you? / Cool! / Is it?*
2 A: I love Spanish and Italian food.
   B: *Really? / Are you? / Do you?*
3 A: My parents have got an apartment in Paris.
   B: *Wow, that's interesting! / Have they? / Are they?*
4 A: There are forty students in my class.
   B: *Is it? / Are there? / Really?*
5 A: I can play the guitar.
   B: *Cool! / Are you? / Can you?*
6 A: I'm passionate about politics.
   B: *Really? / Do you? / Are you?*

5 🔊 1.22 **Listen and decide if the two speakers are similar (✓) or different (✗).**

1 ☐   2 ☐   3 ☐   4 ☐   5 ☐   6 ☐

6 Complete the table.

Statement	Say you're similar	Say you're different
a I'm worried about the world.	Me too.	Are you? ¹*I'm not.*
b I'm not worried about the world.	² _____	Aren't you? I am.
c I love reading poetry.	³ _____	⁴ _____ ? I don't.
d I don't like reading poetry.	Me neither.	Don't you? ⁵ _____ .
e I've got lots of cousins.	⁶ _____	⁷ _____ ? I haven't.
f I haven't got any cousins.	Me neither.	Haven't you? ⁸ _____ .

7 Complete the sentences to make them true for you.

1 I'm really into …
2 I haven't got …
3 I really like …
4 I'm very interested in …
5 I'm not very keen on …
6 I'm not very good at …

8 SPEAKING **Follow the instructions below to make dialogues.**

Student A: Choose a statement from Exercise 7. Say it to Student B.

Student B: Say if you are similar or different. Use the SPEAKING FOCUS to help you.

ROLE-PLAY   Showing interest

▶5 **Watch the video and practise. Then role-play your dialogue.**

1.1 Vocabulary 🔊 4.1

adventurous /əd'ventʃərəs/
bad mood /ˌbæd 'muːd/
be popular with /ˌbi 'pɒpjələ wɪð/
be successful /ˌbi sək'sesfəl/
be the centre of attention /ˌbi ðə ˌsentər əv ə'tenʃən/
caring /'keərɪŋ/
charity /'tʃærəti/
cheerful /'tʃɪəfəl/
confident /'kɒnfədənt/
dependent /dɪ'pendənt/
dishonest /dɪs'ɒnəst/
experience /ɪk'spɪəriəns/
friendly /'frendli/
generous /'dʒenərəs/
hard-working /ˌhɑːd 'wɜːkɪŋ/
honest /'ɒnəst/
impolite /ˌɪmpə'laɪt/
independent /ˌɪndə'pendənt/
insensitive /ɪn'sensətɪv/
irresponsible /ˌɪrɪ'spɒnsəbəl/
kind /kaɪnd/
lazy /'leɪzi/
lonely /'ləʊnli/
look after /ˌlʊk 'ɑːftə/
look cheerful/tired /ˌlʊk 'tʃɪəfəl/'taɪəd/
look forward to /ˌlʊk 'fɔːwəd tə/
mean /miːn/
miserable /'mɪzərəbəl/
outgoing /ˌaʊt'gəʊɪŋ/
polite /pə'laɪt/
popular /'pɒpjələ/
responsible /rɪ'spɒnsəbəl/
selfish /'selfɪʃ/
sensible /'sensəbəl/
sensitive /'sensətɪv/
serious /'sɪəriəs/
shy /ʃaɪ/
silly /'sɪli/
sociable /'səʊʃəbəl/
stupid /'stjuːpɪd/
talkative /'tɔːkətɪv/
tattoo /tə'tuː/
tell lies /ˌtel 'laɪz/
unadventurous /ˌʌnəd'ventʃərəs/
unpopular /ʌn'pɒpjələ/
unwise /ˌʌn'waɪz/
wise /waɪz/

1.2 Grammar 🔊 4.2

admire /əd'maɪə/
be passionate about sth /ˌbi 'pæʃənət əˌbaʊt ˌsʌmθɪŋ/
follow sb on Twitter /ˌfɒləʊ ˌsʌmbɒdi ɒn 'twɪtə/
foreign country /ˌfɒrɪn 'kʌntri/
in person /ˌɪn 'pɜːsən/
inspire /ɪn'spaɪə/
it takes sb a minute/an hour to do sth /ɪt ˌteɪks ˌsʌmbɒdi ə ˌmɪnət/ən aʊə tə 'duː ˌsʌmθɪŋ/
role model /'rəʊl ˌmɒdl/
run a foundation /ˌrʌn ə faʊn'deɪʃən/
work on /'wɜːk ɒn/

1.3 Listening 🔊 4.3

accommodation /əˌkɒmə'deɪʃən/
act /ækt/
active /'æktɪv/
adapt to /ə'dæpt tə/
adaptable /ə'dæptəbəl/
ambitious /æm'bɪʃəs/
communicate /kə'mjuːnɪkeɪt/
communicative /kə'mjuːnɪkətɪv/
developing country /dɪˌveləpɪŋ 'kʌntri/
difficult conditions /ˌdɪfɪkəlt kən'dɪʃənz/
fantastic /fæn'tæstɪk/
farm /fɑːm/
fit /fɪt/
healthy /'helθi/
homeless /'həʊmləs/
hospital /'hɒspɪtl/
imaginative /ɪ'mædʒɪnətɪv/
imagine /ɪ'mædʒɪn/
impress /ɪm'pres/
inspired by /ɪn'spaɪəd baɪ/
library /'laɪbrəri/
make a good impression /ˌmeɪk ə gʊd ɪm'preʃən/
nursery /'nɜːsəri/
old people's home /ˌəʊld 'piːpəlz həʊm/
opportunity /ˌɒpə'tjuːnəti/
personal quality /ˌpɜːsənəl 'kwɒləti/
pessimistic /ˌpesə'mɪstɪk/
prison /'prɪzən/
protect /prə'tekt/
protective /prə'tektɪv/
soup kitchen for homeless people /'suːp ˌkɪtʃən fə ˌhəʊmləs ˌpiːpəl/
sure of yourself /'ʃɔːr əv jəˌself/
team player /'tiːm ˌpleɪə/
voluntary work /'vɒləntəri wɜːk/
volunteer /ˌvɒlən'tɪə/

1.4 Reading 🔊 4.4

adventure /əd'ventʃə/
ambition /æm'bɪʃən/
average age /'ævərɪdʒ eɪdʒ/
be afraid of /ˌbi ə'freɪd əv/
believe in /bə'liːv ɪn/
belong to /bɪ'lɒŋ tə/
can't afford /ˌkɑːnt ə'fɔːd/
care about /'keər əˌbaʊt/
connect with /kə'nekt wɪð/
deal with /'diːl wɪð/
depend on /dɪ'pend ɒn/
enormous /ɪ'nɔːməs/
focus on /'fəʊkəs ɒn/
generation /ˌdʒenə'reɪʃən/
get married /ˌget 'mærid/
get up /ˌget 'ʌp/
gig /gɪg/
go out /ˌgəʊ 'aʊt/
good at /'gʊd ət/
grow up /ˌgrəʊ 'ʌp/
impatience /ɪm'peɪʃəns/
impatient /ɪm'peɪʃənt/
independence /ˌɪndə'pendəns/
listen to /'lɪsən tə/
loneliness /'ləʊnlinəs/
miss out /ˌmɪs 'aʊt/
passion /'pæʃən/

popularity /ˌpɒpjə'lærəti/

popularity /ˌpɒpjə'lærəti/
share /ʃeə/
spend money on /ˌspend 'mʌni ɒn/
spend time /ˌspend 'taɪm/
think about /'θɪŋk əˈbaʊt/
unemployment /ˌʌnɪm'plɔɪmənt/
worry about /ˌwʌri ə'baʊt/

1.5 Grammar 🔊 4.5

avoid /ə'vɔɪd/
can't stand /ˌkɑːnt 'stænd/
casual clothes /ˌkæʒuəl 'kləʊðz/
consider /kən'sɪdə/
decide /dɪ'saɪd/
don't mind /ˌdəʊnt 'maɪnd/
enjoy /ɪn'dʒɔɪ/
get a job /ˌget ə 'dʒɒb/
hate /heɪt/
hoodie /'hʊdi/
identity /aɪ'dentəti/
jacket /'dʒækət/
look good /ˌlʊk 'gʊd/
prefer /prɪ'fɜː/
pretend /prɪ'tend/
priority /praɪ'ɒrɪti/
refuse /rɪ'fjuːz/
second-hand clothes /ˌsekəndˌhænd 'kləʊðz/
skinny jeans /ˌskɪni 'dʒiːnz/
suit /suːt/
sweatpants /'swetpænts/
tie /taɪ/
uniform /'juːnəfɔːm/
winter coat /ˌwɪntə 'kəʊt/

1.6 Use of English 🔊 4.6

be lucky /ˌbi 'lʌki/
busy /'bɪzi/
cook (n) /kʊk/
crowded /'kraʊdɪd/
elderly /'eldəli/
experienced /ɪk'spɪəriənst/
poor /pʊə/
rude /ruːd/
useful /'juːsfəl/

1.7 Writing 🔊 4.7

bad at /'bæd ət/
be crazy about /ˌbi 'kreɪzi əˌbaʊt/
be into/keen on /ˌbe 'ɪntə/'kiːn ɒn/
be involved in /ˌbi ɪn'vɒlvd ɪn/
be mad about /ˌbi 'mæd əˌbaʊt/
be obsessed with /ˌbi əb'sest wɪð/
be serious about /ˌbi 'sɪəriəs əˌbaʊt/
disappointed with /ˌdɪsə'pɔɪntɪd wɪð/
excited about /ɪk'saɪtɪd əˌbaʊt/
interested in /'ɪntrəstɪd ɪn/
unfit /ʌn'fɪt/
useless at /'juːsləs ət/

1.8 Speaking 🔊 4.8

can't wait /kɑːnt weɪt/
do sport /ˌduː 'spɔːt/
have sth in common /ˌhæv ˌsʌmθɪŋ ɪn 'kɒmən/
play the violin/guitar /ˌpleɪ ðə ˌvaɪə'lɪn/ gɪ'tɑː/
socialise with /'səʊʃəlaɪz wɪð/

FOCUS REVIEW 1

VOCABULARY AND GRAMMAR

1 Complete the sentences with personality adjectives. The first letters are given.

1 Shona never smiles and is always depressed. She's a really **m**_____ person.
2 Tim looks after his younger brother when their parents are out. He's so **r**_____ .
3 Zina is such a **s**_____ girl. She cares only about herself.
4 Neil's never made a silly decision. He's such a **s**_____ boy.
5 Has Marion always been so **l**_____ ? She always stays in bed until midday!
6 My grandparents often give me money for the cinema or CDs. They're so **g**_____ .

2 Complete the sentences with the correct form of the words in capitals.

1 My brothers are very _____ . They play sports every day! **ACT**
2 Gino makes new friends easily. He's so _____ . **COMMUNICATE**
3 Carla is sometimes _____ , so I don't believe in her stories. **HONEST**
4 Volunteers work in different conditions, so they must be _____ to changing situations. **ADAPT**
5 Leslie is such an _____ girl. She comes up with stories and writes songs. **IMAGINE**
6 A lot of people decided to help this poor family after that _____ TV programme. **INSPIRE**

3 Complete the questions with the correct form of the verbs in brackets.

1 _____ you ever _____ any problems with your smartphone? (have)
2 What _____ your new friend _____ ? (look like)
3 Who _____ my tablet? It's not on my desk. (use)
4 _____ your grandparents _____ listening to heavy metal? (like)
5 What _____ Amy _____ at the moment? Is it a TV show? (watch)
6 Who _____ your dog when you're on holiday? (look after)

4 Use the prompts to write sentences.

1 My sister / avoid / buy / second-hand clothes.
2 you / ever / refuse / help / your friend?
3 We / not need / wear / a school uniform.
4 They / not afford / buy / a new laptop.
5 I / always / want / dance / in a folk group.
6 you / spend / a long time / study / when you get home from school?

USE OF ENGLISH

5 Choose the correct answer, A, B or C.

1 Johann is _____ boy that he has never been to a school party.
   A so shy
   B such shy
   C such a shy
2 _____ with the project today?
   A Who helps Mary
   B Who is helping Mary
   C Who does help Mary
3 X: I don't enjoy shopping for clothes.
   Y: _____
   A Me too.
   B Me neither.
   C Not me.
4 Sally is _____ . She's been to Thailand twice.
   A such an adventurous
   B such adventurous
   C so adventurous
5 X: My older sister is a charity worker.
   Y: _____
   A Is she?
   B Does she?
   C Has she?

6 Choose the answer, A, B or C that is closest in meaning to the underlined words.

1 Agnes is so <u>friendly and sociable</u>.
   A outgoing
   B lucky
   C responsible
2 <u>What is she like?</u>
   A What kind of person is she?
   B What is her appearance?
   C What is her hobby?
3 Jasper <u>can't stand buying</u> unimportant things.
   A doesn't mind buying
   B doesn't want to buy
   C can't afford to buy
4 Their grandmother is <u>so caring</u>.
   A such a caring woman
   B such caring woman
   C always caring
5 Drake is <u>crazy about</u> sports cars.
   A useless at
   B obsessed with
   C afraid of

LISTENING

7 🔊 **1.23** Listen to a conversation with Tony, who has taken part in an experiment. Then complete the summary with the missing information. Do not use more than three words in each gap. Listen to the recording twice.

Today's guest of the weekly programme is Tony Miller, who studies ¹_____ in Zurich.

Tony volunteered to help a team of ²_____ to do a unique experiment. In the experiment, fifty participants received an amount of money and were divided into two groups. People in Group 1 could only spend the money on themselves, while people in Group 2 – on any ³_____ . During the experiment, the researchers observed those parts of participants' ⁴_____ which are responsible for making decisions and feelings.

Before, during and after the experiment, the participants from both groups were asked how happy they were. The results of the experiment show that when people do not share what they have with others, they feel ⁵_____ generous people.

SPEAKING

8 Do the task in pairs.

Student A

Your friend and you want to create an Internet comic book about matters which interest young people. You're thinking about who the hero should be. Read the role card and have a discussion. You start the conversation.

- Say if you think the hero is a man or a woman and what he/she looks like
- Accept Student B's suggestions about the hero's appearance and say what personality the hero would have
- Add more detail about the superpower
- Suggest a name for the hero.

Student B

Your friend and you want to create an Internet comic book about matters which interest young people. You're thinking about who the hero should be. Read the role card and have a discussion. Student A starts the conversation.

- Disagree with the description of the hero's appearance and suggest a change
- Add some more features of the character of the hero and suggest a superpower he/she has
- Say what he/she is interested in
- Discuss Student A's name of the hero and agree on the name.

9 Look at the photo and choose the most suitable words in the box to describe it. In pairs, describe the photo and answer the questions.

> **Verbs:** belong, carry, clean up, communicate, earn, pick up, protect, run, sing, watch, wear
> **Nouns:** bags, gloves, outfit, phone, rain, rubbish, screen, trees, volunteers, wood

1 Do you think the people in the photo are good voluntary workers? Why?/Why not?
2 Do you get involved in voluntary work? Why?/Why not?
3 Describe a school charity action you took part in or heard of.

WRITING

10 Do the task in pairs.

This semester you're taking part in a student exchange programme in the UK. Write an email to a friend in the USA. Include the following information:

- explain where you are and express your opinion about this place
- talk about the family you're staying with
- describe a friend you met at the new school
- write how you spent the last weekend.

2

Science and technology

Necessity is the mother of invention.

A proverb

URBAN LEGENDS

▶ 6 Watch the BBC video.
For the worksheet, go to page 118.

2.1 VOCABULARY

Online • phones and computers
• word building • collocations

I can use language related to science, technology and inventions.

SHOW WHAT YOU KNOW

1 **Choose the correct verb. Then complete the sentences to make them true for you.**

1 The first thing I do when I *visit / go* online is …
2 The person I'd like to *watch / follow* on Twitter is …
3 The website I *visit / go in* most is …
4 The last music I *downloaded / followed* was …
5 The last comment I *posted / sent* on social media was …
6 The last time I *updated / revised* my social media profile was …

2 **SPEAKING** Compare your sentences with a partner. How much time do you typically spend online each day?

SCIENCE AND TECHNOLOGY QUIZ

1 **Match the years with these digital inventions.**

> 1977   1984   1990   1993   1994

1 The first **web browser** _____
2 The first **search engine** _____
3 The first **laser printer** _____
4 The first **desktop computer** with **keyboard** and **mouse** _____
5 The first **smartphone** _____

BONUS QUESTION: **Which company made the first computer with a mouse?**

2 **Which sciences were these great scientists mostly involved in?**

> astronomy, biology, chemistry, computer science, mathematics, physics

Nicolaus Copernicus	Isaac Newton	Charles Darwin
_____	_____	_____

BONUS QUESTION: **Which scientist won two Nobel Prizes?**

3 🔊 **1.24** Do the Science and Technology Quiz. Then listen and check your answers.

4 🔊 **1.25** Complete sentences 1–5 with the correct scientist in the quiz. Then listen to Part 2 again and check your answers.

1 _____ <u>did</u> experiments with radioactive materials and <u>discovered</u> polonium and radium.

2 _____ <u>did</u> research into gravity, light and many areas of physics, maths and astronomy.

3 _____ <u>invented</u> the idea of a 'Universal Machine' or a computer in 1936.

4 _____ <u>developed</u> the theory that the Earth moves around the Sun.

5 _____ <u>observed</u> nature. He <u>took</u> notes and measurements and <u>collected</u> specimens from around the world.

3

Are statements 1–3 true (T) or false (F)?

1 Albert Einstein failed Mathematics at school. **T / F**

2 An earthquake can shorten the length of a day. **T / F**

3 Some people are left-brained, others are right-brained. **T / F**

BONUS QUESTION: What percentage of our brain do we normally use?

Marie Sklodowska-Curie   Alan Turing

_____   _____

WORD STORE 2A | Phones and computers ⟩

5 🔊 **1.26** Complete WORD STORE 2A with the compound nouns in red in the quiz. Then listen, check and repeat.

6 Complete the questions with compound nouns in WORD STORE 2A.

1 How many _____ messages do you usually send in a day?

2 Do you always use the same _____ name and password online?

3 Have you got a _____ computer or a laptop?

4 Which is the most popular search _____ in your country?

5 Which _____ browser do you normally use?

6 Have you got a reliable _____ connection with fast download speeds?

7 Do you like typing on a smartphone or do you prefer to use a key_____ ?

7 SPEAKING Ask and answer the questions in Exercise 6.

WORD STORE 2B | Word building ⟩

8 🔊 **1.27** Complete WORD STORE 2B with the science subjects in the quiz. Then listen, check and repeat.

9 SPEAKING Discuss the questions.

1 Would you like to be a scientist? Why?/Why not?

2 Which science subject do you find easiest/most difficult to understand?

3 Which science subject do you think will be most useful to you in the future? Why?

WORD STORE 2C | Collocations ⟩

10 🔊 **1.28** Complete WORD STORE 2C with the infinitive form of the underlined verbs in Exercise 4. Then listen, check and repeat.

11 Complete the sentences with the correct verb in Word Store 2C in an appropriate form.

1 Tim has _____ a new program. It will change how people manage databases.

2 Rowena _____ the sky at night. She hopes to _____ a new planet.

3 Lucie _____ wild plants to develop new drugs.

4 Fred is _____ research into laser technology for his doctorate.

5 Lena _____ experiments on plastics to measure how strong they are.

6 George looks at big numbers and _____ notes. He produces formulas to solve problems.

12 SPEAKING What kind of scientist is each person in Exercise 11? Discuss which science you think is the most/least important to society.

1 Tim = a computer scientist

GRAMMAR

Past Continuous and Past Simple

I can use the Past Simple and Past Continuous to describe past events.

1 **SPEAKING** Read what people say about e-books and printed books. Which comments do you agree with? Think of more advantages and disadvantages. Discuss with a partner.

(1) When I go on holiday, I don't have to pack heavy books.

(2) I like the feel of a real book in my hands.

(3) I work with computer screens all day – I don't want to read books on a screen too.

(4) Books are so expensive. E-books are cheaper.

2 Read about E ink. Who was Joe Jacobson and why did he have a 'Eureka' moment?

In 1997 Joe Jacobson was working as a researcher for the Massachusetts Institute of Technology (MIT). One summer, he went on holiday to the coast. He was lying on a beach when he finished his book. Unfortunately, he didn't have another one with him. At that moment, he imagined an electronic book that he could download any time he wanted and read in direct sunlight. It was a 'Eureka' moment. His vision became E ink technology and helped develop the e-readers that we have today.

3 Read the GRAMMAR FOCUS. Complete the examples using the past forms in blue in Exercise 2.

GRAMMAR FOCUS

Past Continuous and Past Simple

- You use the **Past Continuous** to talk about longer actions in progress at a time in the past.
  In 1997 Joe Jacobson ¹_____ as a researcher for MIT.

- You often use the **Past Continuous** with the **Past Simple** – usually when a short action (Past Simple) interrupted a longer action (Past Continuous).
  He ²_____ on a beach when he ³_____ his book.

Past Continuous: was/were + -ing form

+	I was working etc.
–	She wasn't working etc.
?	Were you working? etc.

4 Complete the beginnings of two stories with the Past Simple or the Past Continuous form of the verbs in brackets.

Pearson English **Readers**

David Copperfield
Charles Dickens

It was a terrible stormy night six months after my father's death. My mother ¹was sitting (sit) alone by the fire, waiting for her baby to arrive. She ²_____ (feel) sad and ill. Suddenly she ³_____ (hear) a noise outside. 'There's someone at the door, Peggotty,' my mother ⁴_____ (call). 'Who is it?' Peggotty was her servant and her only real friend. 'I'll go and see,' Peggotty ⁵_____ (reply). She ⁶_____ (go) and ⁷_____ (open) the door.

As the carriage moved quickly along the rough dry road, Jonathan Harker ⁸_____ (look out) at the changing view. Behind him was a land of small, green hills and colourful fields of fruit trees. Now he ⁹_____ (drive) into the Transylvanian mountains through a thick forest. It ¹⁰_____ (get) dark, and the other people in the carriage ¹¹_____ (be) quiet and afraid. A woman opposite him ¹²_____ (reach) towards him and ¹³_____ (put) something in his hand. It ¹⁴_____ (be) a small, silver cross. 'Wear it around your neck,' she said. 'You'll be safe.'

Pearson English **Readers**

Dracula
Bram Stoker

5 **SPEAKING** Which story would you like to continue reading and why? Tell your partner.

6 Complete each sentence with one Past Simple and one Past Continuous verb form. Which sentences are true for you?

1 My parents *were studying* (study) when they *met* (meet).
2 My computer _____ (crash) when I _____ (do) my homework last night.
3 I _____ (watch) a film when my mum _____ (get) home yesterday.
4 It _____ (rain) when I _____ (wake up) this morning.
5 I _____ (burn) myself when I _____ (make) breakfast.
6 A friend _____ (text) me when I _____ (walk) to school.

7 Write questions for the sentences in Exercise 6. Change pronouns where necessary. Then ask your partner as in the example.

A: *Were your parents studying when they met?*
B: *No, they weren't.*

FOCUS VLOG About technology

(► 8) Watch the Focus Vlog. For the worksheet, go to page 119.

Grammar page 135 ▷

LISTENING

2.3

Matching

I can identify key details in a simple recorded narrative about scientists.

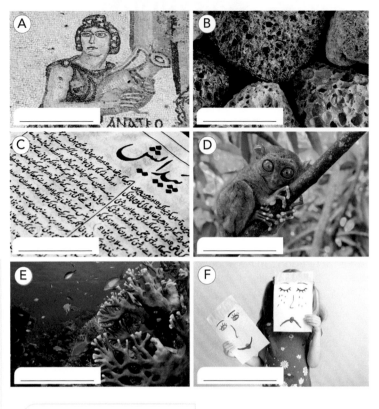

A
ANATEO

B

C

D

E

F

1 🔊 **1.29 Label the photos with the words in the box. Then listen, check and repeat.**

> linguistics geology marine biology
> archaeology psychology conservation

EXAM FOCUS Matching

2 🔊 **1.30 Listen to two conversations and choose the correct answer.**

1 What does the girl want to study in the future?
photo A ☐   photo B ☐   photo D ☐

2 The girl and the boy have both seen one of the documentaries. What was it about?
photo B ☐   photo E ☐   photo F ☐

3 🔊 **1.31 SPEAKING Complete the job descriptions with the jobs in the box. Then listen, check and repeat. Do you know anybody who does one of these jobs? Tell your partner.**

> A linguist   A geologist   A marine biologist
> A psychologist   An archaeologist
> A conservationist

1 _____ studies and often speaks a lot of languages.

2 _____ studies ways of protecting the environment.

3 _____ studies rocks and the history of the Earth.

4 _____ studies how people behave and how their minds work.

5 _____ studies people who lived thousands of years ago.

6 _____ studies, observes and protects oceans.

4 🔊 **1.32 Listen to five speakers talking about why they became scientists. Which job in Exercise 3 does each person do?**

5 🔊 **1.32 Listen again. Match speakers 1–5 with statements A–F. There is one extra statement.**

Speaker 1: ☐   Speaker 3: ☐   Speaker 5: ☐
Speaker 2: ☐   Speaker 4: ☐

A I want to understand how early childhood affects behaviour.

B I'm keen on studying how machines can communicate.

C I want to explore oceans and preserve the ocean environment.

D I'm interested in studying our prehistoric ancestors.

E I want to study the evolution of our planet.

F I want to find solutions to nature's problems.

PRONUNCIATION FOCUS

6 🔊 **1.33 Complete the table. Then listen, check and repeat. Mark the stress.**

Subject	Job
1 archae<u>o</u>logy	*archae<u>o</u>logist*
2 _____	<u>a</u>nalyst
3 conser<u>va</u>tion	_____
4 ge<u>o</u>logy	_____
5 _____	<u>lin</u>guist
6 _____	psy<u>cho</u>logist

7 SPEAKING **Practise the words in Exercise 6 as in the example. Pay attention to the stress.**

A: *What does an archaeologist do?*   **B:** *Archaeology.*

WORD STORE 2D | Collocations

8 🔊 **1.34 Complete WORD STORE 2D with the words in the box. Then listen, check and repeat.**

9 Complete the statements about the speakers with the words and phrases in WORD STORE 2D.

1 The marine biologist wants to collect _____ about global warming.

2 The linguist has published _____ on robot communication.

3 The psychologist loves doing research and analysing _____ .

4 The archaeologist spent _____ in the Egyptian room in the Louvre.

5 The conservationist is doing research into climate change to help protect _____ .

10 SPEAKING **How common is it to study the same subjects as your parents? Think about your friends and family. What will you do? Discuss with a partner.**

1 SPEAKING **Look at the photos of Antarctica. Discuss the questions.**

1 What do you think it's like working there?
2 What kind of jobs do you think people do?

2 **Look at comments from people interested in working in Antarctica. Which of them are suitable in your opinion?**

1 'I don't mind working long hours.' ☐
2 'I don't like the dark.' ☐
3 'I need my own space.' ☐
4 'I'm very fit and healthy.' ☐
5 'I expect to earn lots of money.' ☐
6 'I want to save the planet.' ☐

3 ◄)) 1.35 **Listen to a talk about working in Antarctica. Check your ideas in Exercises 1 and 2.**

4 SPEAKING **Discuss whether you would like to work in Antarctica. Explain why or why not.**

5 **Read an interview with a research scientist and answer the questions.**

1 What is the population of Antarctica?
2 What did Jane Roberts do in her free time in Antarctica?
3 What did she miss most when she was there?

EXAM FOCUS Multiple choice

6 **Read the text again. For questions 1–5, choose the correct answer, A, B, C or D.**

1 The South Pole Station is named after
  A the first person to reach the South Pole.
  B the first person who died after reaching the South Pole.
  C the five people who died after reaching the South Pole.
  D the first two explorers to reach the South Pole.
2 People who work in Antarctica
  A are residents of Antarctica.
  B live in small towns.
  C stay for a period of time in research stations.
  D return to their country in winter.
3 Jane discovered that
  A she likes working in a laboratory.
  B millions of years ago dinosaurs lived on ice.
  C the Antarctic wasn't always cold.
  D research is like doing a jigsaw.
4 The temperature at the South Pole
  A is −80 degrees all year round.
  B is usually above zero in summer.
  C never rises above zero.
  D is too cold to go outside.
5 In the interview, Jane
  A describes her experience of working in Antarctica.
  B encourages tourists to visit Antarctica.
  C explains how researchers apply for jobs in Antarctica.
  D presents her research into the weather in Antarctica.

---

7 ◄)) 1.37 **Match the words in blue in the text with the definitions in the box. Then listen, check and repeat.**

1 several sheets of material on top of one another
  = ___*layers*___
2 the skeleton = _____
3 a place where planes can land = _____
4 organise and manage = _____
5 a place to eat, usually in a school or factory
  = _____
6 a picture cut into small pieces that you put together = _____
7 arrived (at a place) = _____

8 SPEAKING **Complete the questions with the correct form of the words in Exercise 7. Then ask and answer the questions.**

1 How long does it take you to _____ home after school?
2 Do you usually have lunch in the school _____ ?
3 Have you ever completed a 1,000-piece _____ ?
4 Would you like to _____ your own business one day?
5 How many _____ of clothing do you wear when you go outside in winter?
6 Do any museums in your city have dinosaur _____ ?

9 ◄)) 1.38 **Listen to the words and phrases in the box and repeat them. Then complete the text.**

above/below zero   average temperature
(0°) degrees centigrade (Celsius)   plus/minus 10°C
The temperature rises/falls to (+40°/−80°) degrees.

Antarctic weather

The interior of Antarctica is the coldest place on Earth. The hottest month at the South Pole is January with an average temperature of minus 25 [1]_____ centigrade. This is the summer in Antarctica. In fact, the temperature in Antarctica has never risen [2]_____ zero. The warmest temperature ever recorded at the South Pole (on December 25, 2011) was [3]_____ 12.3 degrees [4]_____ . In winter, temperatures [5]_____ to 80 degrees centigrade [6]_____ zero. The coldest month is September.

10 SPEAKING **Tell your partner about the last time you experienced an extreme temperature, hot or cold. Use the questions to prepare.**

1 When did you experience an extreme temperature?
2 Where were you and what were you doing at the time?
3 What was the temperature? How long did it last?
4 How did you manage and what did you do?
5 Do you like extreme temperatures? Why?/Why not?

WORD STORE 2E The temperature

11 ◄)) 1.39 **Complete WORD STORE 2E by arranging the adjectives in order from coldest to hottest. Then listen, check and repeat.**

Science at the **South Pole**

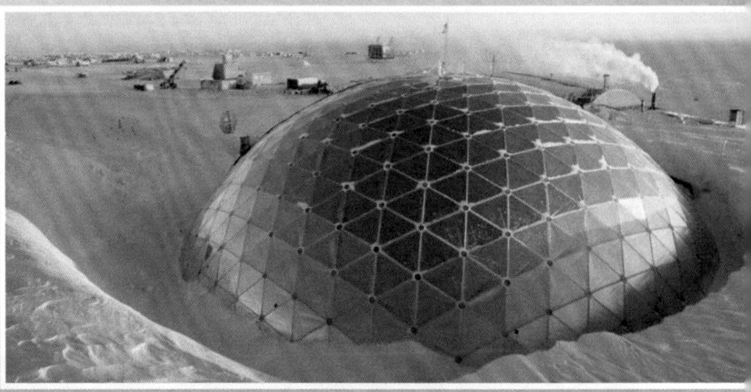

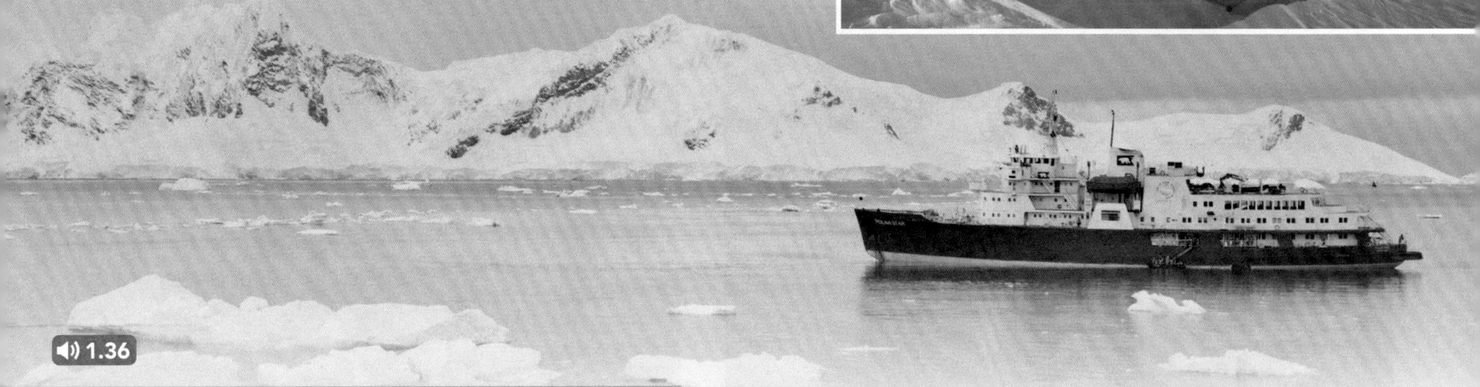

1.36

Jane Roberts is a marine biologist. She worked for two years in Antarctica. Here, she answers your questions.

Is there really a pole at the South Pole?

Yes, there is. It's in front of the Amundsen-Scott South Pole Station. In 1911 a Norwegian explorer called Roald Amundsen was the first person to get there, followed by a British man, Robert Falcon Scott, thirty-four days later. Unfortunately, Scott and his team of five all died on the return journey. When the first explorers **reached** the South Pole there was nothing there. Now, several hundred people work at the Station. There's an **airstrip** for small planes, a **canteen**, hot showers, a post office, a tourist shop, a basketball court and a movie theatre.

Who does Antarctica belong to?

Antarctica doesn't belong to any nation. There's no permanent population, but there are bases that look like small towns. Thirty different countries **run** about seventy research stations in Antarctica. People stay there between three and eighteen months. Most people work only in the summer months, but some stay all year round. The population is around 4,000 in summer and 1,000 in winter.

Why did you want to work in Antarctica?

I was studying in London and I read about an exciting research project in Antarctica. I applied for the job, but thousands of other people also applied. I was lucky!

What exactly were you doing there?

I was doing research into marine life. I collected specimens of ice and examined them in the laboratory. There are **layers** of ice thousands of years old! We found the **remains** of a dinosaur. It was in millions of pieces and we had to put all the pieces together like a **jigsaw**. Our research showed us that millions of years ago the Antarctic was much warmer.

What did you wear in Antarctica?

It's extremely cold all year round. When I was doing experiments outside, I wore three pairs of socks and often five layers of clothing. Winter temperatures fall to −80°C and even summer temperatures are below zero at the South Pole. For several months, there's no sunlight at all. Sometimes it's too cold to go outside.

What did you do in your free time?

When it was snowing, we read lots of books and played games. There isn't much to do in Antarctica, but I enjoy reading and I made some good friends there too.

Did you miss home?

No, but I missed colours – it's very white in Antarctica! But I was working all day and it was really interesting work.

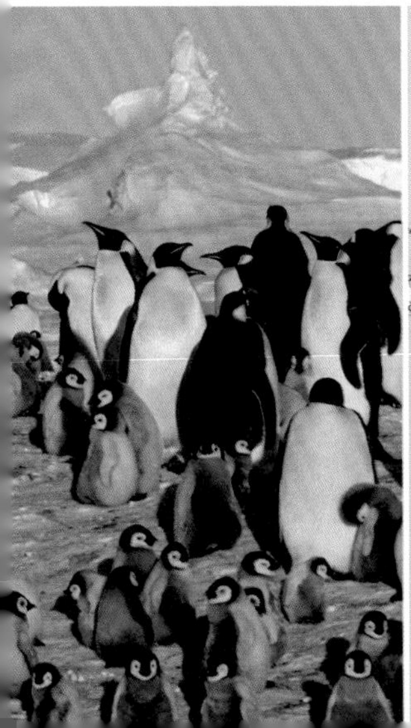

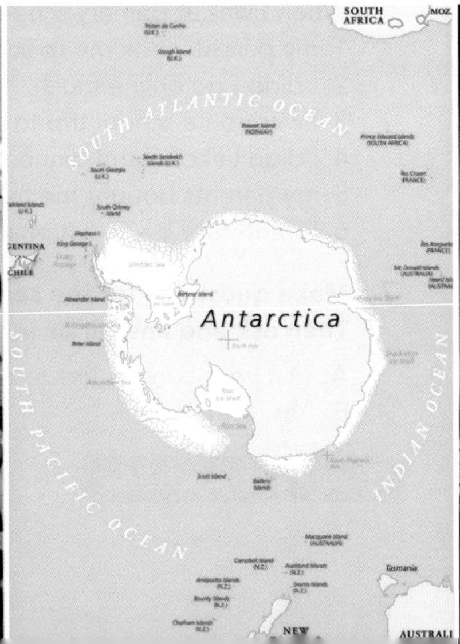

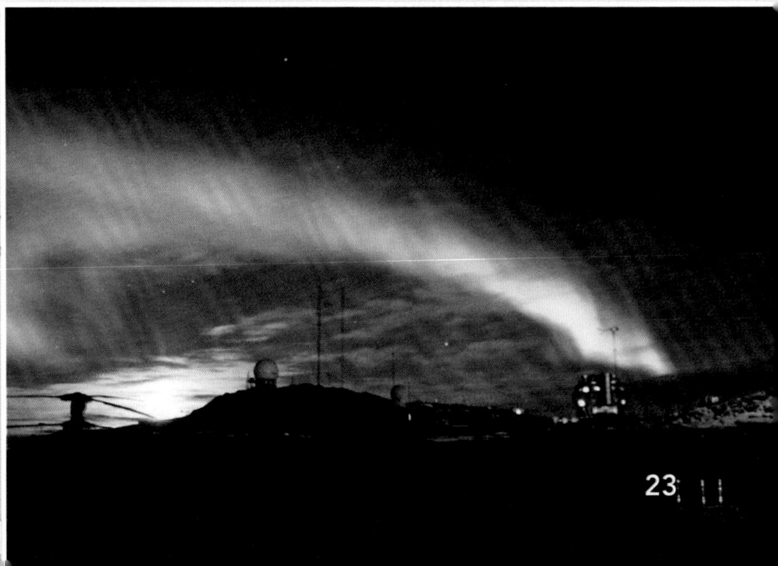

used to

*I can use **used to** to refer to past habits and routines.*

1 SPEAKING **Look at the photos. In what way are these things different today? Discuss with a partner.**

> fashion   friends   music   relationships   school
> technology   travel

2 🔊 **1.40** **Listen to a dialogue between Chris and his granddad. Are the sentences about Chris's granddad true (T) or false (F)?**

1 He used to phone people from the phone in the sitting room. ⬜
2 He used to message people. ⬜
3 He didn't use to live near his friends. ⬜
4 His mum didn't use to like the loud music in his bedroom. ⬜
5 His parents bought him a camera for his sixteenth birthday. ⬜
6 He used to have five or six good friends. ⬜

3 **Read the GRAMMAR FOCUS. Complete the examples using the past forms in blue in Exercise 2.**

GRAMMAR FOCUS

used to

- You use ***used to** + verb* to talk about past states that are no longer true.
  He ¹_____ *have five or six good friends.*

- You use ***used to** + verb* to talk about regular past actions that don't happen anymore.
  He ²_____ *phone people from the phone in the sitting room.*

- You don't use ***used to** + verb* to talk about a past action that only happened once. You use the **Past Simple**.
  His parents ³_____ *him a camera for his sixteenth birthday. (NOT ~~used to buy~~)*

used to + verb

+	I used to work …
–	He didn't use to work …
?	Did they use to work …? Yes, they did./No they didn't.

4 **Complete the sentences with the correct form of the verbs in brackets. Use *used to* + verb or the Present Simple.**

1 People *used to read* (read) maps but now they *use* (use) GPS.
2 People _____ (not/use) their cars much but now they _____ (drive) everywhere.
3 People _____ (update) their online profiles now, but they _____ (write) letters.
4 Children _____ (play) inside now but in the past they _____ (play) outside.
5 Teachers _____ (suggest) books but now they _____ (give out) website addresses.
6 Families _____ (watch) the TV together but now they _____ (watch) it individually.
7 Students _____ (use) Google now, but they _____ (look up) things in encyclopedias.
8 Parents _____ (not/worry) so much but now they _____ (give) children less freedom.

5 SPEAKING **Discuss the statements in Exercise 4. Do you think they are all true?**

6 **Replace the Past Simple with *used to* + verb if possible. Which sentences are true for you?**

When I was at primary school, …
1 my parents took me to school every day.
2 I didn't go online much.
3 I went on a school trip to the Science Museum.
4 I didn't like school dinners.
5 my parents bought me my first mobile phone.
6 I wanted to be an astronaut.

7 **Make questions for the sentences in Exercise 6. Then ask and answer as in the example.**

A: *Did your parents use to take you to school?*
B: *Yes, they did.*

Grammar page 136 ▶

Linkers and time expressions

I can use a range of common linking words and time expressions.

1 🔊 **1.41** SPEAKING **Look at the photo. Discuss what you think the film is about. Use the ideas in the box. Then listen and check.**

> civil rights for black women   computers
> mathematicians   American space projects   robots

2 🔊 **1.41** **Listen again and choose the correct option.**

1 The three women worked for NASA as *mathematicians / astronauts* **during** the 1950s and 60s.

2 **While** they were working for NASA, they earned *more / less* than their white colleagues.

3 Segregation between blacks and whites continued **until** the *mid- / late* 1960s.

4 **When** the film came out, Katherine Johnson – *78 / 98* years old at the time – met the actress who played her.

5 **As soon as** Johnson arrived at the *2016 / 2017* Oscars ceremony, everyone stood up and cheered.

3 **Read the LANGUAGE FOCUS. Complete the information with the words in blue in Exercise 2.**

LANGUAGE FOCUS

Linkers and time expressions

• You use conjunctions **when/while** to link things that happen at the same time. [conjunction + subject + verb]
¹*While they were working for NASA, they earned less than their white colleagues*

• You use conjunctions **after/²_____/before/when** to link things that happen in an order.
[conjunction + subject + verb]
³_____ *the film came out, Johnson met the actress who played her.*

• You use prepositions **during/for/until (till)/by** as follows:
during + noun phrase to say **when** something happens –
⁴_____ *the 1950s and 60s*
until (till) + noun phrase to talk about a state that continues up to a point in time –
Segregation continued ⁵_____ *the mid-1960s.*
by + noun phrase to talk about an action that happens at or before a point in time –
Segregation stopped by the late 1960s.

4 **Choose the correct option. Then change the information to make the sentences true for you.**

1 I haven't been to the cinema *for / during* several weeks.

2 I saw *Hidden Figures during / while* I was on holiday.

3 I learnt a lot about American Civil Rights *during / while* the film.

4 I didn't know that segregation in the USA continued *until / by* 1964.

5 I ate some popcorn *when / after* I was watching the film.

6 *As soon as / While* the film finished, I went home.

5 🔊 **1.42** USE OF ENGLISH **Read the text. Choose the correct answer, A, B or C. Then listen and check.**

KATHERINE JOHNSON

¹*When* Katherine Johnson was a child, she was a maths genius. ²___ she was only 14, she went to university to study Maths. ³___ she was studying at university, her Maths professor told her she should become a research mathematician. ⁴___ she graduated from university she became a teacher. ⁵___ the 1940s she got married and had children. She didn't become a research mathematician ⁶___ she was 35. She got a job as a 'computer' with NASA. Katherine was different from other 'computers' – ⁷___ she was at NASA, she asked a lot of questions. ⁸___ Katherine Johnson started work at NASA, only men went to important meetings. She changed that!

1 A When	B Before	C During
2 A While	B When	C Until
3 A During	B While	C After
4 A Before	B While	C As soon as
5 A Till	B During	C While
6 A until	B by	C during
7 A during	B while	C after
8 A Before	B During	C As soon as

6 **Complete the sentences. Write five true sentences and one false.**

1 While I was going home yesterday, I …

2 As soon as I got home, I …

3 During the evening I …

4 I didn't go to bed until …

5 I was fast asleep by …

7 SPEAKING **Read your sentences in Exercise 6 to your partner for him/her to guess which sentence is false.**

Use of English page 137 ▶

25

WRITING

2.7

A story

I can write a story with a simple linear sequence.

1 SPEAKING **Tell your partner about a surprising or interesting thing that happened to you on holiday.**

Say:
1 where and when it happened.
2 how old you were.
3 what you were doing when it happened.

2 **Read Paul's story and choose the best title, A, B or C.**

A The Holiday of a Lifetime
B Surprise by the Sea
C Beautiful Cornwall

I was twelve years old and my parents and I were on holiday in Cornwall. They are both biologists and we all love nature. One morning, Dad suggested walking along the beach to a distant village.

It was a lovely day for a walk, but after an hour, I noticed some dark clouds. I asked my parents if they thought we should go back. They smiled at each other, and then Mum said we were nearly there.

What was going on? Mum usually made me go indoors during storms. What's more, we were still far away from the village. <u>Anyway</u>, suddenly, there was loud thunder and it started to rain. "Come on, quick!" my father said. "We're almost there."

I noticed a cottage not far away. Dad started running towards it <u>so</u> we ran after him. When we got there, he seemed really excited, which <u>I must admit</u> was a bit strange. Unfortunately, there was no one home. 'That's unlucky,' said Dad 'but wait...' Suddenly, he took a key from his pocket, unlocked the door and pushed it open. He was silent for a moment. Then with a smile he said: "Come in. And welcome home!" What a surprise!

<u>In fact</u>, thinking back to my parents' behaviour <u>during</u> the first part of our holiday, I knew something strange was going on – but I had no idea what! Our new holiday home was the perfect place for nature lovers. It was awesome!

We still live in London, but our cottage in Cornwall is our dream house, and I will never forget the day I first saw it.

3 **Read the story again and put events in the correct order.**

a Nobody answered the door. ☐
b The weather changed. ☐
c The family went into their new holiday home. ☐
d The family went to Cornwall on holiday. ☐
e Paul saw a cottage in the distance. ☐
f The family went for a walk along the coast. ☐

4 **Read the WRITING FOCUS. Complete the examples with the words in purple in the story.**

WRITING FOCUS

A story

• Set the scene:
  I ¹<u>was twelve years</u> old when …
  It was late in the evening when …
  It ²_____ a walk.
  I was in the classroom when …

• Use questions, short dramatic sentences and occasional exclamation marks to show surprise or excitement:
  What was ³_____ on?
  What a ⁴_____ !
  What a nightmare!
  It was ⁵_____ !
  We were in trouble.

• Use adverbs to add interest:
  All of a sudden, / ⁶_____, / ⁷_____, / Luckily,
  … really (good)
  … incredibly (beautiful)
  … completely (lost)

• Use a summarising statement to begin or end your story:
  I'll never forget ⁸_____ I first saw … /
  the time I decided to … / when I first went … /
  … was an event I'll never forget.

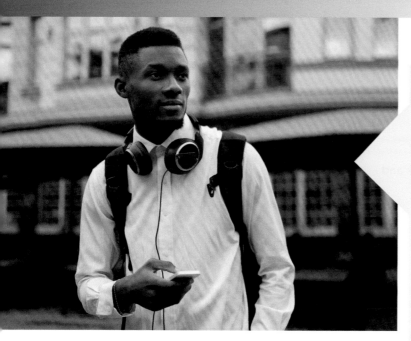

5 Read the extracts from different stories. Find and correct three mistakes in each.

1 I was 14 years old then I first became interested in archaeology. I was looking for fossils one Sunday afternoon when I made the discovery that made me famous. I am never forget the feeling of seeing it there in the ground for the first time. It was awesome?

2 We were in the Chemistry lab at school when we noticed the strange smell. All of a suddenly, there was a loud bang. What is going on? Our teacher walked in from a lab next to ours. Her hair was a mess and her glasses were black with smoke. Lucky, she was more shocked than hurt. 'What happened, Miss?' asked one of my classmates.

3 The school trip to the science museum is a day I'll never remember. We had a great time at the museum. When we were going back to meet the others at the bus to go home, my friend and I got stuck in a lift. The lights went off and the alarm didn't work. We were on trouble. What we were going to do?

6 SPEAKING Choose one of the extracts in Exercise 5 and say what you think happened next.

7 Complete the LANGUAGE FOCUS with the underlined linkers in the story.

LANGUAGE FOCUS

Informal linkers

In narrative stories we often use:
- *I have to say* or [1]*I must admit* to emphasise the next piece of information.
- *Anyhow* or [2]_____ to change the subject or move the story on.
- *Actually* or [3]_____ to show that the next piece of information is surprising.
- *And, but, because,* [4]_____ to join parts of sentences.
- *Then, when, while,* [5]_____ to make the order of events clear.

8 Read the story and choose the correct option.

'This is a bad start', I thought and looked again at the directions on my phone. I was trying to find the city hospital for my first day of work experience in the IT department there. Unfortunately, I was very late and totally lost.

[1]*I have to say/Anyhow* it was my fault. I forgot to check the route the day before. [2]*During/Anyway*, my phone said to turn right, but [3]*in fact/I have to say* there was no right turn, just a wall! What was I going to do? I was already ten minutes late. 'Go back to the main road and try again,' I thought 'and go quickly!' I hurried along as fast as I could. I was turning a corner [4]*then/when* suddenly there was a bang [5]*and/so* everything went black.

[6]*When/I must admit* I opened my eyes, there were four worried faces looking down at me. 'Are you alright?' 'Yes, I think so', I said. My head hurt. [7]*Then/While* I remembered the bang and the darkness. 'What happened?'

'Well, you were hurrying along looking at your phone, and you bumped into that tree. We thought you should go to hospital so we've called an ambulance.'

Luckily, the doctor said I was fine. [8]*Anyway/I must admit* that was not how I expected to arrive at the hospital for my first day of work experience!

SHOW WHAT YOU'VE LEARNT

9 Do the writing task. Use the ideas in the WRITING FOCUS and the LANGUAGE FOCUS to help you.

Your teacher has asked you to write a story ending with: *I was so relieved. It was finally over!*

Use the questions below to help you.
- Where were you?
- When was it?
- Who was with you?
- What happened?
- What could you see and hear?
- How did you feel?
- What did you do next?
- How did it end?

Remember to:
- give your story a title.
- make your story interesting for the reader.
- give your story a strong ending.

It was a chilly autumn morning …

2.8

Telling a story

I can tell a story and show interest in someone's story.

1 SPEAKING Look at the photo of Tom. Then ask and answer the questions.

1 Where was Tom?
2 What was he doing?
3 What was the problem?

2 ◀))1.43 Read and listen to the story. Compare your ideas in Exercise 1.

Lisa: Hi Tom. How was your holiday in Australia?
Tom: It was really good, thanks ... except for the day I nearly died. ⌉¹
Lisa: What happened?
Tom: I was doing some climbing. <u>At first</u> the sun <u>was shining</u> and I was enjoying myself. ⌉²
But <u>all of a sudden</u> the weather changed. It became really foggy and I couldn't see the path. ⌉³
Lisa: Oh dear, <u>that sounds frightening</u>.
Tom: I was pretty worried. I continued for a while, but finally I realised I was lost.
Lisa: What did you do?
Tom: <u>Fortunately</u>, I had my phone with me so I called my father – 9,000 miles away in England! He called the Australian police and told them where I was. Then they called me. <u>Unfortunately</u>, my battery went dead after five seconds. It was dark and cold. I sat under a rock, put on my torch and waited. ⌉⁴
Lisa: Oh no, <u>what a nightmare</u>!
Tom: <u>Eventually</u>, they found me. I was so relieved. I used to go climbing on my own all the time, but <u>I'll never do it again</u>. ⌉⁵

3 There are often five stages in a story. Match stages 1–5 in Tom's story with headings a–e below.

a background ☐ d problem ☐
b final comment ☐ e main events ☐
c introduction ☐

4 Read the SPEAKING FOCUS. Complete the examples with the underlined phrases in the story in Exercise 2.

SPEAKING FOCUS

Telling a story

Use the right tenses
- Past Continuous for the 'background':
  The sun ¹<u>was shining</u> and I was enjoying myself.
- Past Simple for the 'problem' and the 'main events':
  The weather changed. I couldn't see the path.

Use linkers
- **Beginning:** To start with/At ²_____
- **Middle:** Suddenly/All of a ³_____/Luckily/ Fortunately/⁴_____
- **End:** In the end/Finally/⁵_____

Say how you felt
I was excited/frightened/surprised/shocked/worried, etc.

Make a 'final comment'
It was the best/worst day of my life!
I'll never forget the look on his face!
I'll never ⁶_____ .

Listening to a story

Neutral response
Really?/Oh dear./Oh no.

Strong response
That sounds amazing/funny/⁷_____ .
What a great story/⁸a _____ !

Respond with questions
What happened?   What did you do?

5 Follow the instructions to prepare your story.

1 Choose a topic from the box or one of your own ideas.

> a dangerous situation   a mistake
> some good or bad news   some good or bad luck
> a nice surprise   something that happened on holiday
> a problem with technology

2 Think about what you are going to say and make notes under the headings for the five stages of a story in Exercise 3.

6 SPEAKING Follow the instructions below to practise telling your stories. Then act out your dialogue to the class.

Student A: Use your notes in Exercise 5 to tell the story.
Student B: Use the SPEAKING FOCUS to respond to what Student A says.

ROLE-PLAY   Telling a story

▶10 Watch the video and practise. Then role-play your dialogue.

2.1 Vocabulary 🔊 4.9

astronomer /əˈstrɒnəmə/
astronomy /əˈstrɒnəmi/
biologist /baɪˈɒlədʒɪst/
biology /baɪˈɒlədʒi/
broadband /ˈbrɔːdbænd/
camera /ˈkæmərə/
chemist /ˈkemɪst/
chemistry /ˈkeməstri/
collect specimens /kəˌlekt ˈspesəmənz/
computer science /kəmˈpjuːtə ˌsaɪəns/
computer scientist /kəmˌpjuːtə ˈsaɪəntɪst/
desktop computer /ˌdesktɒp kəmˈpjuːtə/
develop a theory /dɪˌveləp ə ˈθɪəri/
digital /ˈdɪdʒətl/
discover /dɪsˈkʌvə/
do an experiment /ˌduː ən ɪkˈsperɪmənt/
do research /ˌduː rɪˈsɜːtʃ/
download music /ˌdaʊnˌləʊd ˈmjuːzɪk/
gravity /ˈɡrævəti/
invent /ɪnˈvent/
keyboard /ˈkiːbɔːd/
laptop /ˈlæptɒp/
laser printer /ˈleɪzə ˌprɪntə/
mathematician /ˌmæθəməˈtɪʃən/
mathematics /ˌmæθəˈmætɪks/
mouse /maʊs/
observe /əbˈzɜːv/
password /ˈpɑːswɜːd/
physicist /ˈfɪzəsɪst/
physics /ˈfɪzɪks/
planet /ˈplænət/
science /ˈsaɪəns/
scientist /ˈsaɪəntɪst/
screen /skriːn/
search engine /ˈsɜːtʃ ˌendʒən/
smartphone /ˈsmɑːtfəʊn/
take measurements /ˌteɪk ˈmeʒəmənts/
take notes /ˌteɪk ˈnəʊts/
text message /ˈtekst ˌmesɪdʒ/
update your profile /ʌpˌdeɪt jɔː ˈprəʊfaɪl/
username /ˈjuːzəneɪm/
visit a website /ˌvɪzət ə ˈwebsaɪt/
web browser /ˈweb ˌbraʊzə/

2.2 Grammar 🔊 4.10

arrive /əˈraɪv/
burn yourself /ˈbɜːn jəˌself/
carriage /ˈkærɪdʒ/
coast /kəʊst/
crash /kræʃ/
direct sunlight /daɪˈrekt ˈsʌnlaɪt/
e-book /ˈiː bʊk/
E ink /ˈiː ɪŋk/
electronic /ˌelɪkˈtrɒnɪk/
e-reader /ˈiː ˌriːdə/
get dark /ˌɡet ˈdɑːk/
get home /ˌɡet ˈhəʊm/
hill /hɪl/
imagine /ɪˈmædʒɪn/
reach towards /ˌriːtʃ təˈwɔːdz/
reply /rɪˈplaɪ/

researcher /rɪˈsɜːtʃə/
rough /rʌf/
servant /ˈsɜːvənt/
silver cross /ˌsɪlvə ˈkrɒs/
text sb /ˈtekst ˌsʌmbɒdi/
thick forest /ˌθɪk ˈfɒrəst/
vision /ˈvɪʒən/
wake up /ˌweɪk ˈʌp/

2.3 Listening 🔊 4.11

affect /əˈfekt/
analyse data/evidence /ˌænəlaɪz ˈdeɪtə/ ˈevədəns/
analysis /əˈnæləsəs/
ancestor /ˈænsəstə/
archaeologist /ˌɑːkiˈɒlədʒɪst/
archaeology /ˌɑːkiˈɒlədʒi/
collect data/evidence /kəˌlekt ˈdeɪtə / ˈevədəns/
conservation /ˌkɒnsəˈveɪʃən/
conservationist /ˌkɒnsəˈveɪʃənɪst/
discovery /dɪsˈkʌvəri/
environment /ɪnˈvaɪrənmənt/
evolution /ˌiːvəˈluːʃən/
exploration /ˌekspləˈreɪʃən/
explore /ɪkˈsplɔː/
find a solution /ˌfaɪnd ə səˈluːʃən/
geologist /dʒiˈɒlədʒɪst/
geology /dʒiˈɒlədʒi/
global warming /ˌɡləʊbəl ˈwɔːmɪŋ/
linguist /ˈlɪŋɡwɪst/
linguistics /lɪŋˈɡwɪstɪks/
marine biologist /məˌriːn baɪˈɒlədʒəst/
marine biology /məˌriːn baɪˈɒlədʒi/
observation /ˌɒbzəˈveɪʃən/
protect the environment /prəˌtekt ði ɪnˈvaɪrənmənt/
protection /prəˈtekʃən/
psychologist /saɪˈkɒlədʒɪst/
psychology /saɪˈkɒlədʒi/
publish a research paper/evidence /ˌpʌblɪʃ ə rɪˈsɜːtʃ ˌpeɪpə/ˈevədəns/
solution /səˈluːʃən/
solve /sɒlv/
spend hours /ˌspend ˈaʊəz/
technology /tekˈnɒlədʒi/

2.4 Reading 🔊 4.12

above zero /əˌbʌv ˈzɪərəʊ/
airstrip /ˈeəstrɪp/
average temperature /ˌævərɪdʒ ˈtemprətʃə/
below zero /bɪˌləʊ ˈzɪərəʊ/
boiling /ˈbɔɪlɪŋ/
canteen /kænˈtiːn/
chilly /ˈtʃɪli/
cold /kəʊld/
degree centigrade /dɪˌɡriː ˈsentəɡreɪd/
fall /fɔːl/
freezing /ˈfriːzɪŋ/
hot /hɒt/
jigsaw /ˈdʒɪɡsɔː/
layer /ˈleɪə/
own (adj) /əʊn/
permanent /ˈpɜːmənənt/

plus/minus 25 degrees /ˈplʌs/ˈmaɪnəs ˈtwenti ˈfaɪv di ˈɡriːz/
reach home/the South Pole /ˌriːtʃ ˈhəʊm/ðə saʊθ ˈpəʊl/
recorded /rɪˈkɔːdɪd/
remains /rɪˈmeɪnz/
return to /rɪˈtɜːn tə/
rise /raɪz/
run a business/research station /ˌrʌn ə ˈbɪznəs/rɪˈsɜːtʃ ˈsteɪʃən/
save /seɪv/
the dark /ðə dɑːk/
warm /wɔːm/

2.5 Grammar 🔊 4.13

astronaut /ˈæstrənɔːt/
give out /ˌɡɪv ˈaʊt/
GPS /ˌdʒiː piː ˈes/
mobile phone /ˌməʊbaɪl ˈfəʊn/
inside /ɪnˈsaɪd/
outside /aʊtˈsaɪd/

2.6 Use of English 🔊 4.14

cheer /tʃɪə/
civil rights /ˌsɪvəl ˈraɪts/
fast asleep /ˌfɑːst əˈsliːp/
graduate from /ˈɡrædʒueɪt frəm/
look up /ˌlʊk ˈʌp/
space /speɪs/
stand up /ˌstænd ˈʌp/

2.7 Writing 🔊 4.15

distant /ˈdɪstənt/
loud thunder /laʊd ˈθʌndə/
fossils /ˈfɒsəlz/
get stuck /ɡet stʌk/
lift /lɪft/
directions /daɪˈrekʃənz/
route /ruːt/
turn a corner /tɜːn ə ˈkɔːnə/

2.8 Speaking 🔊 4.16

all of a sudden /ˌɔːl əv ə ˈsʌdn/
frightened /ˈfraɪtnd/
go dead /ˌɡəʊ ˈded/
nightmare /ˈnaɪtmeə/
put on /ˌpʊt ˈɒn/
shocked /ʃɒkt/
surprised /səˈpraɪzd/
torch /tɔːtʃ/

FOCUS REVIEW 2

VOCABULARY AND GRAMMAR

1 Complete the sentences with the correct form of the verbs in the box. There is one extra verb.

collect develop discover do invent
observe take

1 Edwin Hubble (1889–1953), an American astronomer, _____ galaxies through a telescope.
2 Last month the scientists _____ specimens of some sea spiders from Antarctica.
3 Make sure you _____ notes when we are at the museum.
4 Do you know who _____ the electric guitar?
5 This month two teams of archaeology students _____ research in South Africa.
6 Linguists and psychologists are cooperating to _____ a new theory of language learning.

2 Complete the sentences with the correct form of the words in capitals.

1 Mr Marco works as a _____ at the University of Alaska. **PHYSICS**
2 We all tried to find the best _____ to the problem. **SOLVE**
3 I want to study _____ at university. **CHEMIST**
4 A _____ is someone who works to protect plants and animals. **CONSERVE**
5 Take _____ of your desk before you buy a new computer screen. **MEASURE**
6 The cost of space _____ is very high. **EXPLORE**

3 Use the prompts to write sentences.

1 My computer / crash / while / I / download / a song.
2 Tom / lose / his smartphone / when / he / run / in the park.
3 The first international Internet chat / take place / in February 1989.
4 It / be / so hot yesterday. The temperature / rise / to 38 degrees Celsius.
5 What / you / do / this time last year?
6 I / wait / for the photos from Sandra / last night / but / she / not / send / me any.

4 Choose the correct option.

1 Broadband Internet *didn't use to be / weren't* so popular in the 1980s.
2 Did your grandparents *use to buy / buy* a black and white television in the 1960s?
3 We *did / used to do* a lot of exercises last weekend.
4 My brother *used to spend / was spending* a few hours a day online.
5 Last winter the temperature *used to fall / fell* to minus 28 degrees Celsius.
6 *Did they use to use / Did they use* GPS when they were climbing in the Alps?

USE OF ENGLISH

5 Choose the answer, A, B or C, that is closest in meaning to the underlined words.

1 NASA is running a project on using 3D printers to make food in space.
   A is analysing   B is organising
   C is planning
2 When Anton was a student, he applied for his first job.
   A studied   B was studying
   C used to study
3 Lack of water is a permanent problem in this country.
   A a problem that is always there
   B a problem that is sometimes there
   C a new problem
4 X: When I was a child, I was in a serious car accident and I spent a month in hospital.
   Y: What a nightmare!
   A What a great story!
   B That sounds frightening!
   C Really? That's cool!
5 My sister got lost in the forest, but, luckily, she managed to phone for help.
   A suddenly
   B eventually
   C fortunately
6 We analysed the data while we were talking online.
   A before the online talk
   B after the online talk
   C during the online talk

6 Choose the correct answer, A, B or C, to complete both sentences.

1 She ___ for her bag and took out the phone.
   We ___ home late in the afternoon.
   A asked
   B arrived
   C reached
2 They haven't published their research ___ yet.
   How much ___ do we need to print the documents?
   A paper
   B report
   C ink
3 The radio has warned of ___ temperatures today.
   Cook the pasta in ___ water for about 10 minutes.
   A freezing
   B boiling
   C high
4 I can't believe you've bought a desktop ___ !
   To be a ___ scientist you have to be good at maths.
   A rocket
   B computer
   C space
5 As ___ as they discovered the cave, they started exploring it.
   They reached the top too ___ and spent hours waiting for the sunrise.
   A soon
   B early
   C fast

READING

7 Read three texts about science and technology. Choose the correct answer, A, B or C.

Underwater forest

Several years ago, scuba diver Chas Broughton discovered an underwater forest of massive ancient cypress trees. Located twenty kilometres from the coast of Alabama, in the Gulf of Mexico, it is home for thousands of sea animals. Chas told a local journalist about the discovery, but they kept it secret until 2004, when Hurricane Ivan uncovered some of the trees. Then scientists started exploring the area.

They have suggested that the forest is more than 50,000 years old. In the past, the ocean level in the area was 125 metres lower than today, but when it rose, the water swallowed the trees up. The forest is so unique that conservationists are now working to make it a marine protected area.

1 The scientists
  A found out about the discovery from a local journalist.
  B started visiting the area after the 2004 hurricane.
  C are trying to protect the forest.

Your ideas in 3-D

Are you interested in 3-D printing but don't want to buy another expensive gadget?

Then this offer is for you! Our 3-D printing service will help you produce a figure from your favourite video game, parts for a robot you are building in your basement, beautiful jewellery or decorations for your home. Just choose a design from our catalogue or create your own, decide what material, size and colour you want and send your project to us.

We will print the object and send it to you in no time!
For more information visit our website at:
www.weprint3d.com

2 The advertisement is addressed to people who
  A want to buy a 3-D printer.
  B are professional designers.
  C want to use 3-D printing technology.

Last week I took part in an unusual survey. A psychologist invited forty-four families and asked us different questions about eating habits now and in the past. She wanted to find out why fathers give children less healthy food than mothers. Strange, isn't it? But it's true in my family.

When my mum isn't at home for dinner, Dad orders a pizza. Mum doesn't accept unhealthy food because she feels responsible for what we eat. Dad cares more about my education or hobbies.

According to the survey, in most families the situation was and is similar. Teenagers observe their parents and learn how to behave in the future. My parents used to observe their parents and now I am observing them.

3 The survey the writer took part in shows that
  A mothers and fathers look after families in different ways.
  B fathers don't care about families as much as mothers.
  C teenagers would like to change eating habits in their families.

SPEAKING

8 In pairs, complete the questions with one word in each gap. The first letters are given. Then ask and answer the questions.
  1 W_____ do you use the Internet for?
  2 Do you use s_____ media? Why?/Why not?
  3 What i_____ do you find the most useful? Why?
  4 What were you doing y_____ at 8 p.m.?

9 In pairs, write down five words to describe the photo.

10 Imagine you are one of the people in the photo. Answer the questions.
  1 When was it?
  2 What was the weather like?
  3 Who were you with?
  4 What were you doing? What happened?
  5 How did you feel about it in the end?

11 When was the last time you got lost? What happened? Discuss with a partner.

WRITING

12 Read the writing task and write the story.

You agreed to write a story for the *Me and Technology* section of your school newspaper. The title of your story is: *The day technology saved me.* Remember to:

- explain when and where the situation happened.
- describe the events and show their sequence using the correct past tenses.
- make the story interesting for the reader.
- give your story an interesting ending.

3

The arts

Beauty is in the eye of the beholder.

A proverb

BBC

THE MUSKETEERS

▶ 11 Watch the BBC video.
For the worksheet, go to page 120.

VOCABULARY

Watching habits • TV programmes
• adjectives • elements of a film/TV drama

*I can use language related to films,
film-making and TV.*

SHOW WHAT YOU KNOW

1 **Put the words and phrases in the box under an appropriate verb.**

> the telly   Internet radio stations   my favourite rock album
> ~~blogs on my laptop~~   fashion magazines   horror movies
> music on my mobile   e-books   YouTube clips

Read	Watch	Listen to
blogs on my laptop		

2 SPEAKING **Think of three more words and phrases for each verb. Which of them do you do? Tell your partner.**

I read blogs on my laptop.

One episode is never enough

I have an <u>embarrassing</u> confession to make – I am a TV binge watcher! Of course I don't mean traditional TV programmes – **documentaries**, **chat shows**, **reality TV** and the old **soap operas** my grandmother likes to watch. They're boring. No – I mean the on-demand TV series that are so <u>engaging</u> and <u>addictive</u>.

When I was a teenager, before on-demand TV, I was a bookworm. I used to sit down with a <u>gripping</u> novel, and read chapter after chapter, sometimes a whole book in a day. Now, I'm twenty-seven and I do the same with TV.

3 SPEAKING **Complete the sentences to make them true for you. Then discuss your TV habits with a partner.**

1 I usually watch TV *with my family / on my own / …*
2 I watch most TV programmes *live / on demand / …*
3 I usually watch TV programmes on *my phone / the TV / …*
4 Each day I watch TV for around *fifteen minutes / one hour /…*
5 I also watch other things such as *YouTube clips / music videos / …*
6 My favourite TV programme at the moment is
_____ .

4 **Read the text. What is a 'TV binge watcher'?**

5 SPEAKING **Discuss the questions.**

1 Are you a TV binge watcher?
2 What's the longest single time you've ever spent watching TV?
3 What is the best TV series you've ever seen?

TV audiences are becoming more difficult to please, so TV channels are producing better dramas more quickly. The best drama series have complex plots and fascinating characters. I just have to watch the next episode.

My greatest weakness? I really like dramas that are funny and moving with brilliant acting. But my absolute favourite type of series is **fantasy** or **science fiction**. I love the imaginative costumes and amazing special effects. The series I watch on TV are excellent. I never go to the cinema these days.

WORD STORE 3A | TV programmes

6 🔊 1.44 **Complete WORD STORE 3A with the words in red from the text. Then listen, check and repeat.**

7 SPEAKING **Think of an example of each type of TV programme in WORD STORE 3A. Which programmes do you never/rarely/sometimes/often binge watch? Tell your partner.**

WORD STORE 3B | Adjectives

8 🔊 1.45 **Complete WORD STORE 3B with the underlined adjectives in the text. Add a translation. Then listen and repeat.**

9 **Put the adjectives from WORD STORE 3B on the line according to how positive or negative you think they are. Some can be both, depending on the context.**

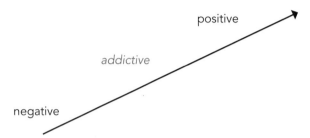

positive

addictive

negative

WORD STORE 3C | Elements of a film/TV drama

10 🔊 1.46 **Complete WORD STORE 3C only with vowels. Use these definitions to help you. What is the mystery word? Listen, check and repeat.**

1 artificially created images or sound in a drama
2 what actors do in a drama
3 clothes an actor wears
4 the events in the story of a drama
5 the written words of a drama
6 the main people in a drama
7 the place where or time when a drama happens
8 the music that is played during a drama
9 the way a drama finishes

11 🔊 1.47 **Listen to Lucy talking about her favourite TV series and write her answers. Then listen again and check.**

1 What is your favourite TV series?
_____

2 How or where do you watch it?
_____

3 How many episodes have you watched?
_____

4 What kind of series is it?
_____

5 What is the setting?
_____

6 What is the plot or main storyline?
_____

7 What do you like most about it?
_____

12 SPEAKING **Discuss your favourite TV series using the questions in Exercise 11.**

GRAMMAR

3.2

Comparative and superlative adjectives

I can use all forms of comparative and superlative adjectives to make comparisons.

1 🔊 **1.48** **Do the Quick Culture Quiz. Then listen and check.**

QUICK CULTURE QUIZ

True or False?

① Shakespeare's play *Romeo and Juliet* isn't as long as *Hamlet*. ☐

② Singer Mariah Carey has a **better** vocal range **than** Christina Aguilera. ☐

③ **The biggest** music festival in the world is the Glastonbury Festival in the UK. ☐

④ **The best-selling** film soundtrack of all time is *The Bodyguard*. ☐

⑤ The Palace Museum in Beijing is **a bit busier than** the Musée du Louvre in Paris. ☐

⑥ The *Harry Potter* films were **far more expensive** to make **than** *Pirates of the Caribbean*. ☐

2 **Read the GRAMMAR FOCUS. Complete the examples using the comparative and superlative adjectives in blue in Exercise 1.**

GRAMMAR FOCUS

Comparative and superlative adjectives

	Comparative	Superlative
Short adjectives long big busy	longer (than) bigger (than) ² _____ (than)	the longest ¹ _____ the busiest
Long adjectives expensive	³ _____ expensive (than)	the most expensive
Irregular adjectives good bad far	⁴ _____ (than) worse (than) further (than)	the best the worst the furthest

- You use **(just) as + adjective + as** to say things are equal and you use **not as + adjective + as** to make negative comparisons.
  Romeo and Juliet isn't ⁵_____ *long as Hamlet.*
  = Hamlet is longer than Romeo and Juliet.
- You use **a bit** or **much/far** to modify comparisons.

3 **Complete the table with the comparative and superlative forms of the adjectives in the box.**

bad far fat funny high lucky
popular simple talented thin

SPELLING RULE	COMPARATIVE ADJECTIVES	SUPERLATIVE ADJECTIVES
Add *-er / -r*	*higher*	
Double letter + *-er*		
Delete *-y*, add *-ier*		
more + adjective		
Irregular		

4 SPEAKING **Complete the questions with the comparative or superlative forms of the adjectives in brackets. Then discuss the questions.**

1 What is __the worst__ (bad) song you've ever heard?
2 What band is _____ (great) than the Beatles?
3 What is _____ (thick) book you've ever read?
4 Where is _____ (near) theatre to your house?
5 Is it _____ (good) to watch a concert live or on telly?
6 Where is _____ (exciting) nightlife in your city?
7 Who is _____ (funny) – your mother or your father?

5 SPEAKING **Complete the statements with *as*, *more*, *the* or *than*. Then discuss the statements.**

1 Music downloads are a bit cheaper __than__ CDs.
2 Jazz is not as popular _____ rock.
3 American pop music is _____ best in the world.
4 Live music is far _____ exciting than recorded music.
5 Lady Gaga is just _____ talented as Adele.
6 Male actors usually have much more interesting roles _____ female actors.
7 The violin is _____ most difficult instrument to play.
8 Who is _____ most talented musician among your friends?

6 SPEAKING **Make sentences comparing things now with the same things five years ago. Use the prompts. Then compare your sentences with a partner.**

cinema tickets pop music mobile phones sharing videos	is are	a bit much just as not as	cheap/ expensive good/bad big/small easy/difficult	than as	five years ago

Cinema tickets are a bit more expensive than five years ago.

Grammar page 138

LISTENING

3.3

Multiple choice

I can understand the key points about a radio programme on a familiar topic.

1 SPEAKING Discuss the questions. Use the words and phrases in the table.

1 What kind of art do you like/not like?
2 When was the last time you saw some art?
3 Where did you go and what did you see?

Type of artist	painter photographer sculptor
Type of art	black and white photographs classic oil paintings landscapes modern abstract paintings portraits sculpture street art
Where to see it	at a museum in an art gallery in public places pasted on walls and buildings

A
Brazil – the 'favelas' (slums)

B
Paris – the city centre

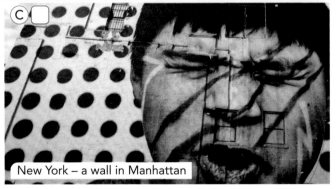

C
New York – a wall in Manhattan

2 SPEAKING Look at three works of art (A–C) by French street artist JR. Which words in Exercise 1 can you use to describe his work?

3 🔊 1.49 Listen to a radio programme about JR and check your ideas in Exercise 2. Number the photos (A–C) in the order in which you hear about them.

EXAM FOCUS Multiple choice

4 🔊 1.49 Listen to the radio programme again. For questions 1–6, choose the correct answer, A, B or C.

1 Katy West is
   A a guest artist of the week.
   B an artist in her studio.
   C the editor of a photography magazine.
2 Because most of his work is illegal, JR
   A doesn't want people to know his name.
   B doesn't want people to see his face.
   C uses his full name.
3 JR prefers to have exhibitions in
   A the Pompidou Centre in Paris.
   B public places.
   C art galleries and museums.
4 In Brazil he took photographs of women because
   A they have beautiful eyes.
   B the rest of the world wants to hear their story.
   C they don't have a chance to tell their story.
5 He pastes portraits of
   A famous people on buildings.
   B unusual people in ordinary places.
   C ordinary people in surprising places.
6 Which statement describes JR and his work?
   A He is interested in people and their identity.
   B He wants to have exhibitions everywhere.
   C He only likes taking photographs of women.

5 SPEAKING Discuss the questions.

1 What photos or pictures do you see every day?
2 What kind of pictures are they and what/who are the subjects?

PRONUNCIATION FOCUS

6 🔊 1.50 Complete the table. Then listen and repeat. Mark the stressed syllable for each word. In which cases does the word stress change syllable?

Country	Nationality	Country	Nationality
1 Brazil	*Brazilian*	4 Mexico	_____
2 Italy	_____	5 Hungary	_____
3 Egypt	_____	6 Poland	_____

WORD STORE 3D | Art and artists ⟩

7 🔊 1.51 Complete WORD STORE 3D with the words in the box. Then listen, check and repeat.

READING

3.4

Matching

I can understand the main points in simple descriptive text on a familiar topic.

1 **◀))1.52 Translate these types of books. Use a dictionary if necessary.**

1 autobiography = _____
2 biography = _____
3 classic novel = _____
4 comic book = _____
5 crime novel = _____
6 fairy tale = _____
7 fantasy novel = _____
8 historical fiction = _____
9 horror fiction = _____
10 poem = _____
11 science fiction = _____
12 short story = _____
13 thriller = _____

2 **SPEAKING Discuss your taste in books. Use the phrases and the words in Exercise 1.**

• I love … • I'm into … • I quite like …
• I'm not into … • I can't stand …

3 **SPEAKING Read the list of comic book and film superheroes and their special superpowers. Discuss the questions.**

1 Which superheroes have you read about/seen in films?
2 Which superpower would you most like to have?

SUPERHEROES
AND THEIR SUPERPOWERS

Captain America never gets tired.

Batman is super intelligent.

Hulk is super strong.

X-men can mutate (change shape), control the weather or read minds.

Hulk

Wonder Woman can fly and is super fast.

Spiderman can shoot spider webs from his wrists.

Iron Man is super strong, can fly and become invisible.

Superman is super strong, can fly and has X-ray vision.

4 **Read the article about superhero films and choose the best title.**

1 It's a hard life being a superhero
2 Why we love superheroes
3 The psychology of a superhero fan

---

5 **Read the article again. Match questions 1–6 with paragraphs A–E that answer the questions. There is one extra question.**

1 How do we know that superhero movies are popular?
2 Why are superhero movies and westerns different?
3 Why are superhero movies so popular?
4 Which superheroes had problems before becoming stronger?
5 What are typical storylines for superhero movies?
6 Which superheroes show that they are weak?

6 **SPEAKING Discuss questions 1–6 in Exercise 5.**

7 **◀))1.54 Match the words in blue in the article with the definitions. Then listen, check and repeat.**

1 all the most popular or famous film stars, musicians, etc. = ____*A-list*____
2 a book or film that is very good or successful = _____
3 the place in a theatre, cinema, etc. where tickets are sold = _____
4 images made using computer programs = _____
5 a particular type of art, writing, music, etc. = _____
6 an advertisement for a new film or television show = _____

8 **Complete the sentences with the words in blue in the article.**

1 One of my favourite film _____ is romantic comedy.
2 I don't like Hollywood _____ . I prefer small-budget films.
3 I think the best _____ actor is Leonardo DiCaprio.
4 I don't think amazing special effects with _____ are as important as good acting.
5 I don't watch film _____ because they show all the best scenes.
6 The last film I saw wasn't very successful at the _____ , but I thought it was good.

9 **SPEAKING Change the sentences in Exercise 8 to make them true for you. Then compare your sentences with a partner.**

WORD STORE 3E | Phrasal verbs ▷

10 **◀))1.55 Complete WORD STORE 3E with the base forms of the underlined phrasal verbs in the article. Then listen, check and repeat.**

Iron Man

Wonder Woman

Batman

🔊 1.53

A ☐

One of the most popular cinema genres of the twenty-first century so far is the superhero movie. Some people say that superhero movies are the new westerns. Both genres have similar themes: the good guys fighting the bad guys, protecting the innocent 5 and giving up their life for the good of others.

B ☐

When a new superhero movie comes out, it dominates the box office for weeks. The trailer for *Captain America: Civil War* was one of the most downloaded trailers ever and A-list actors are keen to take on 10 superhero roles.

Many superhero films have had Oscar nominations, and fan events like Comic-Con* keep fans excited about the latest blockbusters.

C ☐

First of all, there's the adventure, the action and the 15 costumes, the great soundtracks, the special effects and computer-generated images. They're fun and entertaining, and we love the escapism. But is that enough?

You have to look deeper to find out why people love 20 them. Superheroes have feelings. They cope with human experiences that we can relate to. In other words, they are not so different from regular people. Psychologist Mary Tavost has written books about the psychology of superheroes, and she thinks that they 25 inspire their fans because their goals in life are similar to human goals.

They want peace, justice and love, just as we do. The lives of superheroes reflect real life as we know it.

D ☐

Batman dedicates himself to fighting crime after 30 somebody murders his parents in front of him. In real life, people who experience a trauma often decide to help others. But he also shows a very human side because love is his motivation. In *The Dark Knight*, his love for Rachel makes him weak. As a result, he often 35 makes bad decisions. When Hulk is angry, he causes terrible destruction. He finds it difficult to control his angry feelings, and then he feels guilty when he loses control. This is easy to understand — extreme anger is a very human emotion. 40

E ☐

Superheroes cope with problems and find meaning in loss and trauma. When they discover their powers they use them for a good purpose. X-Men are 'mutants' — people reject them because they are different and 'weird' — but they use their powers 45 to stand up for the innocent. They inspire us to accept ourselves and be proud of who we are. Before Spiderman had superpowers, his classmates bullied him at school. Later, he uses his abilities to protect people who can't protect themselves. These 50 superheroes may be larger than life, but we have no problems identifying with their human side.

*Comic-Con – a conference for comic book and film character fans

Present Perfect with *just*, *already*, *(not) yet* and Past Simple

I can use the Present Perfect with just and already.

1 SPEAKING **What are your musical tastes? Note down your favourites. Then compare with a partner.**

- Favourite band
- Favourite female singer
- Favourite male singer

2 **Read about The BRIT School in London. What do Leona Lewis, Adele and Jessie J all have in common?**

★ A SCHOOL FOR STARS ★

The BRIT School opened in 1991. Over the years, it has produced many successful graduates. Leona Lewis, Adele and Jessie J are three former students – they have sold millions of albums between them. In 2006, Leona Lewis **won** *The X Factor* and she has already sold more than ten million albums worldwide. Adele has had No 1 hits in the British and American charts including the single *Hello* from her album *25*, the best-selling album of 2015. Singer and songwriter Jessie J **has already won** numerous music awards and she's written songs for other international artists such as Miley Cyrus.

Another term **has just ended** at the BRIT School. Have they produced new stars? Probably! We **haven't heard** of them **yet**, but we will!

3 **Read the GRAMMAR FOCUS. Complete the examples using the verb phrases in blue in Exercise 2. Then underline five more Present Perfect sentences in the text.**

GRAMMAR FOCUS

Present Perfect with *just*, *already*, *(not) yet* and Past Simple

- You use the **Present Perfect** to talk about finished actions in time 'up-to-now'. You never say exactly 'when' they happened.
  Time expressions: *ever, never, since then, just, already* (usually affirmative), *(not) yet* (usually negative or questions)
  just = has happened very recently
  Another term ¹_____ just _____ at the BRIT School.

  (not) yet = hasn't happened but probably will happen
  We ²_____ of them yet.

  already = has happened earlier than expected
  She ³_____ already _____ numerous music awards.

- You use the **Past Simple** to talk about finished actions in past time. You usually say 'when' they happened.
  In 2006, Leona Lewis ⁴_____ The X Factor.

4 **Choose the correct time expressions and write them in the correct place in the sentences. Which sentences are true for you?**

1 I lent my iPod to my sister but she hasn't given it back *yet*. (*yet* / *just*)
2 I've updated my Facebook profile with some new photos. (*just* / *yet*)
3 I want to learn the guitar but I haven't found a teacher. (*already* / *yet*)
4 I got my favourite band's new album recently and I've learnt all the words. (*already* / *yet*)
5 I've finished a really good book. (*already* / *just*)

5 **Complete the text with the Present Perfect or the Past Simple forms of the verbs in brackets.**

Adele Laurie Blue Adkins ¹*grew up* (grow up) in London with her mum and ²_____ (begin) singing when she was four. She ³_____ (graduate) from the BRIT School in 2006. Adele ⁴_____ (already earn) millions of pounds, but according to her friends, she ⁵_____ (not changed). She's still the same girl they ⁶_____ (know) before she was famous. She ⁷_____ (write) her first two albums about two relationships that ended badly, but continued to write good songs while she was happily married. Adele says, 'I don't know what's going to happen if my music career goes wrong, I ⁸_____ (not have) a proper job yet!'

6 **Read *6 Cultural Things to Do*. Write one sentence with *already* and one with *yet* for each one. Which sentences are true for you?**

6 Cultural Things to Do Before You Are 18

- see a live band
- visit a big art gallery
- listen to a Beethoven symphony
- act in a play
- read a classic novel
- write a poem or a short story

I've already seen a live band.
I haven't seen a live band yet.

7 SPEAKING **Ask your partner about *6 Cultural Things to Do*. If the answer is 'yes', ask three more questions beginning with *who*, *where* and *what*.**

A: *Have you seen a live band yet?*   B: *Yes, I have.*
A: *Who did you see?*   B: *I saw Imagine Dragons.*

FOCUS VLOG London attractions

▶ 14 Watch the Focus Vlog. For the worksheet, go to page 121.

Grammar page 139

USE OF ENGLISH

3.6

too and *not enough*

I can express sufficiency and insufficiency with *enough* **and** *too.*

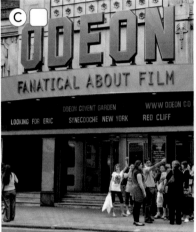

1 🔊 **1.56** Listen to four conversations between people who have just been to the places in the photos. Match conversations 1–4 with photos A–D.

2 🔊 **1.56** Listen again and choose the correct option.
1 I think I fell asleep. It was *too / enough* long for me.
2 Her voice wasn't *loud enough / enough loud.*
3 There were far *too many / too much* people in there.
4 The room was *very crowded / too crowded* to see it properly.
5 She didn't sing *enough / too much* hits.

3 Read the LANGUAGE FOCUS. Complete sentences 1–7 by putting the word in capitals in the correct place in the sentence.

LANGUAGE FOCUS

too and *not enough*

You use **too** and **not enough** to show there is a problem with something.

* **too** + adjective/adverb or
  not + adjective/adverb + **enough**:
  The music was too quiet.
  They didn't play loudly enough.

* **too much/many** + noun or **not enough** + noun:
  There were too many people.
  There wasn't enough space.

Note: You also use **not too** and **enough** to say that something is possible.

This song is not too hard to learn.
This song is easy enough to learn.

1 There are many talent shows on TV these days. **TOO**
2 The dialogue is never loud when you watch a film on the TV. **ENOUGH**
3 People spend much time watching on-demand TV series. **TOO**
4 The plots in modern thrillers are often complex to follow. **TOO**
5 Actors in crime dramas don't usually speak clearly. **ENOUGH**
6 Period dramas are slow and boring for young people to watch. **TOO**
7 There isn't comedy on TV any more. **ENOUGH**

4 SPEAKING Discuss if you agree or disagree with the statements in Exercise 3.

5 Complete the sentences with *too* or *not enough* and the adjectives in brackets. Are any of the sentences true for you?
1 I'm <u>not old enough</u> to watch X-rated films. You have to be eighteen. (old)
2 I don't go to the cinema much: tickets are _____ . (expensive)
3 I'm _____ to perform on the stage. (shy)
4 I'm _____ to remember music from the 1990s! (young)
5 I'm _____ to learn a musical instrument. (talented)
6 I don't download films. My Internet connection is _____ (fast).

6 USE OF ENGLISH Complete the second sentence so that it has a similar meaning to the first.
1 Our music teacher speaks too softly. I can't hear her. **ENOUGH**
   Our music teacher _____ . I can't hear her.
2 There are too many Arts students compared to Science students. **NOT**
   There _____ compared to Arts students.
3 I don't have enough free time to take on a role in the school play. **BUSY**
   I'm _____ to take on a role in the school play.
4 The old school hall wasn't big enough to put on concerts. **TOO**
   The old school hall _____ to put on concerts.

Use of English page 140 ▶

WRITING

A film review

I can write a simple review of a film.

1 **SPEAKING** What is the best or worst film you've seen? Discuss with a partner.

2 In the film review on the left, Simon talks about the film *Blade Runner 2049*. Before you read, make a list of the things you think he might include.

plot, actors, special effects, ...

3 Read the film review and check your answers in Exercise 2.

4 Read the film review again and answer the questions.

In which paragraph does the writer:
a give his opinions about the film? ☐
b give a summary of his opinions and his recommendation? ☐
c give background information? ☐
d describe the plot and the main characters? ☐

5 Complete the WRITING FOCUS with the phrases in purple in the film review.

BLADE RUNNER 2049

1 **Directed by** Denis Villeneuve and **starring** Ryan Gosling and Harrison Ford, this action-adventure film is the **sequel** of the 1982 science-fiction film *Blade Runner* by Ridley Scott. It is **set** thirty years after the events of the original film.

2 The action takes place in the Los Angeles of the future, a city where there are flying cars and gigantic adverts in the form of holograms. People use replicants (androids) for work. **Unfortunately**, some of these replicants have become dangerous to humans. Ryan Gosling stars as K, a replicant who works for the Los Angeles Police Department as a 'blade runner'. His job is to find and kill these dangerous replicants. One day he discovers a secret that could put the future of humans at risk.

3 Ryan Gosling is excellent as K, and Harrison Ford also gives a great **performance** as the retired blade runner Rick Deckart, who helps K find the answers he is looking for. The special effects and photography are as <u>stunning</u> as in the original film, the soundtrack is <u>superb</u> and the screenplay **holds your attention** from beginning to end.

4 For me the word that best **describes** this movie is *awesome*. It's one of the best science-fiction films I've ever seen and in my view it's suitable for adults and teenagers alike.

Simon

WRITING FOCUS

A film review

- **Background information:**
  [1]*Directed by* Denis Villeneuve ...
  [2]_____ Ryan Gosling and Harrison Ford.
  The film was nominated for/was awarded the ...
  This action-adventure/romantic comedy/thriller/historical drama/animated feature film ...
  The film is a [3]_____ of/a remake of/an adaptation of ...
  It is based on the true story of/the novel ...
  It is [4]_____ 30 years later/during the ...
  The action takes place in the future/in a village/in ...
  Ryan Gosling/the actor stars as ...

- **Plot:**
  At first/Then/After that/Later on ...
  [5]_____ , some of these replicants have become dangerous ...
  Eventually, the police catch the terrorists.

- **Main characters:**
  The characters are skilfully played/aren't very convincing.
  Harrison Ford (also) gives a great [6]_____ as ...

- **Different aspects of the film:**
  The screenplay [7]_____ from beginning to end.
  The special effects are amazing.
  The plot is fascinating/a bit boring/slow-moving.
  The photography/soundtrack is amazing.

- **Summary of opinion and recommendation:**
  For me the word that best [8]_____ this movie is ...
  It's one of the best (science fiction) films I've ever seen.
  In my view, it's suitable for adults and teenagers/kids alike.

Film Review: Pitch Perfect

Pitch Perfect is a 2012 musical comedy, ¹d_____ by Jason Moore and ²s_____ Anna Kendrick and Rebel Wilson. The film is an ³a_____ of a non-fiction book by Mickey Rapkin. It was ⁴a_____ MTV Movie Awards for Wilson's performance and for best musical moment.

The ⁵p_____ focuses on Beca Mitchell, a college student who would like to be a music producer. At university she meets Barden Bellas, an all-girl *a capella* group, who want Beca to sing with them and help them win the national singing competition. At first Beca doesn't want to join the group. ⁶E_____, she agrees and it all begins …

Anna Kendrick gives a superb ⁷p_____ as a rather shy but rebellious student, and the rest of the actresses are really convincing playing the Bellas. The ⁸s_____ is cleverly written and extremely engaging. The plot is a bit predictable but it's still a pleasure to watch. And, of course, the soundtrack is <u>brilliant</u>! The film was so popular that it has now two ⁹s_____: *Pitch Perfect 2* (2015) and *Pitch Prefect 3*, which came out in 2017.

The word that best ¹⁰d_____ this movie is *fun*. It is both amusing and very <u>inspiring</u> to those who dream of performing. In my view, it is ¹¹s_____ for teenagers and adults alike, and I believe that everyone will find something interesting in the *Pitch Perfect* series.

6 Complete the review of the film *Pitch Perfect* with words and phrases from the WRITING FOCUS.

7 SPEAKING **Discuss the questions.**

1 Have you seen *Blade Runner 2049* or *Pitch Perfect*? If so, do you agree with the opinions in the reviews?
2 If you haven't seen these films, would you like to? Why/Why not?

8 Complete the LANGUAGE FOCUS with the underlined adjectives in the reviews in Exercise 3 and Exercise 6.

LANGUAGE FOCUS

Adjectives to describe films, plots, screenplays etc.
We use:
- ¹*superb*, ²_____ and ³_____ to mean fantastic, wonderful.
- *engaging* to mean something pleasant that makes you interested, curious.
- *amusing* to mean funny.
- ⁴_____ to mean something that makes you excited and makes you want to do something important.
- *convincing* to mean something which makes you believe something is true or right.
- *predictable* to mean something not surprising, something you expected to happen.

9 Complete the sentences with the correct adjectives from the LANGUAGE FOCUS. Sometimes more than one answer is possible.

1 The story of that film was really _____ – it held my attention for over two hours non-stop.
2 I love musicals, and I think the soundtrack from *The Phantom of the Opera* was simply _____.
3 We prefer films which are _____ – which make people get up from the sofa and go change the world.
4 I don't think the actor playing Jesse was very _____ – he's in his 30s and he played the role of a teenager.
5 Did you also think that film was _____? Everybody in the cinema laughed and I couldn't understand why.
6 That thriller was really _____ – we knew who the killer was after just fifteen minutes!

10 SPEAKING **Discuss the questions with a partner.**

1 Have you ever seen a truly horrible film?
2 What's the most brilliant film soundtrack you can think of?
3 Have you ever seen a really inspiring film? Why was it inspiring?
4 When you go to the cinema, does the film have to be amusing?

SHOW WHAT YOU'VE LEARNT

11 **Do the writing task. Use the ideas in the WRITING FOCUS and the LANGUAGE FOCUS to help you.**

Think of a film you've seen recently and write a review for an online teen magazine. Include the following information:
- background information on the film
- the plot and main characters
- your opinion
- a summary of your opinion and recommendation.

A few days ago I saw the latest film directed by …

1 SPEAKING **Look at the photos and discuss the questions.**

1 Who are the people?
2 Where are they?
3 What are they doing?

2 **Complete sentences 1–3 in as many ways as possible with the adjectives in the box. Some adjectives can be used more than once.**

bored   crowded   empty   excited   famous   shy
friendly   frightened   happy   irritated   miserable
nervous   noisy   proud   quiet   tired   young

1 (describing people)   He or she is …
2 (describing feelings)   He or she is feeling …
3 (describing places)   It is …

3 🔊 **1.57** **Listen to a description and decide which photo it describes. Explain your decision.**

4 🔊 **1.57** **Complete the description with words and phrases in the SPEAKING FOCUS. Then listen again and check.**

¹*In this photo I can see* a street artist drawing a portrait on the pavement. ²_____ there are some people watching him. They're wearing shorts and T-shirts, so ³_____ it's summer. The street is quite crowded, so perhaps this is a tourist area. The street artist has got dark hair and he's wearing jeans and a bright green T-shirt. ⁴_____ quite young. ⁵_____ him is a picture and he's copying it. ⁶_____ he's a very good artist. ⁷_____ he's going to collect money from the people who are watching him. ⁸_____ , I'd give him some money because I think he's done a good job.

SPEAKING FOCUS

Beginning a description
In this photo, I can see …/there is …/there are …
This photo shows …
Saying where (place)
There are … so I think they're in a street/in an art gallery/ at a concert, etc.
Saying where (in the photo)
in the background/in the middle/in the foreground/ on the left/on the right/in front of/behind/next to
Speculating
He/She looks shy/bored/tired, etc. She's probably …
Perhaps/Maybe/I imagine/I'm sure he's very proud.
Giving your opinion
I think …   I don't think …   Personally, …   In my opinion, …

5 SPEAKING **Discuss the questions about Photo C.**

1 Who do you think the man sitting on the right is?
2 Describe a time when you saw a street artist.
3 Do you give money to street artists or other street performers? Why?/Why not?

6 SPEAKING **Work in pairs. Student A: describe Photo A. Student B: describe Photo B. Use the SPEAKING FOCUS to help you.**

7 🔊 **1.58** **Listen to model descriptions of Photos A and B. Then do Exercise 6 again.**

8 SPEAKING **Follow the instructions below.**

Student A: Ask Student B the following questions:
• What kind of music do you enjoy listening to and who is your favourite band or singer?
• Describe a time when you saw live music.

Student B: Ask Student A the following questions:
• What kind of art do you like and why?
• Describe a time when you visited a gallery or museum.

3.1 Vocabulary 🔊 4.17

acting /ˈæktɪŋ/
addictive /əˈdɪktɪv/
animation /ˌænəˈmeɪʃən/
audiences /ˈɔːdiənsɪz/
binge watcher /ˈbɪndʒ ˌwɒtʃə/
bookworm /ˈbʊkwɜːm/
chapter /ˈtʃæptə/
character /ˈkærəktə/
chat show /ˈtʃæt ˌʃəʊ/
clip /klɪp/
comedy /ˈkɒmədi/
complex /ˈkɒmpleks/
confession /kənˈfeʃən/
cooking programme /ˈkʊkɪŋ
  ˌprəʊɡræm/
costume /ˈkɒstjuːm/
(crime/TV) drama /(ˈkraɪm/ˌtiː ˈviː)
  ˌdrɑːmə/
disappointing /ˌdɪsəˈpɔɪntɪŋ/
documentary /ˌdɒkjəˈmentəri/
drama series /ˈdrɑːmə ˌsɪəriːz/
embarrassing /ɪmˈbærəsɪŋ/
ending /ˈendɪŋ/
engaging /ɪnˈɡeɪdʒɪŋ/
entertaining /ˌentəˈteɪnɪŋ/
episode /ˈepəsəʊd/
excellent /ˈeksələnt/
factual /ˈfæktʃuəl/
fantasy /ˈfæntəsi/
fascinating /ˈfæsɪneɪtɪŋ/
game show /ˈɡeɪm ˌʃəʊ/
gripping /ˈɡrɪpɪŋ/
horror /ˈhɒrə/
imaginative /ɪˈmædʒɪnətɪv/
inspiring /ɪnˈspaɪərɪŋ/
light entertainment /ˌlaɪt
  ˌentəˈteɪnmənt/
live /laɪv/
movie /ˈmuːvi/
moving /ˈmuːvɪŋ/
musical /ˈmjuːzɪkəl/
news bulletin /ˈnjuːz ˌbʊlətɪn/
novel /ˈnɒvəl/
on-demand TV /ɒn dɪˌmɑːnd ˌtiː ˈviː/
period drama /ˈpɪəriəd ˌdrɑːmə/
plot /plɒt/
reality TV /riˈæləti ˌtiːˈviː/
romantic comedy /rəʊˌmæntɪk
  ˈkɒmədi/
science fiction /ˌsaɪəns ˈfɪkʃən/
script /skrɪpt/
setting /ˈsetɪŋ/
sitcom /ˈsɪtkɒm/
soap (opera) /ˌsəʊp (ˈɒpərə)/
soundtrack /ˈsaʊndtræk/
special effects /ˌspeʃəl əˈfekts/
talent show /ˈtælənt ˌʃəʊ/
telly /ˈteli/
thriller /ˈθrɪlə/
travel show /ˈtrævəl ʃəʊ/
TV series /ˌtiːˈviː ˌsɪəriːz/
weakness /ˈwiːknəs/
weather forecast /ˈweðə
  ˌfɔːkɑːst/

3.2 Grammar 🔊 4.18

best-selling /ˌbestˈselɪŋ/
busy /ˈbɪzi/
play /pleɪ/
record /rɪˈkɔːd/
vocal range /ˌvəʊkəl ˈreɪndʒ/

3.3 Listening 🔊 4.19

art gallery /ˈɑːt ˌɡæləri/
at a museum /ət ə mjuːˈziəm/
black and white /ˌblæk ən ˈwaɪt/
classic oil painting /ˌklæsɪk ˈɔɪl ˌpeɪntɪŋ/
colour /ˈkʌlə/
editor /ˈedɪtə/
exhibition /ˌeksəˈbɪʃən/
landscape /ˈlændskeɪp/
modern abstract painting /ˌmɒdn
  ˈæbstrækt ˌpeɪntɪŋ/
ordinary /ˈɔːdənəri/
painter /ˈpeɪntə/
paste on walls/buildings /ˌpeɪst ɒn
  ˈwɔːlz/ˈbɪldɪŋz/
photo/photograph /ˈfəʊtəʊ/ˈfəʊtəɡrɑːf/
photographer /fəˈtɒɡrəfə/
photography /fəˈtɒɡrəfi/
portrait /ˈpɔːtrət/
public place /ˌpʌblɪk ˈpleɪs/
sculptor /ˈskʌlptə/
sculpture /ˈskʌlptʃə/
slum /slʌm/
street art /ˈstriːt ˌɑːt/

3.4 Reading 🔊 4.20

A-list actors /ˈeɪ lɪst ˌæktəz/
anger /ˈæŋɡə/
autobiography /ˌɔːtəbaɪˈɒɡrəfi/
biography /baɪˈɒɡrəfi/
blockbuster /ˈblɒkˌbʌstə/
box office /ˈbɒks ˌɒfəs/
bully /ˈbʊli/
cause /kɔːz/
classic novel /ˌklæsɪk ˈnɒvəl/
come out /ˌkʌm ˈaʊt/
comic book /ˈkɒmɪk ˌbʊk/
computer-generated images
  /kəmˌpjuːtə ˌdʒenəreɪtɪd ˈɪmɪdʒɪz/
cope with /ˈkəʊp wɪð/
crime novel /ˈkraɪm ˌnɒvəl/
dedicate yourself to sth /ˈdedəkeɪt
  jɔːˌself tə ˈsʌmθɪŋ/
destruction /dɪˈstrʌkʃən/
escapism /ɪˈskeɪpɪzəm/
fairy tale /ˈfeəri teɪl/
fantasy novel /ˌfæntəsi ˈnɒvəl/
find out /ˌfaɪnd ˈaʊt/
genre /ˈʒɒnrə/
give something up /ˌɡɪv ˌsʌmθɪŋ ˈʌp/
have X-ray vision /ˌhæv ˈeks reɪ ˌvɪʒən/
historical fiction /hɪˌstɒrɪkəl ˈfɪkʃən/
horror fiction /ˈhɒrə ˌfɪkʃən/
innocent /ˈɪnəsənt/
invisible /ɪnˈvɪzɪbəl/
loss /lɒs/
poem /ˈpəʊɪm/
purpose /ˈpɜːpəs/
reject /rɪˈdʒekt/

relate to /rɪˈleɪt ˌtə/
scene /siːn/
science fiction /ˌsaɪəns ˈfɪkʃən/
short story /ˌʃɔːt ˈstɔːri/
stand up for /ˌstænd ˈʌp fə/
take on (a role) /ˌteɪk ˌɒn ə ˈrəʊl/
thriller /ˈθrɪlə/
trailer /ˈtreɪlə/
weird /wɪəd/

3.5 Grammar 🔊 4.21

gig /ɡɪɡ/
music award /ˈmjuːzɪk əˌwɔːd/
proper /ˈprɒpə/
the charts /ðə ˈtʃɑːts/

3.6 Use of English 🔊 4.22

perform /pəˈfɔːm/
put on (a play) /ˌpʊt ɒn (ə ˈpleɪ)/
softly /ˈsɒftli/
stage /steɪdʒ/
X-rated /ˈeks ˌreɪtəd/

3.7 Writing 🔊 4.23

adaptation of /ˌædæpˈteɪʃən əv/
amusing /əˈmjuːzɪŋ/
brilliant /ˈbrɪljənt/
convincing /kənˈvɪnsɪŋ/
directed by /ˌdaɪˈrektɪd baɪ/
engaging /ɪnˈɡeɪdʒɪŋ/
holds your attention /həʊldz jər
  əˈtenʃən/
inspiring /ɪnˈspaɪərɪŋ/
masterpiece /ˈmɑːstəpiːs/
performance /pəˈfɔːməns/
predictable /prɪˈdɪktəbəl/
remake of /ˈriːmeɪk əv/
screenplay /ˈskriːnpleɪ/
sequel of /ˈsiːkwəl əv/
starring /ˈstɑːrɪŋ/
stunning /ˈstʌnɪŋ/
suitable for /ˈsuːtəbəl fə/
superb /suːˈpɜːb/

3.8 Speaking 🔊 4.24

in the background /ˌɪn ðə ˈbækɡraʊnd/
in the foreground /ˌɪn ðə ˈfɔːɡraʊnd/
look bored/tired /ˌlʊk ˈbɔːd/ˈtaɪəd/
pavement /ˈpeɪvmənt/

VOCABULARY AND GRAMMAR

1 Choose the odd one out in each group.

1 documentary, opera, thriller, game show
2 biography, fantasy novel, landscape, fairy tale
3 plot, gallery, museum, painting
4 band, sitcom, symphony, soundtrack
5 songwriter, photographer, sculptor, character
6 entertaining, fascinating, embarrassing, imaginative

2 Complete the sentences with the correct form of the words in capitals.

1 My favourite _____ is Claude Monet. **ART**
2 Tom Holland played in the _____ *Billy Elliot* when he was 11. **MUSIC**
3 Don't take flash photographs of _____ in the gallery. **PAINT**
4 A _____ drama is a film about true events and people from the past. **HISTORY**
5 What's the most _____ film you've ever watched? **MOVE**
6 Almost every actor would like to get an Oscar for _____ . **ACT**

3 Complete the second sentence using the word in capitals so that it has a similar meaning to the first. Do not change the word in capitals.

1 Both TV binge watching and playing video games are addictive. **AS**
  TV binge watching _____ playing video games.
2 My father paid €30 for the ticket but I paid only €5. **MUCH**
  My father paid _____ me for the ticket.
3 I've never seen a film with such amazing special effects. **MOST**
  The film had _____ I've ever seen.
4 The plot in a comedy is not as gripping as the plot in a thriller. **THAN**
  The plot in a thriller _____ the plot in a comedy.
5 I think painting a landscape is easier than painting a portrait. **DIFFICULT**
  I think painting a portrait _____ painting a landscape.
6 We spent a long time in the museum but only ten minutes in the souvenir shop. **FAR**
  We spent _____ in the museum than in the souvenir shop.

4 Use the prompts and *yet, already* or *just* to write sentences.

1 the new *Star Wars* episode / not come out
2 Evelyn / see / the exhibition at the Tate Modern
3 Lottie / call / you
4 Howard / take on / the role / in the new sitcom?
5 Jeff / finish / download / the soundtrack
6 We / not buy / the tickets for the concert in Edinburgh

USE OF ENGLISH

5 Choose the correct answer, A, B or C.

1 X: We didn't go to the cinema ____.
  Y: Why not?
  A yet
  B since then
  C last night
2 X: What a disappointing film!
  Y: Yes, the plot was ____.
  A too funny
  B too complex
  C too inspiring
3 X: What do you think about this portrait?
  Y: The girl looks OK, but the ____ is too dark.
  A background
  B centre
  C foreground
4 X: Adele's new song is so inspiring.
  Y: Yes, it's as ____ her previous hits.
  A great as
  B better than
  C the best of
5 X: Why do the boys in the photo look so miserable?
  Y: Because the exhibition is ____ for them.
  A not interesting enough
  B too exciting
  C quite entertaining
6 X: What's ____ soundtrack you've ever heard?
  Y: Probably *The Dark Knight*.
  A bad
  B worse
  C the worst

6 Read the text and choose the correct answer, A, B or C.

HAVE YOU BEEN TO BRATISLAVA?

If visiting art galleries is ¹___ for you, in Bratislava, the capital city of Slovakia, you can see attractive art when you walk round the Old Town. Full-sized bronze ²___ of people show up suddenly at street corners or on benches. They ³___ one of the main tourist attractions in the city. One of the ⁴___ popular is the statue of Ignac Lamar, a cheerful old man wearing elegant clothes and holding a hat in his hand. The legend says that Lamar was ⁵___ poor to visit restaurants or coffee shops, but he always greeted people in the street and kissed ladies' hands. It's an ⁶___ idea to take a photo with the statue and have a great souvenir of your visit to Bratislava.

1 A too expensive   B not expensive enough
  C more expensive
2 A sculptors   B sculptures   C portraits
3 A have become   B became   C used to become
4 A enough   B more   C most
5 A than   B too   C enough
6 A excellent   B addictive   C imaginative

7 Match the headings (A–F) with the paragraphs (1–4). There are two extra headings.

A Dealing with clients
B A modest artist in the background
C Art is not for sale
D Two definitions
E A photographer's perspective
F A famous person in the foreground

Art or craftsmanship?

1 ☐

Are photographers artists or only craftspeople? What is the difference? A craftsperson creates useful objects by hand and then sells them. An artist creates things just to express emotions, entertain or tell a story. But is it really so simple?

2 ☐

Let's take Annie Leibovitz, for example, who is now the most famous portrait photographer in the world. She has photographed well-known actors, singers, Olympic champions and designers. Her photographs always tell an emotional story and are true pieces of art. But she also earns money on them.

3 ☐

The backgrounds for her portraits are created by another person, Sarah Oliphant. Her works include huge landscapes, abstract paintings or small objects. She says she is a craftsperson, not an artist, because everything she makes is useful to other people and they pay her for it. But people can see her work as art too.

4 ☐

So what is the answer? I am a photographer and I know that people who work in the photography business are almost always craftspeople. They produce images for money on their clients' orders. But sometimes they use their talent, tools and skills to create something personal. And then they become artists.

What do you think?

8 Look at the photo and choose the most suitable words from the box to describe it. Then describe the photo.

> ambitious ballet room dancer easy mirror music professional purple singer stretch teenage girl theatre trainers

9 In pairs, answer the questions. Which question refers directly to the photo in Exercise 8?

1 Is the activity easy for the girl to do? Why?/Why not?
2 What artistic skills would you most like to learn? Why?
3 Tell us about an artistic competition you watched or took part in.

10 Read the writing task and write the review.

> You have decided to take part in the *Film Fan* online writing competition. Write a review of a film you have seen recently. Include the following information:
> * background information about the film (e.g. the director, cast)
> * the plot and the characters
> * your opinion about the film
> * your recommendations.

4

Home sweet home

Home is where the heart is.
A proverb

BBC

CAVE HOUSES

▶ 15 Watch the BBC video.
For the worksheet, go to page 122.

SHOW WHAT YOU KNOW

1 **Think about your house and complete the task in five minutes.**
   - List all the different rooms in your house.
   - List at least six items you can find in each room – furniture, decoration, objects, etc.

2 **Compare your lists with a partner. What is your total number of different words for rooms and items in rooms?**

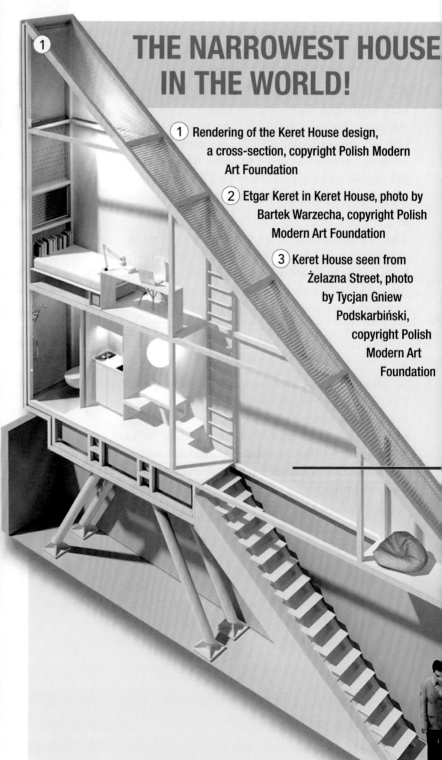

THE NARROWEST HOUSE IN THE WORLD!

1. Rendering of the Keret House design, a cross-section, copyright Polish Modern Art Foundation

2. Etgar Keret in Keret House, photo by Bartek Warzecha, copyright Polish Modern Art Foundation

3. Keret House seen from Żelazna Street, photo by Tycjan Gniew Podskarbiński, copyright Polish Modern Art Foundation

3 ◀))2.1 Listen and answer the questions.

1 Where is Keret House?
2 What does Etgar Keret think of the house?
3 How wide is Keret House?
4 How many floors are there?
5 How many people can live in it?

4 SPEAKING Discuss whether or not you would like to live in the Keret house. Give reasons for your answers.

WORD STORE 4A | Describing houses ⟩

5 ◀))2.2 Complete WORD STORE 4A with the words and phrases in the box. Then listen, check and repeat.

> ~~a block of flats~~ brick concrete cosy glass
> the ground floor historic in the city centre metal
> modern open-plan spacious upstairs

6 Replace the underlined phrases with words or phrases with a similar meaning in WORD STORE 4A. Which sentences are true for you?

I know someone who lives in a …
1 detached house with only one floor. _a bungalow_
2 house which is joined to a neighbour's house.
_____
3 house on the edge of the city. _____
4 small, traditional house in a village. _____
5 modern house in an area with other similar houses.
_____
6 flat that is very warm and comfortable. _____
7 large flat that is without many interior walls.
_____ _____
8 flat at the top of a building in the middle of the city.
_____ _____

7 SPEAKING Describe a flat or house that you know to your partner.

WORD STORE 4B | Inside a house ⟩

8 ◀))2.3 Translate the words in WORD STORE 4B into your language. Which of the items can you see in Keret House? Listen and repeat.

9 ◀))2.4 We asked three people: 'Would you like to live in Keret House?' Listen and complete the table.

	Answer	Reasons
Speaker 1	Yes / No / Maybe	
Speaker 2	Yes / No / Maybe	
Speaker 3	Yes / No / Maybe	

WORD STORE 4C | _make or do_ ⟩

10 ◀))2.5 Complete WORD STORE 4C with the nouns in the box. Then listen, check and repeat.

> ~~the washing~~ dinner the ironing the gardening
> the washing-up a mess a noise the shopping

11 SPEAKING Complete the questions with the correct form of _make_ or _do_. Then ask and answer the questions.

1 Did you _____ your bed this morning?
2 Do your neighbours ever _____ a noise?
3 Do you like _____ the washing-up?
4 Who _____ the cooking in your house?
5 Have you ever _____ dinner for somebody?
6 Where does your family usually _____ the shopping?

47

Present Perfect with *for* and *since*

I can use the Present Perfect with for and since to talk about duration.

1 SPEAKING **Tick the places where you have slept. What was the most unusual place? Tell your partner.**

- in my bed ☐
- on a floor ☐
- on a couch ☐
- in a hotel ☐
- on a train ☐
- other ☐

2 SPEAKING **Read US TODAY. What is couchsurfing? Discuss whether you would like to do it. Give reasons for your answers.**

US TODAY

We asked CS employee, Dan, about the world's largest travel community.

What is it?
A worldwide travel network connecting travellers with people who offer free accommodation.

Who is it for?
People who don't want to stay in hotels but want to meet local people and experience new cultures.

How much does it cost?
Nothing! It's free.

How long have **you** worked for CS?
I've been here since it started in 2004. I've worked with people from all over the world for more than ten years. Together we want to create a global community.

3 **Read the GRAMMAR FOCUS. Complete the examples using the Present Perfect forms in blue in Exercise 2.**

GRAMMAR FOCUS

Present Perfect with *for* and *since*

You use the **Present Perfect** to talk about unfinished situations that started in the past and continue in time 'up to now'.

- You use **How long** to ask about the length of time 'up to now'.
  How long ¹_____ you _____ for CS?

- You use **since** when the answer is a point in time:
  e.g. *since 1998, since last week, since I was born.*
  I ²_____ here *since it started in 2004.*

- You use **for** when the answer is a period of time:
  e.g. *for six hours, for a few days, for a long time.*
  I ³_____ with people from all over the world *for more than ten years.*

4 🔊 2.6 **Choose *for* or *since* and complete the comments with the Present Perfect form of the verbs in brackets. Then listen and check.**

Couchsurfer

I ¹*'ve been* (be) a member ²*for / since* three years now. ³*For / Since* I became a member, I ⁴_____ (stay) in thirty-two countries in different types of accommodation. I ⁵_____ (sleep) in a luxury studio apartment in Manhattan, on a houseboat in Amsterdam and in a basement flat in London – all for free!

Host

I ⁶_____ (be) a couchsurfing host ⁷*for / since* two years now and I ⁸_____ (already/meet) more than thirty people. At the moment, Miki is visiting from Tokyo. I ⁹_____ (only know) her ¹⁰*for / since* a week, but I'm sure we'll remain friends. Miki is happy too – she ¹¹_____ (study) English ¹²*for / since* ten years, but she ¹³_____ (never/have) the chance to speak with a native speaker before. She ¹⁴_____ (be) here ¹⁵*for / since* nearly a week, but she ¹⁶_____ (not feel) homesick because she says I make her feel at home.

5 **Complete the second sentence so that it has a similar meaning to the first.**

1 My dad was born in our house.
   My dad *has lived* (live) in our house *since* he was born.
2 My dad gave my mum this watch when she was forty.
   My mum _____ (have) this watch _____ she was forty.
3 I met my best friend two years ago.
   I _____ (know) my best friend _____ two years.
4 I bought these trainers last Christmas.
   I _____ (not buy) any new trainers _____ last Christmas.
5 I joined this English class three months ago.
   I _____ (be) in this English class _____ three months.
6 I had breakfast at 7 a.m.
   I _____ (not eat) anything _____ 7 a.m.

6 **Write true sentences from the prompts. Use the Present Perfect and *since* or *for*.**

1 I/know/(name of your neighbour) …
2 I/live in/(name of your neighbourhood) …
3 I/like/(name of your favourite band) …
4 I/have/(make of your phone) …
5 I/be interested in/(name of a subject) …
6 My dad/have/(type of your dad's car) …

7 SPEAKING **Use the sentences in Exercise 6 to make dialogues. Then ask and answer as in the example.**

A: *Who is your neighbour?* B: *Barry.*
A: *How long have you known him?* B: *For five years.*

FOCUS VLOG Where people live

▶ 17 **Watch the Focus Vlog. For the worksheet, go to page 123.**

Grammar page 141

Matching

*I can identify key details in
a simple narrative about
teenagers' rooms.*

1 SPEAKING **Look at the photo. How different or
similar is the bedroom to your own? Discuss with
a partner. Think about:**

1 **the size:** bigger/smaller, more/less spacious,
the same

2 **the decoration:** more/less modern, colour of
walls/curtains/carpet, posters, etc.

3 **the furniture:** bookcase, bed, wardrobe, desk, etc.

4 **other details:** more/less tidy, clothes, musical
instruments, computer, etc.

2 ◀)) **2.7** **Listen to five teenagers describing their
rooms. Are statements 1–5 true (T) or false (F)?**

1 Speaker 1 lives in a quiet house. ◯

2 Speaker 2 isn't like her sister. ◯

3 Speaker 3 doesn't like music. ◯

4 Speaker 4 is often out. ◯

5 Speaker 5 never invites her friends round. ◯

EXAM FOCUS Matching

3 ◀)) **2.7** **Listen to the teenagers again. Match
speakers 1–5 with statements A–F. There is one
extra statement.**

Speaker 1: ◯ Speaker 3: ◯ Speaker 5: ◯

Speaker 2: ◯ Speaker 4: ◯

A uses his/her room as a creative space.

B likes to escape to his/her room and have private
time.

C spends time with friends in his/her room.

D likes having an untidy room.

E just does homework and sleeps in his/her room.

F shares his/her room with someone.

4 SPEAKING **Discuss which teenager's attitude is most
similar to your own.**

5 ◀)) **2.8** **Listen to two teenagers talking about their most
treasured possessions and complete the information.**

DAFYDD

1 a laptop: has had it for _____ ,
a _____ present

2 a guitar: has had it for _____ ,
it belonged to his _____

3 a Welsh flag: he feels _____
of being Welsh

KAREN

1 a collection of animals: has had them
since she _____ , her favourite is
_____

2 a bedside lamp: a present from her
_____ , brought from _____

3 a collection of shells: they are souvenirs from
_____ , she has collected them since
she _____

6 ◀)) **2.8** **Choose the correct preposition and try to
complete the sentences from memory. Then listen again
and check.**

1 Dafydd's _____ is *on / next to* his desk.

2 His _____ is *on / in* the corner *above / next to* the
bookcase.

3 His _____ is *onto / on* the wall *onto / above* his
bed.

4 Karen's _____ is *on top of / above* the wardrobe.

5 Karen's _____ is *on / in* her bedside table.

6 Her _____ is *in / on* the bottom shelf of her
bookshelves, which are *opposite / in front of* her bed.

7 SPEAKING **What are your own most treasured
possessions? Where is everything in your room?
Tell your partner.**

PRONUNCIATION FOCUS

8 ◀)) **2.9** **Listen and repeat the words with long vowel
sounds. Then put them in an appropriate column in the
table.**

art calm floor free meet new room sea
start surf third true wall warm work

/iː/	/uː/	/ɔː/	/ɜː/	/ɑː/
				art

9 ◀)) **2.10** **Listen, check and repeat.**

WORD STORE 4D | Phrasal verbs ⟩

10 ◀)) **2.11** **Complete WORD STORE 4D with the particles in
the box. Then listen, check and repeat.**

People who don't live in traditional houses

🔊 2.13

1 SPEAKING **Look at the photos and discuss the questions.**

  1 What are the advantages of living in each place?

  2 What are the disadvantages?

  3 Would you like to live there? Why/Why not?

I suppose one advantage of living in the trees is that you would have fantastic views …

2 🔊 2.12 **Which words in the box describing landscape features can you see in the photos? Use your dictionary if necessary. Then listen and repeat.**

> a cave a crater an island a rainforest
> rocks ruins stilts a treehouse
> a turquoise ocean a volcano

3 **Read the text and answer the questions.**

  1 Why do the Korowai Tribe build their houses in trees?

  2 Why do people in Coober Pedy prefer living underground?

  3 Why do people on Aogashima want to live in a volcano?

  4 Why do the Bajau people feel uncomfortable on land?

  5 Why have most people recently moved from Petra to a nearby village?

EXAM FOCUS Gapped text

4 **Read the text again. Complete gaps 1–5 with sentences A–F. There is one extra sentence.**

  A Alternatively, you can take a helicopter and it only takes two hours.

  B This means that they have better access to water, electricity and Wi-Fi.

  C In fact, income from tourism is helping to keep their traditions alive.

  D It has to be strong because sometimes a family of twelve people live there.

  E However, if you look closer, you can see chimneys on the surface of the dry landscape.

  F Also, they start hunting when they're just eight years old.

1 Living in trees

The Korowai Tribe of Papua New Guinea are strong and good at climbing. They have to be! They live in treehouses, sometimes forty-five metres above the ground. The dense rainforest is **hot and humid**; there are insects and dangerous animals. Treehouses protect the 5 tribe from these dangers on the ground. They use material from the forest to build the houses. They cut off the top of a tree and build the floor first. ¹___ They use a ladder to get up and down. Imagine the **breathtaking views** from one of these treehouses!

2 Living underground

In the desert of Southeast
10 Australia, 500 miles away from
the nearest city, is a **mining
town** called Coober Pedy. On
the sandy surface, there isn't
much to see. ²___ Almost all
15 of the 3,500 residents live
underground and work in the
opal mines. To escape from
<u>scorching</u> temperatures,
they have created an impressive underground world where you'll find
20 everything from a bookstore to a church, and even a hotel.

3 Living in a volcano

Aogashima is a Japanese
island in the Philippine
Sea. Over 230 years ago,
a volcanic eruption killed half
25 of its population. Now about
200 people live in the old
<u>volcanic</u> crater. They try not
to worry too much about
another eruption. They love
30 living on the island – there
are no **traffic jams** or crowds of people. Fishing, hiking, camping and
swimming are popular activities. Aogashima's natural <u>hot</u> springs and
<u>lush</u> vegetation **attract** a lot of **visitors**, but the island is not so easy to
reach. You can take a fourteen-hour boat trip from Tokyo. ³___

4 Living on the sea

35 The Bajau /ˈbɑːdʒaʊ/ people
of Borneo in Southeast Asia,
also called sea gypsies, live
on boats or houses on stilts in
the turquoise Pacific Ocean.
40 When they go on land, they
feel 'landsick'. Bajau children
don't go to school on land. But
from an early age they learn to
swim and dive. ⁴___ The best
45 Bajau divers can dive twenty metres to the bottom of the ocean to
search for fish. Young Bajau children spend so much time in the ocean
that their eyes develop excellent underwater vision.

5 Living in caves

The <u>ancient</u> city of Petra is a
popular tourist destination. It
50 is located in the rose-coloured
mountains of south-western
Jordan and was once a busy
trading centre. Then, its
residents abandoned the city
55 and for thousands of years
only the Bedouin, a <u>nomadic</u>
tribe, lived in caves among
the spectacular historic ruins. However, the government has recently
decided to move them to a nearby village to protect Petra. But the
60 Bedouins' way of life has not changed much. ⁵___ Some of them work
in Petra, selling souvenirs or transporting tourists on horses, camels
and donkeys around the **historic monuments**.

---

5 Match 'clues' 1–3 with their function a–c in
a text.

1 *she, he, it, her, him, one, this, that, here,
there*
2 *But, However, Alternatively, Instead*
3 *Also, In addition, For example, In fact*

a they introduce additional information ◯
b they introduce contrasting information ◯
c they refer back to something in the text ◯

6 Underline examples of 'clues' in sentences
A–F in Exercise 4. Do they 'add', 'contrast'
or 'refer'?

7 ◀) 2.14 Complete the phrases with the
words in blue in the text. Then listen,
check and repeat.

1 attract _____
2 breathtaking _____
3 historic _____
4 hot and _____
5 mining _____
6 trading _____
7 traffic _____

8 Complete the questions with the words in
Exercise 7.

1 Are there any _____ monuments in
your city?
2 Is your city a busy _____ centre?
3 Which parts of your country _____
a lot of visitors?
4 Where can you see breathtaking
_____ ?
5 Does it ever get hot and _____ in
your country?
6 Are there any _____ towns in your
country?
7 Where in your city are the worst
_____ jams?

9 SPEAKING Ask and answer the questions
in Exercise 8.

WORD STORE 4E | Collocations ⟩

10 ◀) 2.15 Complete WORD STORE 4E with
the words in the box. Then listen, check
and repeat. Write an example sentence for
each collocation.

GRAMMAR

4.5

Future forms: Present Continuous, *be going to* and *will*

I can talk about the future using the Present Continuous, going to and will.

1 SPEAKING **What makes a good house party? Add your own ideas to the ones below and put them in order of importance. Then compare your ideas with a partner.**

decoration ☐ food and drink ☐ furniture ☐
lighting ☐ music ☐ people ☐ theme ☐

2 🔊 2.16 **Read and listen to the dialogue. Then answer the questions.**

1 Why is Tony having a party?
2 Where and when is he having it?
3 How is Luisa going to help?

Tony: *I'm having* a birthday party on the 25th. Can you come?
Luisa: That's next Saturday, right? Yes, that sounds great. Are you having it at home?
Tony: No, our apartment isn't big enough. I'm using my aunt and uncle's house. They're really nice – they say it's fine.
Luisa: That's kind of them – do they know how many friends you've got?
Tony: Not yet. *I'm going to tell* them later. We'll probably use the basement. It's huge.
Luisa: A basement? Are you going to decorate it?
Tony: I suppose so. I'm not very good at that sort of thing.
Luisa: Don't worry, *I'll help* you. What are you doing later?
Tony: I'm going to text everybody with the invitation now, but after that I'm free.

3 **Read the GRAMMAR FOCUS. Complete the examples using the future forms in blue in Exercise 2. Then underline more examples of each future form in the text.**

GRAMMAR FOCUS

Future forms: Present Continuous, *be going to* and *will*

- You use the **Present Continuous** for future arrangements. You often mention a time, a date or a place.
  I ¹_____ a birthday party on the 25th.

- You use *be going to* for future intentions. You have already decided to do something and you tell people about it.
  I ²_____ *tell* them later.

- You use *will* for spontaneous decisions. You often use expressions like: *I think I'll …, I'll probably … , Don't worry, I'll … Don't worry, I* ³_____ *help* you.

4 🔊 2.17 **Choose the most appropriate future form. Then listen and check.**

Tony: Two of my friends ¹*are helping / will help* me prepare the room on Saturday afternoon. We ²*'re going to hang / 'll hang* sheets on the walls and the ceiling. Then we ³*'re going to put / 're putting* coloured lights everywhere. We ⁴*'ll have / 're having* a band and a DJ from eight to midnight. I've already booked them.
Aunt: Okay, I think I ⁵*'ll warn / 'm going to warn* the neighbours!
Tony: We've decided to have a fancy dress theme – everybody ⁶*will come / is coming* as their favourite film character.
Uncle: Oh good, I think I ⁷*'ll come / 'm going to come* as Captain Jack Sparrow!
Aunt: No, we ⁸*'ll go out / 're going out* to the theatre, remember? I told you yesterday.
Uncle: I know, I was joking. Now, what are you ⁹*eating / going to eat*?
Tony: That's all arranged. Mum ¹⁰*will make / is making* some pizzas.
Aunt: And what about the cleaning the next day?
Tony: Oh, erm … Don't worry, I ¹¹*'ll do / 'm doing* that with my friend Luisa. She won't mind!

5 **Complete the email with appropriate future forms in gaps 1–6 and your own ideas in gaps a–c.**

Hi Amy

You know I ¹*'m moving* (move) house next week. Well, I've decided that I ²_____ (have) a house-warming party in the new house. The theme is Superheroes, so I ³_____ (dress up) as ᵃ_____ . You know my mum's a fantastic cook so she ⁴_____ (make) ᵇ_____ . I think everybody ⁵_____ (like) that. I'm not sure about the music. I think I ⁶_____ (get) a DJ and ask him to play lots of ᶜ_____ .

6 SPEAKING **You are responsible for organising an end-of-term party for your school year. Discuss with a partner. Follow the instructions.**

1 Make some decisions about location, food and drink, music, decoration, theme, etc.
2 Write an email to the class to explain your ideas. Use all three future forms.

As a class, decide whose party ideas are best.

Grammar page 142

Adverbs

I can form adverbs and qualify them with really/quite/very.

1 SPEAKING **Look at the photos. What are the advantages and disadvantages of each place? Where would you like to spend the weekend? Discuss with a partner.**

2 🔊 **2.18** **Listen to Robbie trying to decide which place to go to. How many of your ideas in Exercise 1 does he mention? What does he decide to do and why?**

3 🔊 **2.18** **Listen again and choose the correct option.**
1 She doesn't speak *French very well / very well French*.
2 I speak *more well / better* than she does.
3 I stay up *late / lately*.
4 That sounds *extreme / extremely* boring.
5 Everybody goes to bed *really early / real early*.
6 Time goes *unbelievably slowly / unbelievably slow* in the country.

4 **Read the LANGUAGE FOCUS. Form appropriate adverbs from the adjectives in bold in sentences 1–6 below. Then put the words in the correct order to make sentences.**

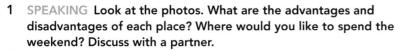

LANGUAGE FOCUS

Adverbs
- You use adverbs to modify verbs, adjectives and other adverbs.
- You form adverbs by adding **-ly**, **-y**, **-ily** to adjectives:
  slow → *slow**ly**, unbelievable* → *unbelievab**ly**, lucky* → *luck**ily***.
  Note: Some adverbs and adjectives have the same spelling:
  hard, fast, late, early.
  He is a fast runner./He runs fast.
- You never put an adverb between a verb and its object.

  VERB   OBJECT
  *He speaks English **well**.* NOT ~~He speaks well English.~~
- Use adverbs of degree to modify adjectives and adverbs.

WEAKER   STRONGER

a little/a bit/slightly	quite/rather/pretty	really/extremely/completely
She's **a little shy**.	My French is **pretty bad**.	Everybody goes to bed **really early**.

- You form comparative adverbs with *more*:
  *Alice speaks **more clearly** than John.*
  Note: Some comparative adverbs are irregular:
  well → *better, badly* → *worse, hard* → *harder*.

1 go to bed / I / at the weekend / **real late**
2 eat / I / quite **healthy**
3 I / my money / **wise** / spend
4 **extreme easy** / new words / learn / I
5 **pretty fast** / drives / My father / his car
6 understand / My parents / I do / English / than / **good**

5 **Change the sentences in Exercise 4 to make them true for you.**

6 USE OF ENGLISH **Complete the second sentence with option A, B or C so that it has a similar meaning to the first.**
1 My house is not very far from the school.
  My house is ___ near the school.
  A very   B quite⟲
  C completely
2 My cousin really hates meeting people.
  My cousin is ___ shy.
  A extremely   B a little
  C slightly
3 I don't get up early during the holidays.
  I get up ___ during the holidays.
  A late   B lately
  C more late
4 I don't sing as well as my best friend.
  My best friend sings ___ than me.
  A well   B good
  C better
5 I have to make more effort in English.
  I have to work ___ in English.
  A hardly   B more harder
  C harder

7 SPEAKING **Make the sentences true for you. Then compare your sentences with a partner.**
1 The countryside near my house is …
  [adverb] + [adjective]
  The countryside near my house is extremely beautiful.
2 The streets in my neighbourhood are …
  [adverb] + [adjective]
3 The capital city is …
  [adverb] + [adjective]
4 My school is … [adverb] + [adjective]
5 I usually get to school … [comparative adverb] … my schoolmates
6 I speak English … [adverb] + [adverb]

▸ Use of English page 143

WRITING

4.7

A blog entry

I can write a description of a recent trip.

1 In pairs, list as many British cities as you can think of in sixty seconds.

2 Read a blog about Bath. Which topics does the blogger mention?

a Art and culture
b Food and drink
c Entertainment and nightlife
d General information
e Shopping
f Tourist highlights

3 SPEAKING Would you like to visit Bath? Why?/ Why not? Discuss with a partner.

13 January

Last weekend, I visited my cousin in Bath, Somerset, in the southwest of England. Bath is a popular tourist destination and is famous for its historic sites. Today's blog entry is about my visit.

I met my cousin on Saturday morning and we walked around the city. Bath is a <u>lovely</u> place. The centre is small, so most people <u>tend</u> to visit it on foot. It was very busy, but we saw some really beautiful architecture. For visitors, a walk along the river is a must.

We stopped for lunch in a traditional tearoom. One of the local specialities is the Sally Lunn Bun. It was <u>delicious</u>! After lunch, we went shopping. Bath has a wide selection of shops. According to fashion magazines, Bath is 'Britain's best fashion secret'. I bought a cool T-shirt, some sunglasses and a hat.

In the evening, we went to the Roman Baths. It is the most popular attraction in the city. If you're tired after a long day, I would definitely <u>recommend</u> relaxing in the thermal waters of Bath Spa. I thought it was <u>wonderful</u>!

Comments (8)

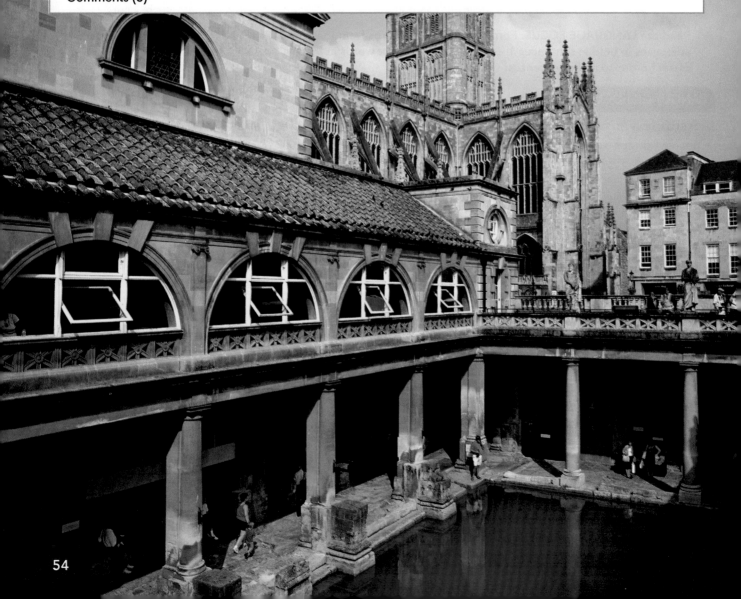

4 🔊 **2.19** Match the words and phrases in purple in the blog with the definitions below. Then listen, check and repeat.

1 an interesting thing to see or do = _____
2 choice or range = _____
3 food that you can only find here = _____
4 places that were important in the past = _____
5 something you should definitely see or do = _____

5 Read the WRITING FOCUS. Complete the examples with the underlined words in the blog in Exercise 2.

> **WRITING FOCUS**
>
> **A blog entry**
>
> **1 Say when and/or why you visited**
> *Last week/weekend/month, etc. I went to …/I visited my cousin/friend/aunt in …*
>
> **2 Introduce the place**
> *… is a small/large city in …*
> *… is a popular tourist destination.*
> *… is famous for its …*
>
> **3 Give impressions or opinions**
> *It is a busy/interesting/[1] lovely place.*
> *Most people seem to/[2]_____ to …*
> *According to …*
> *I thought it was great/[3]_____/a bit boring.*
> *It (the food) was [4]_____ !*
>
> **4 Make recommendations**
> *I would (definitely) [5]_____ (doing something).*
> *For visitors, … is a must.*

6 SPEAKING Complete these sentences to describe your own town or region. Then compare your answers with a partner.

1 _____ is famous for _____ .
2 For visitors, _____ is a must.
3 _____ is probably the most popular attraction.
4 One of the local specialities is _____ .
5 I would recommend _____ .

7 Read the LANGUAGE FOCUS. Complete with examples of comma use in the blog.

> **LANGUAGE FOCUS**
>
> **Punctuation – commas**
> • Put a comma between the names of cities and states or countries: [1] *Bath, Somerset*
> • Use commas to separate three or more nouns in a list – [2] _____
> • Use commas to separate clauses in a sentence when they are joined by *but* or *so*: [3] _____
> • Use a comma to separate an *if*-clause from the main clause when the *if*-clause is the first one in a sentence: [4] _____
> • Use a comma after time expressions at the beginning of a sentence: [5] _____

8 Add commas to the text about the Lake District.

The Lake District

The Lake District Cumbria is the UK's most popular national park. Every year 15 million people visit the area. The landscape is wonderful – there are lakes mountains beaches and breathtaking views. The Lake District is the wettest place in England but the dramatic skies are part of the attraction. Lake Windermere is eleven miles long and is a must for all visitors. If you enjoy walking hiking climbing or water sports the Lake District is an ideal place for a holiday.

SHOW WHAT YOU'VE LEARNT

9 Do the writing task. Use the ideas in the WRITING FOCUS and the LANGUAGE FOCUS to help you.

Write a blog entry in which you describe your impressions after visiting a well-known tourist destination. Include the following information:

• introduce the place and write when you were there
• write what you did there and what you saw
• present your impressions and your opinion about this place
• give some advice to the readers.

A few months ago, I visited …

Making suggestions

I can make suggestions and respond to them politely.

1 SPEAKING Imagine you are visiting London. Discuss which of these activities you would like to do. Give reasons for your answers.

SIX OF THE BEST THINGS TO DO IN LONDON

London by speedboat
▶ 7 days a week, all year
▶ Suitable for all ages!
▶ £35 for 50 minutes

Shopping
▶ Oxford Street shops: 8.30 a.m.–9 p.m., Sun 11.30 a.m.–6 p.m.
▶ Camden Market: Clothes, music, souvenirs. 10 a.m.–6 p.m. daily

The London Eye
Get the best view of London.
▶ 10 a.m.–9 p.m. every day
▶ Adult: £19, 15 and under: £10

The London Dungeon
Prepare to be scared!
▶ Tours from £20
▶ 10 a.m.–4 p.m. on Mon, Tue, Wed, Fri, 10 a.m.–5 p.m. on Sun, 10 a.m.–6 p.m. on Sat, 11 a.m.–4 p.m. on Thur

Shakespeare's Globe Theatre
▶ Experience *Romeo and Juliet* in Shakespeare's own theatre!
▶ Tickets: £20–£45
▶ Standing tickets from £5 only

Madame Tussauds
Come and see the Royal Family!
▶ 9 a.m.–6 p.m. daily
▶ Adult: £30 – save 50% when you book online

2 🔊 **2.20** Listen to Marcus and Ann. What do they decide to do? Which activities do they reject and why?

3 🔊 **2.20** Listen again and tick the expressions you hear.

SPEAKING FOCUS

Making suggestions
Do you fancy (going) …? ☑
Let's (go) … ☐
How about (going) …? ☐
We could (go) … ☐
(I think) we should (go) … ☐
What about (going) …? ☐
Why don't we (go) …? ☐

Agreeing with suggestions
(That's a) good/great idea! ☐
(That) sounds good/great! ☐
Why not! ☐

Disagreeing with suggestions
(I'm sorry) I'm not keen on … ☐
I don't really like … ☐
I'd rather (go) … ☐
I'm not sure about that. ☐
Let's (go) … instead. ☐

4 🔊 **2.21** Complete each expression in the dialogue with an appropriate word from the SPEAKING FOCUS. Then listen and check.

A: Do you fancy ¹_____ to the cinema tonight?
B: That's a good ²_____ ! What do you want to see?
A: The new film with Jennifer Aniston.
B: Oh no, I'm not ³_____ on romantic comedy. I'd ⁴_____ see an action film.
A: Okay, let's see the new James Bond ⁵_____ .
B: Great. How ⁶_____ having a burger before we go?
A: Why ⁷_____ ! We ⁸_____ try that new burger bar in town.

5 SPEAKING You are planning a day out in Edinburgh. Look at the tourist information. Follow the instructions below to prepare a dialogue. Use the SPEAKING FOCUS to help you.

A: Suggest an activity for the morning.
B: Agree and suggest something for the afternoon.
A: Disagree and suggest something different for the afternoon.
B: Disagree and suggest something else for the afternoon.
A: Agree and suggest something for the evening.
B: Agree.

National Museum of Scotland
10 a.m.–5 p.m.
Botanic Gardens
10 a.m.–6 p.m.
Climb a hill to get great views of the city
2 hours to climb up
Visit Edinburgh Castle
9.30 a.m.–5 p.m.
Comedy at 'Comedy Club'
8.30 p.m.–midnight
Ghost tour 'Dark secrets of old Edinburgh'
3 p.m.
Learn to do Scottish dancing
7 p.m.–midnight
Eat seafood in waterfront restaurants
7 p.m.–midnight

6 SPEAKING Practise your dialogue. Then act it out to the class.

ROLE-PLAY Making suggestions

🎬 **19** Watch the video and practise. Then role-play your dialogue.

4.1 Vocabulary 🔊 4.25

accommodation /əˌkɒmə'deɪʃən/
basement /'beɪsmənt/
bedside table /ˌbedsaɪd 'teɪbəl/
block of flats /ˌblɒk əv 'flæts/
bookcase /'bʊk-keɪs/
brick /brɪk/
bungalow /'bʌŋgələʊ/
carpet /'kɑːpət/
chest of drawers /ˌtʃest əv 'drɔːz/
comfortable /'kʌmftəbəl/
concrete /'kɒŋkriːt/
cooker /'kʊkə/
cosy /'kəʊzi/
cottage /'kɒtɪdʒ/
cupboard /'kʌbəd/
desk /desk/
detached house /dɪˌtætʃt 'haʊs/
do the cooking /ˌduː ðə 'kʊkɪŋ/
do the gardening /ˌduː ðə 'gɑːdnɪŋ/
do the housework /ˌduː ðə 'haʊswɜːk/
do the ironing /ˌduː ði 'aɪənɪŋ/
do the shopping /ˌduː ðə 'ʃɒpɪŋ/
do the washing /ˌduː ðə 'wɒʃɪŋ/
do the washing-up /ˌduː ðə ˌwɒʃɪŋ 'ʌp/
do your homework /ˌduː jɔː 'həʊmwɜːk/
downstairs /ˌdaʊn'steəz/
fridge /frɪdʒ/
front door /ˌfrʌnt 'dɔː/
glass /glɑːs/
in a village /ˌɪn ə 'vɪlɪdʒ/
in the city centre /ˌɪn ðə ˌsɪti 'sentə/
in the countryside /ˌɪn ðə 'kʌntrisaɪd/
in the suburbs /ˌɪn ðə 'sʌbɜːbz/
interior wall /ɪnˌtɪəriə 'wɔːl/
kitchen sink /ˌkɪtʃən 'sɪŋk/
ladder /'lædə/
make a complaint /ˌmeɪk ə kəm'pleɪnt/
make a decision /ˌmeɪk ə dɪ'sɪʒən/
make a mess /ˌmeɪk ə 'mes/
make a noise /ˌmeɪk ə 'nɔɪz/
make dinner /ˌmeɪk 'dɪnə/
make your bed /ˌmeɪk jɔː 'bed/
metal /'metl/
modern /'mɒdn/
narrow /'nærəʊ/
natural light /ˌnætʃərəl 'laɪt/
near the sea /ˌnɪə ðə 'siː/
neighbour /'neɪbə/
on a housing estate /ˌɒn ə 'haʊzɪŋ ɪˌsteɪt/
on the edge of the city /ˌɒn ði 'edʒ əv ðə 'sɪti/
on the first floor /ɒn ðə ˌfɜːst 'flɔː/
on the ground floor /ɒn ðə ˌgraʊnd 'flɔː/
on the second floor /ɒn ðə ˌsekənd 'flɔː/
on the top floor /ɒn ðə ˌtɒp 'flɔː/
open-plan /ˌəʊpən 'plæn/
radiator /'reɪdieɪtə/
semi-detached house /ˌsemidɪˌtætʃt 'haʊs/
shelf /ʃelf/
spacious /'speɪʃəs/

stairs /steəz/
stone /stəʊn/
terraced house /ˌterəst 'haʊs/
traditional /trə'dɪʃənəl/
upstairs /ˌʌp'steəz/
wardrobe /'wɔːdrəʊb/
wide /waɪd/
wood /wʊd/
wooden floor /ˌwʊdn 'flɔː/

4.2 Grammar 🔊 4.26

community /kə'mjuːnəti/
couch /kaʊtʃ/
feel at home /ˌfiːl ət 'həʊm/
feel homesick /ˌfiːl 'həʊmˌsɪk/
free /friː/
host /həʊst/
houseboat /'haʊsbəʊt/
luxury /'lʌkʃəri/
member /'membə/
neighbourhood /'neɪbəhʊd/
studio apartment /'stjuːdiəʊ əˌpɑːtmənt/

4.3 Listening 🔊 4.27

come round /ˌkʌm 'raʊnd/
get away from /ˌget əˌweɪ 'frəm/
keep sb out /ˌkiːp 'sʌmbɒdi 'aʊt/
lamp /læmp/
let sb in /ˌlet ˌsʌmbɒdi 'ɪn/
shell /ʃel/
show sb around /ˌʃəʊ 'sʌmbɒdi ə'raʊnd/
souvenir /ˌsuːvə'nɪə/
stay in /ˌsteɪ 'ɪn/

4.4 Reading 🔊 4.28

abandon /ə'bændən/
ancient /'eɪnʃənt/
attract /ə'trækt/
breathtaking view /ˌbreθteɪkɪŋ 'vjuː/
busy /'bɪzi/
camel /'kæməl/
cave /keɪv/
crater /'kreɪtə/
dense /dens/
desert /'dezət/
develop underwater vision /dɪ'veləp ˌʌndə'wɔːtə 'vɪʒən/
dry /draɪ/
electricity /ɪˌlek'trɪsəti/
historic monument /hɪˌstɒrɪk 'mɒnjəmənt/
hot springs /ˌhɒt 'sprɪŋz/
humid /'hjuːmɪd/
impressive /ɪm'presɪv/
island /'aɪlənd/
landscape /'lændskeɪp/
lush /lʌʃ/
mining /'maɪnɪŋ/
mountain /'maʊntən/
move (house) /ˌmuːv ('haʊs)/
nomadic tribe /nəʊˌmædɪk 'traɪb/
population /ˌpɒpjə'leɪʃən/
rainforest /'reɪnfɒrəst/
rock /rɒk/
ruins /'ruːɪnz/
scorching /'skɔːtʃɪŋ/

stilt /stɪlt/
tourist destination /'tʊərɪst destəˌneɪʃən/
trading centre /'treɪdɪŋ ˌsentə/
traffic jam /'træfɪk ˌdʒæm/
treehouse /'triː haʊs/
turquoise ocean /ˌtɜːkwɔɪz 'əʊʃən/
vegetation /ˌvedʒɪ'teɪʃən/
volcanic /vɒl'kænɪk/
volcano /vɒl'keɪnəʊ/

4.5 Grammar 🔊 4.29

ceiling /'siːlɪŋ/
house-warming party /'haʊswɔːmɪŋ ˌpɑːti/
sheet /ʃiːt/
warn /wɔːn/
dress up as /ˌdres 'ʌp əz/

4.6 Use of English 🔊 4.30

a little/a bit/slightly /ə 'lɪtl/ə 'bɪt/'slaɪtli/
badly /'bædli/
completely /kəm'pliːtli/
extremely /ɪk'striːmli/
luckily /'lʌkɪli/
quite/rather/pretty /kwaɪt/'rɑːðə/'prɪti/
really /'rɪəli/
stay up /ˌsteɪ 'ʌp/
unbelievably /ˌʌnbə'liːvəbli/
well /wel/

4.7 Writing 🔊 4.31

a must /ə 'mʌst/
according to /ə'kɔːdɪŋ tə/
architecture /'ɑːkətektʃə/
attraction /ə'trækʃən/
be famous for /bi 'feɪməs fə/
delicious /dɪ'lɪʃəs/
entertainment /ˌentə'teɪnmənt/
historic site /hɪˌstɒrɪk 'saɪt/
local speciality /ˌləʊkəl ˌspeʃi'æləti/
lovely /'lʌvli/
nightlife /'naɪtlaɪf/
on foot /ˌɒn 'fʊt/
recommend /ˌrekə'mend/
selection of /sə'lekʃən əv/
tend to /'tend tə/
tourist highlight /ˌtʊərɪst 'haɪlaɪt/
wonderful /'wʌndəfəl/

4.8 Speaking 🔊 4.32

adult /'ædʌlt/
castle /'kɑːsəl/
daily /'deɪli/
hill /hɪl/
river /'rɪvə/
royal family /ˌrɔɪəl 'fæməli/
suitable /'suːtəbəl/
waterfront restaurant /ˌwɔːtəfrʌnt 'restərɒnt/

VOCABULARY AND GRAMMAR

1 Complete the sentences with the words in the box. There are two extra words.

bungalow cupboard drawers estate
temperatures trading vegetation

1 There is a new housing _____ in the suburbs of the city. You can get there by bus.
2 Last month my family moved to a modern _____ with a large garden.
3 This chest of _____ is too small for my clothes. I need a big wardrobe.
4 Singapore is an important _____ centre in Asia. That's why the port there is so big.
5 Many popular tourist destinations have scorching _____ in summer.

2 Complete the sentences with the correct form of the words in capitals.

1 The Eiffel Tower is probably the most popular tourist _____ in Paris. **ATTRACT**
2 This is a _____ costume worn by young men on special occasions. **TRADITION**
3 My room in the new house is much more _____ than in the old flat. **SPACE**
4 The room was cosy with _____ stairs leading up to the next floor. **WOOD**
5 Our neighbours play loud music nearly every night. We've made several _____ . **COMPLAIN**

3 Complete the second sentence using the word in capitals so that it has a similar meaning to the first. Do not change the word in capitals.

1 They moved to Venice in 2016. **LIVED**
They _____ 2016.
2 Liz started working for a coachsurfing service two years ago. **WORKED**
Liz _____ for a couchsurfing service for two years.
3 They last saw Paul in January. **SINCE**
They _____ January.
4 When did you first meet Karen? **KNOWN**
How long _____ Karen?
5 I stopped travelling abroad three years ago. **FOR**
I _____ three years.

4 Complete the sentences with the correct future forms of the verbs in brackets.

1 Are you moving house on Saturday? I _____ you if you like. (help)
2 I'm sorry I can't come. I _____ a language course this evening. (start)
3 We _____ on Friday night, but we still don't know where exactly. (meet)
4 Hi, Jack! It's Sue. What time _____ you _____ tomorrow? (come)
5 'Was that the doorbell?' 'Yes, I _____ it!' (answer)
6 I _____ probably _____ in tonight. I feel so tired. (stay)

USE OF ENGLISH

5 Choose the correct answer, A, B or C.

1 X: What are your neighbours like?
Y: We haven't got any close neighbours. We live in a ___ house in the countryside.
A terraced
B detached
C semi-detached
2 X: Do you fancy going to the cinema?
Y: I'm not sure about that. ___ go swimming.
A How about
B Let's
C I would recommend
3 X: How long have you lived here?
Y: Not very long. ___ .
A For a few weeks.
B Since I was born.
C A few weeks ago.
4 X: Is Tamara going to the party?
Y: No, she isn't ___ dancing and is a bit shy.
A rather
B like
C keen on
5 X: Has your uncle seen your new house?
Y: I don't think so. ___ .
A I'll keep him out.
B I won't let him in.
C He's coming round tomorrow.
6 X: Do most people you know tend to eat ___ ?
Y: Yes, they try to avoid fast food.
A healthy
B healthily
C unhealthily

6 Choose the correct answer, A, B or C, to complete both sentences.

1 I'll ___ dinner. What would you like?
Can you tidy your room, please, and ___ your bed?
A do   B make   C prepare
2 What ancient ___ would you like to visit?
Do you fancy walking around in the ___ centre?
A city   B monument   C trading
3 There are a lot of places to ___ the shopping in my town.
It's best to ___ the washing-up right after the meal.
A do   B go   C make
4 I'd ___ take a taxi to the suburbs.
Put on a coat – it's ___ cold outside.
A quite   B like   C rather
5 We were ___ surprised when we heard the news.
There was ___ table next to the sofa.
A a little   B slightly   C so
6 The shops aren't ___ on Sunday afternoons.
We used to live in a(n) ___-plan flat.
A working   B closed   C open

7 🔊 **2.22** Listen to four people talking about living in the suburbs. Match the speakers (1–4) with the statements (A–E). There is one extra statement. Listen to the recording twice.

The speaker:

A feels like a member of the community in the suburbs. ☐

B has changed his/her opinion about living in the suburbs. ☐

C is not going to live in the suburbs all his/her life. ☐

D addresses people who don't want to live in the city centre. ☐

E presents people's opinions about living in the suburbs. ☐

SPEAKING

8 Your family and you are going to spend a month of your summer holiday somewhere in England. You are looking through different types of accommodation available. In pairs, discuss which accommodation you would prefer for a month-long holiday and why.

Think about:
- location
- surroundings
- attractions
- price

9 In pairs, describe the photo and answer the questions.

1 What are the family doing, in your opinion?
2 How do you help with the housework in your home?
3 Tell us about a situation when you or someone you know had to tidy up a garage or basement.

WRITING

10 Read the writing task. Decide in what order the sentences (a–d) should be used in the blog post.

> You've recently been on a school trip to one of the cities in your country. Share your impressions of this city in a blog post. Include the following information:
> - say what city you visited and when
> - express and explain your opinion about this city
> - write what you recommend seeing in the city you visited
> - describe an unexpected problem you had on the trip and how it was solved.

a Lyon is a beautiful, historic city. ☐
b Unfortunately, we missed our train back to Paris. ☐
c I would recommend visiting Parc de la Tête d'Or. ☐
d Last month we went on a class trip to Lyon. ☐

11 Write the blog post.

5

Time to learn

Tell me and I forget, teach me and I remember, involve me and I learn.

Benjamin Franklin

BBC

SOUTH KOREAN SCHOOLS

▶ 20 Watch the BBC video.
For the worksheet, go to page 124.

VOCABULARY

5.1

Places in school • education • phrasal verbs • collocations

I can use language related to school life and equipment.

SHOW WHAT YOU KNOW

1 SPEAKING **Look at the words and discuss your favourite/least favourite place in school. Where do you spend most time?**

> canteen/cafeteria classroom corridor gym library playground reception school hall school office science lab sports field staff room

2 **Look at the photos and read three descriptions of different school systems. Decide which text describes a school in Brazil, Finland and Japan. For the answers, go to page 157.**

School systems

1 Our school is quite informal – we can call our teachers by their first names. We don't <u>move up</u> to secondary school when we're eleven because we attend the same comprehensive school from seven to sixteen. All our classes are mixed ability. The curriculum includes academic subjects but also Art, Music and PE, with only about thirty minutes of homework every day. We're lucky – we don't have to pay tuition fees to do a degree at university.

2 English is my favourite subject, but I can't <u>keep up with</u> all the homework! We have to learn lists of vocabulary by heart. At elementary school, the timetable includes earthquake practice. If there's an earthquake when children are outside, they have to <u>line up</u> in the playground. At the end of the day, we have to clean our classroom. Most of my classmates will go to university. In my country, 50 percent of the population are university graduates.

3 Compare the descriptions with your own school system. Find a piece of information for each line in the table.

This is true for me/my school	In our school system we also have two terms.
This isn't true for me/my school	
I like this	
I don't like this	
This is interesting, strange or unusual	

4 🔊 **2.23** Listen to a UK school head teacher. What did she change in her school and why?

5 🔊 **2.23** Listen again. Which three problems were the result of sleepiness?
1 Students dropped subjects.
2 Students thought that teachers set too much homework.
3 Students didn't hand in their homework on time.
4 Students skipped lessons.
5 Students couldn't pay attention in class.
6 Students made lots of mistakes.

6 SPEAKING Prepare a timetable for a 'perfect school day'. Compare it with your classmates. Who has the best day?

3 School is compulsory between the ages of six and fourteen. Our school terms are from February to June and August to December. We break up in December for our summer holiday. I set off for school very early because my lessons start at 7 a.m. and finish at 12.

My school's open all day to cope with the high numbers of students. There are three sessions, from 7 to 12, 12 to 5 and 5 to 10 o'clock in the evening. In the afternoon I do after-school activities like football or music. When I finish high school, I'll take an entrance exam to get into university.

WORD STORE 5A Education

7 🔊 **2.24** Complete WORD STORE 5A by matching the correct form of the words or phrases in red in the text with their definitions. Then listen, check and repeat.

8 Complete the sentences with words or phrases in WORD STORE 5A. Which sentences are true for you?
In my school …
1 it's _____ to wear a school uniform.
2 the school year starts in September and is divided into three _____ .
3 students at the same level learn together. There are no _____ classes.
4 we focus on _____ . Personally, I prefer subjects like Drama and PE.
5 our English teacher gives us long lists of vocabulary to _____ .
6 the History _____ only covers the twentieth century.
7 the _____ includes a break in the morning and a long break for lunch.
8 I get on really well with all my _____ .

WORD STORE 5B Phrasal verbs

9 🔊 **2.25** Complete WORD STORE 5B with the base form of the underlined phrasal verbs in the text and in Exercise 5. Then listen, check and repeat.

10 Complete the sentences with the correct particle and your own ideas. Then compare your sentences with a partner.
1 We break _____ for summer on [date] _____ .
2 The last piece of homework I handed _____ was [subject] _____ .
3 It's hard to keep up _____ all the homework in [subject] _____ .
4 Next year I'll move _____ to [year/school] _____ .
5 If you want to get _____ university, you have to pass [name/type of exam] _____ .
6 The thing I find most difficult to cope _____ at school is [your idea] _____ .

WORD STORE 5C Collocations

11 🔊 **2.26** Complete WORD STORE 5C with the base form of the highlighted words in the text and in Exercise 5. Then listen, check and repeat.

12 SPEAKING Complete the statements with the correct verb. Sometimes more than one answer is possible. Discuss whether you agree or disagree with the statements.
1 Parents should pay a fine if their children _____ lessons.
2 It's impossible to _____ attention in class straight after lunch.
3 You shouldn't have to _____ university tuition fees. All education should be free.
4 English teachers don't _____ enough homework. We want more!
5 You have to go to university and _____ a degree if you want a good job.
6 Students should be able to _____ a subject if they are not interested in it.

GRAMMAR

5.2

First Conditional

I can use the First Conditional to predict possible results of actions or situations.

1 SPEAKING **Read UK TODAY. What is a gap year? Discuss whether you think it's a good thing to do. Give reasons for your answers.**

UK TODAY

Did you know that about 10 percent of students in the UK do a gap year between leaving school and going to university?

What do they do?
• travel abroad   • go backpacking   • do voluntary work

Where do they go?
• Africa   • Southeast Asia
• Australia and New Zealand   • South America

How much does it cost?
Usually about £4,000.

He'll waste a year if he goes travelling.

If he **goes** to South America next year, he**'ll go** to university the year after.

2 🔊 **2.27** **Look at the photo of Ricky's parents and read the sentences. Who do you think is in favour of Ricky doing a gap year and who is against? Listen and check.**

3 **Read the GRAMMAR FOCUS. Complete the examples using the First Conditional forms in blue in Exercise 2.**

GRAMMAR FOCUS

First Conditional

• You use the **First Conditional** to predict the future result of an action.

action	→	future result
***if* + Present Simple**		***will/won't* + verb**

If he ¹_____ *to South America next year, he* ²_____ *to university the year after.*
*If he **doesn't go** to university, he **won't get** a decent job.*

• You can put the *if*-clause after the main clause.
*He**'ll waste** a year if he **goes** travelling.*

4 🔊 **2.27** **Match the halves of the sentences from the conversation. Then listen again and check.**

1 If Ricky doesn't go to university this year, ☐
2 He'll get a lot out of it ☐
3 He'll do bungee jumps and get a tattoo ☐
4 If he goes away on his own, ☐
5 If he doesn't do anything on his own, ☐

a if he does a gap year.
b he'll never go.
c he'll get into trouble.
d he'll never be independent.
e if he goes to South America.

5 🔊 **2.28** **What other reasons might Ricky have for going to South America? Listen and check your ideas.**

6 🔊 **2.28** **Complete the sentences with the correct form of the verbs in brackets. Then listen again and check.**

1 He thinks if I _____ (go) travelling,
I _____ (not go) to university when I come back.
2 If I _____ (tell) them the truth, they definitely _____ (not let) me go.
3 You _____ (not learn) any Spanish if you _____ (visit) her!
4 If my dad _____ (not agree), I _____ (not able) to go.
5 If your mum _____ (think) it's a good idea, she _____ (convince) your dad.

7 SPEAKING **Work in groups of three. Look at the prompts and practise the conversation as in the example.**

A (student's wish)	B (positive parent)	C (negative parent)
1 live abroad	new culture	miss friends
2 join a band	have a lot of fun	not do schoolwork
3 part-time job	earn money	get up early

A: *I want to live abroad.*
B: *Great! If you live abroad, you'll learn about a new culture.*
C: *Oh dear. If you live abroad, you'll miss all your friends.*

Grammar page 144

1 SPEAKING **Read the tips for dealing with exam stress. Which tips do you usually follow? Can you add any more tips? Discuss with a partner.**

Get rid of exam stress

☐ Create a revision schedule – and follow it!

☐ Don't get exhausted – get plenty of sleep.

☐ Study in a group from time to time.

☐ Be positive – imagine yourself passing the exam.

☐ Take regular breaks – do things you enjoy.

☐ Remember, it's only an exam. You won't die if you fail!

2 🔊 **2.29 Listen to Grace and Tom talking about exams. Tick the tips in Exercise 1 that Grace mentions.**

3 **Read statements 1–6 in Exercise 4. Match the underlined words and phrases with the words and phrases in the box.**

alone	☐3	blame Grace	☐
enjoy himself	☐	marks	☐
nervous	☐	take it easy	☐

EXAM FOCUS True/False

4 🔊 **2.29 Listen to the conversation again. Are statements 1–6 true (T) or false (F)?**

1 Tom doesn't usually get good <u>grades</u> at school. ☐

2 Grace thinks Tom will get sick if he doesn't <u>relax</u>. ☐

3 Grace thinks Tom should spend less time <u>on his own</u>. ☐

4 Grace doesn't get <u>stressed</u> about exams. ☐

5 Grace tells Tom to go out and <u>have a good time</u>. ☐

6 Tom will <u>say it's Grace's fault</u> if he fails his exams. ☐

5 **Do you have to take an entrance exam to get into university in your country? Read the information about British universities. Is the missing word a noun or a number?**

How to get a place at University in Britain

1 Apply for a place at university when you're in your last year of secondary school: Year _____ .

2 You can apply to _____ universities.

3 To get into university, you have to get good _____ in three or four A levels.

4 To get into Oxford or Cambridge University, you have to take an entrance _____ .

5 Last year _____ students applied for 400,000 university places.

6 You have to pay university tuition fees up to £_____ a year.

Notes:
A levels = Advanced level exams. Students usually do A levels at eighteen.

6 🔊 **2.30 Listen and complete the information sheet in Exercise 5.**

7 **In groups, write an information sheet which explains how to get a place at university in your country.**

PRONUNCIATION FOCUS

8 🔊 **2.31 Listen and choose the number you hear. Then listen again and repeat.**

1	15.1	50.1	4	18.18	80.18
2	170	117	5	14,440	40,414
3	13,990	30,919	6	660,000	616,000

9 **Write six similar numbers. Take it in turns to dictate them to your partner. Check your answers.**

WORD STORE 5D get

10 🔊 **2.32 Complete WORD STORE 5D. Put the collocations and phrasal verbs with *get* under the correct heading. Then listen, check and repeat.**

READING

Matching

I can scan a short text to locate specific information.

1 SPEAKING **Look at the photos and the title of the article. Discuss the questions.**

1 What do you know about the people? What are they famous for?

2 What do you think the text is about?

3 Which of the words and phrases in the box do you expect to see in the text?

> ability animals autism dyslexia food
> hard work help learning disorders money
> strong successful support

2 **Read the text and check your ideas in Exercise 1.**

EXAM FOCUS **Matching**

3 **Read the text again. Match questions 1–6 with the people described in the text. Write MP, TG, KK or RB.**

1 Which person's teacher changed his/her life in a positive way? _____

2 Who is able to concentrate on his/her strengths because of his/her learning disorder? _____

3 Who became better at something when learning about his/her favourite subject? _____

4 Who changed in a positive way thanks to getting over his/her learning difficulties? _____

5 Who did something to help others understand a learning disorder? _____

6 Which person got over his/her difficulties to have a job of his/her dreams? _____

Different, not less

🔊 2.33

Many people have learning disorders. They suffer in school: other children bully them or *make fun of them and call them 'slow'*. However, people can get over their learning disorders and have successful careers
5 **with the help and support of family, teachers and doctors, as these examples prove.**

At school, **Michael Phelps** could not sit still and found it difficult to concentrate. His teachers said he couldn't *focus on anything.* But then he found his passion for sport.
10 His mother encouraged him and *helped him to develop his swimming ability.* His reading improved when he read books about sport. And his Maths improved when the problems reflected his interests, for example, 'How long will it take to swim 500 metres if you swim three metres
15 per second?' Through hard work and never missing a day's practice, Michael became an Olympic champion, winning twenty-eight medals, twenty-three of them gold.

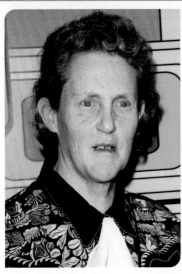

In the world of autism, **Dr Temple Grandin** is an
20 important voice. Autistic herself, she is an expert on how to teach people with autism, and she *has written six books about the condition*. She describes
25 herself as a visual thinker and says that *her mind is like Google Images*. School was difficult for her
30 because she didn't think in the same way as other children. But one summer, she worked on a farm and discovered that she 'understood animals'. At school,
35 her science teacher became her mentor. With *his help and support*, Grandin became interested in animal science. She later became a professor of animal science at Colorado State University.

Keira Knightley found out
40 she had dyslexia at the age of six and she remembers other children calling her stupid. She believes that her *problems with reading and*
45 *writing* made her strong. Knightley struggled with reading and writing, but she dreamt of being an actress, so she had to read scripts.
50 She had to *work harder than other children* to improve her literacy, but she finished school with top grades.

Richard Branson is one
55 of the most successful entrepreneurs in the world. He says that because of his dyslexia, he has learnt to keep things simple, ignore
60 difficulties and focus on what he is good at. However, he grew up at a time when dyslexia was misunderstood – his
65 teachers *made the mistake of thinking* that he was lazy or 'not very clever'. His head teacher at secondary school told him: 'I predict
70 that you will either go to prison or become a millionaire.' He was right.

So don't worry if you are different – you never know where your differences could lead you.

---

4 🔊 **2.34** Look at the words in blue in the text and note how the phrases in italics can help you understand their meaning. Match the words with the definitions. Then listen, check and repeat.

1 try to hurt or frighten someone who is weaker = ___bully___
2 a very experienced person who helps a less experienced person = _____
3 think very carefully about something you are doing = _____
4 someone who has special knowledge of a subject = _____
5 to give someone the confidence to do something = _____
6 try very hard to achieve something that is difficult = _____
7 not liked by other people in a way that is unfair = _____
8 someone who imagines words as pictures = _____

5 Complete the gaps with words in Exercise 4. Then complete the sentences with your own ideas.

1 I find it difficult to _____ when …
2 The best way of dealing with someone who _____ you is …
3 The school subject I _____ with most is …
4 A good way to _____ students to work harder is …
5 A person I know who I'd like as a _____ is …
6 I'd like to become an _____ on …

I find it difficult to concentrate when somebody has the TV on too loud …

6 SPEAKING **Compare your sentences in Exercise 5 with a partner. How similar or different are you?**

WORD STORE 5E | *of and for*

7 🔊 **2.35** Complete WORD STORE 5E with *of* or *for*. Use the underlined words in the text. Then listen, check and repeat.

GRAMMAR

5.5

Defining relative clauses

I can use who/that/which in basic defining relative clauses.

1 SPEAKING **Read an extract from *The British Students' Manifesto*. How is this school similar or different to your school? Discuss with a partner.**

> The <u>school</u> that we'd like is: A <u>school</u> which is for everybody, with <u>boys and girls</u> who come from all backgrounds and abilities, a <u>place</u> where we don't compete against each other, but just do our best.

2 **Read the GRAMMAR FOCUS. Complete the rules using the relative pronouns in blue in Exercise 1.**

GRAMMAR FOCUS

Defining relative clauses

- You use ¹_____ or *that* for people.
- You use ²_____ or *that* for things.
- You use ³_____ to refer to a place.

The relative pronoun usually comes immediately after the person, thing or place it refers to. You can leave out **that**, **which** or **who** when it comes before a noun or a pronoun.

3 **Read *The British Students' Manifesto*. Underline the nouns that relative pronouns 1–10 refer to. Choose the correct relative pronoun.**

4 **Complete these definitions of words from the *Manifesto* with an appropriate relative pronoun.**

1 An *uncluttered* classroom is a classroom <u>which/that</u> is tidy with no unnecessary things in it. ☐
2 A *beanbag* is a large cushion _____ forms a comfortable shape when you sit on it. ☐
3 A person _____ scrapes their knees may get small cuts. ☐
4 *Chill out* is an informal expression _____ means 'to relax'. ☐
5 *Blinds* are like curtains _____ you use to keep out the light. ☐
6 A *swipe card* is a plastic card _____ works like a key and lets you in or out. ☐
7 A *rigid* timetable is a timetable _____ you can't change. ☐
8 A *relevant* school is a school _____ lessons are directly connected with real life. ☐

5 **Tick the sentences in Exercise 4 where you can leave out the relative pronoun.**

6 SPEAKING **Work in groups. Prepare a manifesto about your ideas for a perfect school. Think about:**

1 classrooms and study areas
2 gardens and sports grounds
3 equipment and technology
4 school uniforms
5 canteen.

7 SPEAKING **Present your manifesto to the rest of the class.**

FOCUS VLOG About education

🎬 **23** **Watch the Focus Vlog. For the worksheet, go to page 125.**

Grammar page 145

The British Students' Manifesto
We, the school pupils of Britain, have a voice.

This is what we say.

The school that we'd like is:

A beautiful school ¹*where / that* the classrooms are uncluttered and the walls are brightly coloured.

A comfortable school with sofas and beanbags, cushions on the floors, tables ²*who / that* don't scrape our knees, and quiet rooms ³*where / which* we can chill out.

A light school with huge windows ⁴*that / where* let the sunshine in, but blinds ⁵*who / which* keep out the sun when we want to watch something on a screen.

A safe school with swipe cards for the school gate, anti-bully alarms, first aid classes, and someone ⁶*where / that* we can talk to about our problems.

A flexible school without rigid timetables or exams, without compulsory homework, ⁷*where / who* we can follow our own interests and spend more time on the subjects ⁸*who / which* we enjoy.

A relevant school ⁹*who / where* we learn through experience, experiments and exploration, with field trips to historic sites and other places of interest.

A school that is for everybody with students ¹⁰*which / who* come from all backgrounds and abilities, a place where we don't compete against each other, but just do our best.

The British Students' Manifesto was the result of a nationwide survey of over 15,000 students in England and Wales.

5.6 USE OF ENGLISH

Future time and conditional clauses

I can use conjunctions in the Present Simple with future reference.

1 SPEAKING **Look at the list of team sports. Discuss the questions.**

1 Which of these sports do you play/have you played?
2 What other sports do you play/have you played?
3 How much time a week do you spend doing sport?

TOP 6 TEAM SPORTS IN UK SCHOOLS

Football
Rugby
Cricket
Netball
Hockey
Basketball

2 2.36 **Listen to Isabel and Monica discussing their hockey team and answer the questions.**

1 How much of her free time does Isabel spend playing hockey?
2 How does she feel about it?
3 What does she agree to do?

3 SPEAKING **Do you know anyone who spends all their free time training for something? Tell your partner.**

4 2.36 **Complete the sentences from the conversation with the correct form of the verbs in brackets. Then listen again and check.**

1 **If** you ___________ (leave) the team, we ___________ (not win) our next match.
2 I ___________ (not have) time to do anything else **unless** I ___________ (give up) hockey.
3 **As soon as** I ___________ (get) home tonight, I ___________ (change) into my hockey kit.
4 I ___________ (call) her **when** I ___________ (have) a minute.
5 **Before** I ___________ (decide), I ___________ (discuss) it with the rest of the team.

5 **Read the LANGUAGE FOCUS and choose the most appropriate conjunction in sentences 1–5 below.**

LANGUAGE FOCUS

Future time and conditional clauses

- When you are talking about the future, you use the present tense after the conjunctions ***if***, ***when***, ***as soon as***, ***unless*** (=if not), ***before*** and ***after***.
  __After__ you get your own place, you'll need money to live.
  You won't pass your exams __unless__ you do some work.
- The clause with the conjunction can come before or after the main clause. When it comes before, you need a comma to separate the two clauses.

1 *When / If* school finishes today, I'll probably go straight home.
2 *As soon as / Unless* I get home, I'll change into my football kit.
3 I won't get into the school team *if / unless* I train hard.
4 *Before / If* I finish training, I'll do some shooting practice.
5 *After / Before* I finish training, I'll have a shower.

6 USE OF ENGLISH **Complete the second sentence with the appropriate conjunction so that it has a similar meaning to the first.**

1 Start revising now or you'll fail your exams.
You won't pass your exams _________ you start revising now.
2 Learn your vocabulary. At home I'll test you.
I'll test you on your vocabulary _________ we get home.
3 First I'll pass my exams. Two weeks later I'll go on holiday.
I'm going to go on holiday _________ I pass my exams.
4 The moment I get my exam result, I'll apply to university.
I'll apply to university _________ I get my exam results.
5 First he wants to have a break for a year, and then he plans to go to university.
He thinks he'll do a gap year _________ he goes to university.

7 SPEAKING **Complete the sentences with your own ideas. Then compare your sentences with a partner.**

1 When this term ends, …
When this term ends, I'll be very happy!
2 I'll stop studying English as soon as …
3 If I fail any of my end-of-school exams, …
4 Unless I keep up with my schoolwork, …
5 My parents will go mad unless …

Use of English page 146

WRITING

5.7

An enquiry

I can write a formal email requesting information.

1 You want to do an English course in the UK. Read the ad and write down three questions you would like to ask about the school.

Paddington School Online | Paddington School Group

Q | LIVE CHAT | CONTACT US | BOOK NOW

PADDINGTON ENGLISH SCHOOL

Central London location, ideal for shops, art galleries and museums.

We offer English courses for all levels and all exams:

IELTS, TOEFL, CAMBRIDGE, PTE

Excellent teachers, competitive prices.

Contact us: call **00 44 208 44 44 44**

or write to
enquiry@paddingtonenglish.co.uk

Dear Sir or Madam,

I am a seventeen-year-old Italian student, and **I am writing to enquire about** doing an English course at your school next summer. I am particularly interested in doing the Cambridge First Certificate exam. I got good marks in my English exam this year, and I think I am B2 level. **Could you tell me** how long I will need to study and how much it will cost?

I would also like to know if you can arrange accommodation for me. Could you tell me what kind of accommodation you provide, and how much it costs?

Finally, **I would be grateful if you could** send me details of how to book a course and how to pay for it.

I look forward to hearing from you.

Yours faithfully,

Analisa Bargellini

---

2 Read Analisa's email of enquiry. Did she ask any of the questions you wrote down?

3 Put the sentences summarising the email in the order they appear (1–3).

a polite questions about the information you need ☐

b what you would like the reader to do ☐

c information about yourself and why you are writing the email ☐

4 Read the WRITING FOCUS. Complete the examples with the phrases in purple in the email in Exercise 2.

5 Read the LANGUAGE FOCUS. Complete with examples in the email in Exercise 2.

6 Complete the indirect questions.

1 Does your school have a canteen? →
   Could you tell me _____ ?
2 Can my friend stay with the same host family? →
   I would like to know _____ .
3 How far is the school from the nearest tube station?
   → Could you tell me _____ ?
4 How many students are there in a class? →
   I would like to know _____ .
5 Could you send me an application form? →
   I would be grateful if _____ .

7 Rewrite the email so that it is more formal. Use the WRITING FOCUS and the LANGUAGE FOCUS to help you.

Hi

I'm coming to London in July and I'd like to attend your school and improve my English. Please tell me how I can register with your school.

Do you have a space for me? I'm seventeen years old and I'm from Spain. How much does it cost? I don't have anywhere to stay in London – can you help me with accommodation?

I hope you reply soon.

Thanks.

SHOW WHAT YOU'VE LEARNT

8 Do the writing task. Use the ideas in the WRITING FOCUS and the LANGUAGE FOCUS to help you.

ST JOHN'S SCHOOL

Study English in the beautiful, peaceful village of Amberley. Small groups, experienced staff, excellent host-family accommodation.
For information about exams, fees and availability, please call 00 44 543 43 32 21 or write to Mary Johnson at mary@stjohn.edu

You've read the advertisement and you want to learn English at St John's School. Write an email to the school asking for more details. Include the following information:

- introduce yourself and explain why you're writing
- ask for the information about the exam, the nearest city and public transport
- ask about the accommodation and say that you're expecting a reply.

Dear Sir or Madam,

I am a sixteen-year-old Turkish student and I am writing ...

SPEAKING

5.8

Giving an opinion • agreeing and disagreeing

I can express belief, opinion, agreement and disagreement politely.

1 **SPEAKING** Why do some students choose to leave school early and not go to university? Discuss with a partner.

2 ◀) **2.37** Listen to a dialogue between Tom and Susie. Look at the statements. Do Tom and Susie agree (A) or disagree (D)?

	Tom	Susie
1 Robert should leave school if he wants to be an actor.		
2 He doesn't need to do A levels.		
3 He might need to get a proper job.		
4 Robert's good-looking and talented.		
5 He should do his A levels first.		

3 ◀) **2.37** Listen again and number the expressions in the order you hear them.

SPEAKING FOCUS

Giving an opinion

I think he …	☐
I don't think it's …	☐ 1
Personally, I think …	☐
I really believe …	☐
In my opinion, …	☐
If you ask me, …	☐

Agreeing

I couldn't agree more.	☐
That's a good point.	☐

Disagreeing politely

I see what you mean, but …	☐
That's true, but …	☐
I'm not so sure.	☐

Disagreeing

I totally disagree!	☐
Oh come on! That's nonsense.	☐

4 Choose the correct option.

1. **A:** What do you think about single-sex schools?
   B: *I don't think / Personally, I think* they're a good idea. It isn't normal to separate boys and girls.
2. **A:** If you ask me, I think we get too much homework.
   B: *I'm not so sure. / I couldn't agree more.* I never have time to do sport or relax in the evenings.
3. **A:** I don't think my pronunciation is very good.
   B: *I really believe it, / I see what you mean, but* if you practise, I'm sure you'll improve.
4. **A:** I think the food in the school canteen is too expensive.
   B: *Oh come on! That's nonsense. / That's a good point.* If you go to a restaurant in town, you'll pay much more.
5. **A:** In my opinion, it's a waste of time going to university – I want to get a job and earn some money.
   B: *I totally disagree. / I couldn't agree more.* If you go to university, you'll get a much better job.

5 **SPEAKING** Discuss the subjects in the box.

> leaving school at sixteen
> having extra lessons after school
> learning by heart   playing sport at school
> wearing a uniform   doing a gap year
> skipping lessons

A: Ask what your partner thinks.
B: Give your opinion.
A: Agree or disagree and say why.

6 **SPEAKING** Your school has received a donation of €5,000. Photos 1, 2 and 3 show three possible ways your school could spend the money. Follow the instructions below and present your choice to the class. Use the SPEAKING FOCUS to help you.

1. Choose the option which, in your opinion, is the best for the school.
2. Support your choice with some reasons.
3. Explain why you have rejected the other options.

I think the school should spend the money on computers because …
I don't think the school should choose option … because …

ROLE-PLAY   Giving an opinion

▶ 24 **Watch the video and practise. Then role-play your dialogue.**

5.1 Vocabulary 🔊 4.33

ability /ə'bɪləti/
academic subject /ˌækə'demɪk 'sʌbdʒɪkt/
after-school activity /ˌɑːftə ˌskuːl æk'tɪvəti/
attend/go to school /ə'tend/ˌɡəʊ tə 'skuːl/
break up /ˌbreɪk 'ʌp/
classmate /'klɑːsmeɪt/
compulsory /kəm'pʌlsəri/
cope with /ˌkəʊp 'wɪð/
curriculum /kə'rɪkjʊləm/
do a degree /ˌduː ə dɪ'ɡriː/
do/take an exam /ˌduː/ˌteɪk ən ɪɡ'zæm/
drop a subject /ˌdrɒp ə 'sʌbdʒɪkt/
elementary school /ˌelə'mentəri skuːl/
entrance exam /'entrəns ɪɡˌzæm/
fail an exam /ˌfeɪl ən ɪɡ'zæm/
finish school /ˌfɪnɪʃ 'skuːl/
get a degree /ˌget ə dɪ'ɡriː/
get into university /ˌget ˌɪntə ˌjuːnə'vɜːsəti/
get on well with /ˌget ɒn 'wel wɪð/
hand in homework /ˌhænd ˌɪn 'həʊmwɜːk/
have a degree /ˌhæv ə dɪ'ɡriː/
keep up with /ˌkiːp 'ʌp wɪð/
learn by heart, memorise /ˌlɜːn baɪ 'hɑːt/'meməraɪz/
learn from mistakes /ˌlɜːn frəm mɪ'steɪks/
leave school /ˌliːv 'skuːl/
line up /ˌlaɪn 'ʌp/
make mistakes /ˌmeɪk mɪ'steɪks/
mark homework /ˌmɑːk 'həʊmwɜːk/
miss/skip lessons /ˌmɪs/ˌskɪp 'lesənz/
mixed-ability class /ˌmɪkst əˌbɪləti 'klɑːs/
move up /ˌmuːv 'ʌp/
Music /'mjuːzɪk/
pass an exam /ˌpɑːs ən ɪɡ'zæm/
pay attention /ˌpeɪ ə'tenʃən/
PE /ˌpiː 'iː/
playground /'pleɪɡraʊnd/
revise for an exam /rɪˌvaɪz fər ən ɪɡ'zæm/
school uniform /ˌskuːl 'juːnəfɔːm/
secondary school /'sekəndəri skuːl/
set homework /ˌset 'həʊmwɜːk/
start school /ˌstɑːt 'skuːl/
take a subject /ˌteɪk ə 'sʌbdʒɪkt/
term /tɜːm/
timetable /'taɪmˌteɪbəl/
tuition fee /tjuːˈɪʃən fiː/
university graduate /ˌjuːnə'vɜːsəti 'ɡrædʒuət/

5.2 Grammar 🔊 4.34

be in favour of /ˌbi ɪn 'feɪvər əv/
decent job /ˌdiːsənt 'dʒɒb/
do a bungee jump /ˌduː ə 'bʌndʒi ˌdʒʌmp/
gap year /'ɡæp jɪə/
go away /ˌɡəʊ ə'weɪ/
go backpacking /ˌɡəʊ 'bækˌpækɪŋ/
go/live abroad /ˌɡəʊ/ˌlɪv ə'brɔːd/
join a band /ˌdʒɔɪn ə 'bænd/
part-time job /ˌpɑːt taɪm 'dʒɒb/
schoolwork /'skuːlwɜːk/
waste /weɪst/

5.3 Listening 🔊 4.35

A levels /'eɪ ˌlevəlz/
apply for (a place) /ə'plaɪ fər ə 'pleɪs/
be positive /ˌbi 'pɒzətɪv/
field trip /'fiːld trɪp/
get a job /ˌget ə 'dʒɒb/
get a lot out of sth /ˌget ə 'lɒt aʊt əv ˌsʌmθɪŋ/
get a place at university /ˌget ə ˌpleɪs ət ˌjuːnə'vɜːsəti/
get a tattoo /ˌget ə tə'tuː/
get exhausted /ˌget ɪɡ'zɔːstɪd/
get good grades /ˌget ɡʊd 'ɡreɪdz/
get ill /ˌget 'ɪl/
get into trouble /ˌget ˌɪntə 'trʌbəl/
get nervous /ˌget 'nɜːvəs/
get rid of sth /ˌget 'rɪd əv ˌsʌmθɪŋ/
get stressed about sth /ˌget 'strest əˌbaʊt ˌsʌmθɪŋ/
grade/mark /ɡreɪd/mɑːk/
have a good time /ˌhæv ə ɡʊd 'taɪm/
on your own /ˌɒn jɔːr 'əʊn/
revision /rɪ'vɪʒən/
schedule /'ʃedjuːl/
take a break /ˌteɪk ə 'breɪk/
take it easy /ˌteɪk ɪt 'iːzi/
your fault /ˌjɔː 'fɔːlt/

5.4 Reading 🔊 4.36

ability /ə'bɪləti/
be an expert on /ˌbi ən 'ekspɜːt ɒn/
be/become a professor of /bi/bɪˈkʌm ə prə'fesər əv/
bully /'bʊli/
concentrate /'kɒnsəntreɪt/
condition /kən'dɪʃən/
dream of /'driːm əv/
encourage /ɪn'kʌrɪdʒ/
get over a difficulty with the support of /ˌget ˌəʊvə ə'dɪfɪkəlti wɪθ ðə sə'pɔːt əv/
have/find a passion for /ˌhæv/ˌfaɪnd ə 'pæʃən fə/
help sb to do sth /ˌhelp ˌsʌmbɒdi tə 'duː ˌsʌmθɪŋ/
ignore /ɪɡ'nɔː/
learning disorders /'lɜːnɪŋ ˌdɪs'ɔːdəz/
make fun of /ˌmeɪk 'fʌn əv/
make the mistake of doing sth /ˌmeɪk ðə mɪˌsteɪk əv 'duːɪŋ ˌsʌmθɪŋ/
mentor /'mentɔː/
misunderstand /ˌmɪsʌndə'stænd/
struggle with /'strʌɡəl wɪð/
visual thinker /ˌvɪʒuəl 'θɪŋkə/

5.5 Grammar 🔊 4.37

background /'bækɡraʊnd/
beanbag /'biːnbæɡ/
blinds /blaɪndz/
bright /braɪt/

chill out /ˌtʃɪl 'aʊt/

chill out /ˌtʃɪl 'aʊt/
compete against /kəm'piːt əˌɡenst/
cushion /'kʊʃən/
first aid /ˌfɜːst 'eɪd/
flexible /'fleksəbəl/
follow your own interests /ˌfɒləʊ jɔːr əʊn'ɪntrəsts/
manifesto /ˌmænɪ'festəʊ/
nationwide /ˌneɪʃən'waɪd/
relevant /'reləvənt/
rigid /'rɪdʒəd/
school gate /ˌskuːl 'ɡeɪt/
scrape /skreɪp/
swipe card /'swaɪp kɑːd/
uncluttered /ˌʌn'klʌtəd/

5.6 Use of English 🔊 4.38

cricket /'krɪkɪt/
give up /ˌɡɪv 'ʌp/
hockey /'hɒki/
kit /kɪt/
netball /'netbɔːl/
rugby /'rʌɡbi/

5.7 Writing 🔊 4.39

application form /ˌæplɪ'keɪʃən fɔːm/
arrange /ə'reɪndʒ/
availability /əˌveɪlə'bɪləti/
do a course /ˌduː ə 'kɔːs/
enquire about /ɪn'kwaɪər ə'baʊt/
grateful /'ɡreɪtfəl/
provide /prə'vaɪd/
register (v) /'redʒəstə/
staff /stɑːf/

5.8 Speaking 🔊 4.40

donation /dəʊ'neɪʃən/
single-sex school /ˌsɪŋɡəl seks 'skuːl/
waste of time /ˌweɪst əv 'taɪm/

VOCABULARY AND GRAMMAR

1 Choose the correct option.

1 It is now harder for new college *classmates / experts / graduates* to find a good job than in the past.

2 I have to attend PE classes because PE is a(n) *academic / after-school / compulsory* subject.

3 You'll learn more if you pay *attention / tuition fees / the bills* in classes.

4 Josh *skipped / dropped / took* the Science class again. Is he going to get into trouble?

5 If they change the *curriculum / timetable / academic subjects*, we'll start lessons at 8 o'clock every day.

6 My father used to *bully / encourage / struggle* with Maths and Physics at school, but now he is an engineer.

2 Complete the text with words which mean the same as the expressions in brackets. The first letters are given.

The second **¹t**_____ (*one part of an academic year*) was much worse for Barrett than the first one. He got a lot of poor **²g**_____ (*marks*) and he **³f**_____ (*didn't pass*) three tests. He says he got exhausted by all the **⁴s**_____ (*the work that a student does at school or at home*), but the truth is that he didn't concentrate enough on learning and **⁵s**_____ (*didn't attend*) the classes he wasn't keen on. If he wants to be successful in the final exams, he has to start **⁶r**_____ (*preparing for exams*) now.

3 Complete the First Conditional sentences with the correct form of the verbs in brackets.

1 If I _____ (take) a gap year, I _____ (get) a lot of experience.

2 If Stella _____ (not hurry), we _____ (miss) the first lesson.

3 _____ (your parents/get) angry if you _____ (not get) into university?

4 He _____ (not pass) his exams if he _____ (not take) extra lessons.

5 I _____ (not/help) you with Maths if you _____ (not/help) me with English.

4 Choose the correct answer, A, B or C.

1 Any student ___ hasn't finished their homework, please see me after the lesson.
   A who   B which   C where

2 This is the canteen ___ we eat our lunch.
   A that   B which   C where

3 Students ___ only revise the night before an exam don't usually get good grades.
   A who   B which   C where

4 It was a gap year ___ seemed to last forever.
   A who   B that   C where

5 There are lots of schools in the world ___ don't have water or electricity.
   A who   B which   C where

6 Oxford was the university ___ she did her degree.
   A who   B that   C where

USE OF ENGLISH

5 Choose the answer, A, B or C, which has the same meaning as the underlined phrase in each sentence.

1 The head teacher will close the canteen <u>unless the chef changes</u> the menu.
   A after the chef changes
   B if the chef doesn't change
   C before the chef changes

2 <u>If you ask me, I think</u> our school doesn't spend enough money on computers.
   A That's true, but
   B In my opinion
   C I agree that

3 I have to <u>learn</u> these maths rules <u>by heart</u> for tomorrow.
   A memorise
   B explain
   C hand in

4 We will wear school uniforms <u>when they become</u> compulsory.
   A before they become
   B unless they become
   C as soon as they become

5 It's a single-sex school for ambitious boys <u>that</u> offers the best learning conditions.
   A which
   B where
   C who

6 X: I think that going to school every day is boring.
   Y: <u>That's true</u>, but not all schools are the same.
   A I see what you mean
   B That's complete nonsense
   C I couldn't agree more

6 Read the text and choose the correct answer, A, B or C.

Should I take a gap year?

I'll have to make an important decision **¹**___ the academic year ends. My parents want me to continue my studies at university, but I'd rather do something more adventurous. I like the idea **²**___ a gap year. I want to study Spanish in the future, but I'd like to practise the language first, so I'm thinking of going to South America and working with children **³**___ can't read or write. I'm tired of a rigid timetable and all the schoolwork. I feel that a gap year **⁴**___ me some freedom. My parents know that most of my classmates are going to go to university when they **⁵**___ school. If they accept my decision, I'll go abroad for ten months. Could you tell me **⁶**___ to convince them?

1 A while	B before	C unless
2 A of	B on	C at
3 A who	B which	C where
4 A give	B gives	C will give
5 A take off	B leave	C go
6 A what can I do	B what should I do	C what I should do

7 Match the headings (A–F) with the paragraphs (1–4). There are two extra headings.

A school on every doorstep

1 ◯ In India there are 1.4 million children aged six–eleven who do not attend any school. That is why in 1988, two passionate teachers, Ranjani Paranjpe and Bina Lashkari, started a non-formal education project, *Door Step School*, for fifty children in a small slum in Mumbai. A year later the project became an official educational programme aiming to teach children to at least read and write.

2 ◯ At the beginning, the teachers walked from door to door looking for children who did not go to school, speaking to parents and asking them to send the children to their school. They arranged classrooms everywhere: in marketplaces, on pavements, at railway stations and even in a bus.

3 ◯ The idea spread very quickly to neighbouring communities. More and more teachers as well as volunteers decided to join the programme. Now, the *Door Step School* has a team of 1,000 teachers and volunteers across eight districts in India and deals with more than 70,000 students every year.

4 ◯ Since 1988, the teaching conditions in the *Door Step School* have changed a lot. Now, buses called *School on Wheels* serve as libraries and mobile classrooms with computers, TVs and DVD players. Apart from learning basic skills such as reading, writing and arithmetic, children also have lessons on hygiene or health and safety.

A Growing numbers of teachers and students
B Trying to solve the literacy problem
C Teaching in the slums around India
D Modern classrooms and new subjects
E Keeping children safe and healthy
F Teaching in strange places

8 Read the text again. Complete the gaps in the email to Matthew with the correct information. Don't write more than three words in each gap.

From: Emma Clark
To: Matthew Jones
Subject: interesting article!

Hi Matthew,

I've just read a very interesting article. It's about the *Door Step School* – an educational initiative in India, which in 1989 became ¹_____ . The idea came from ²_____ who wanted children from a small slum in Mumbai to learn how to read and write. It started with only fifty children but now the numbers of teachers, ³_____ involved in the project are much higher. Children also study new subjects and the teaching conditions are ⁴_____ those in 1988.

Really interesting! I can send you a link if you like.

Love, Emma

9 Do the task in pairs.

You are studying in a secondary school in England for six months. You are taking part in a survey about the most effective methods of learning Science subjects, such as Physics.

- Choose the photo which, in your opinion, shows the most effective method. Explain why.
- Explain why you rejected the other option.

10 Ask and answer the questions.

1 Some people say that Science should be the most important subject at school. Do you agree? Why?/ Why not?
2 What are the advantages of using computers for learning?

11 Read the task and write the email.

During holiday you'd like to take part in a two-week-long photography course in the UK, which every year is very popular among photography students. Write an email to the organisers. Include the following information:

- introduce yourself and write what course you're interested in
- describe your photography experience
- ask to be sent information about the signing-in process and payment
- ask what types of accommodation are available and how much they cost.

6

Just the job

Choose a job you love, and you will never have to work a day in your life.

Confucius

WINDOW CLEANING

🔴 25 Watch the BBC video.
For the worksheet, go to page 126.

VOCABULARY

Jobs • collocations • describing jobs • phrasal verbs

I can use language related to job descriptions and types of work.

SHOW WHAT YOU KNOW

1 Complete the names of jobs below with suffixes *-er, -or, -ian, -ist* or *-ant*. Then add three more jobs.

> build_er_ account___ doct___ electric___ flight attend___
> hairdress___ shop assist___ swimming instruct___
> reception___ scient___ politic___ plumb___

2 SPEAKING Complete the table with the jobs in Exercise 1. Then compare your ideas with a partner.

Jobs I would be good at	Jobs I might or might not be good at	Jobs I would not be good at

What's your worst work experience?

We interviewed four people who run very successful companies. We wanted to find out about the jobs they did before they became their own bosses and we asked them about their worst work experiences.

1

EVA

- **applied for a job** during her school holidays
- **was badly paid**
- **worked long hours**
- didn't enjoy **dealing with** customers
- almost **got the sack** for offering a customer a bigger size

2

MARCUS

- had a **part-time job**
- **was responsible for** washing the machines
- didn't find the job <u>challenging</u>
- <u>put up with</u> a horrible smell

3 Read about four people's worst work experiences. Match jobs A–D with people 1–4.

A A postman/postwoman ☐
B A shop assistant ☐
C A cleaner in a factory ☐
D A warehouse assistant ☐

4 🔊 **3.1** Listen and check your ideas in Exercise 3. Who do you think had the worst work experience?

5 🔊 **3.1** Answer the questions. Then listen again and check your answers.

1 Who is self-employed now and rarely has a day off?
2 Who is always nice to people who bring the post?
3 Who was motivated to pass some exams and get a better job?
4 Who left a summer job because he/she got fired?

6 SPEAKING Discuss whether you would like to be your own boss. Give reasons for your answers.

3

CHRIS

• worked **night shifts**
• found the job boring and <u>repetitive</u>
• **had to stand for hours**
• had two managers who came up with different tasks at the same time

4

AMY

• had to **get up** very early
• couldn't turn up for work one minute late
• **worked outdoors**
• had to answer difficult questions and found it really <u>stressful</u>

WORD STORE 6A | Collocations ⟩

7 🔊 **3.2** Complete WORD STORE 6A with the words and phrases in red in the text and in Exercise 5. Then listen, check and repeat.

8 Complete the statements with an appropriate verb in WORD STORE 6A. Sometimes more than one answer is possible.

1 You can _____ self-employed.
2 You generally _____ outdoors.
3 You usually _____ long hours.
4 You sometimes have to _____ night shifts.
5 You _____ responsible for lots of workers.
6 You need a university degree to _____ for this job.

9 SPEAKING Discuss which statements in Exercise 8 could describe the jobs in Exercise 1.

Well, a lot of builders are self-employed. They generally work outdoors. They start work early, but I don't think they do particularly long hours …

WORD STORE 6B | Describing jobs ⟩

10 🔊 **3.3** Complete WORD STORE 6B with the underlined adjectives in the text. Then listen, check and repeat.

11 SPEAKING Decide where to put the adjectives in WORD STORE 6B on the line according to how positive or negative you think they are in a job.

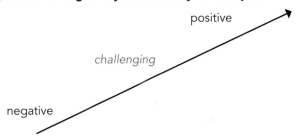

positive

challenging

negative

WORD STORE 6C | Phrasal verbs ⟩

12 🔊 **3.4** Complete WORD STORE 6C with the base form of the highlighted phrasal verbs in the text. Then listen, check and repeat.

13 SPEAKING Choose the correct particle. Then finish the sentences and compare your ideas with a partner.

In my ideal job …
1 I turn *off* / *up* for work at …
2 My employer only takes *on* / *up* people who …
3 I'm not prepared to put *out* / *up* with …
4 If I come *up* / *into* with a good idea, my boss …
5 Nothing puts me *down* / *off* my work except …

75

1 SPEAKING **How can students earn money in your country? Make a list of part-time jobs. Which jobs would you like/not like to do? Why? Discuss with a partner.**

2 **Look at the questionnaire. Choose the answer that is best for you and find out what your ideal part-time job is.**

Your ideal part-time job

1 If I had a day off tomorrow, I'd spend the day with a friend. We'd …
A go swimming.   B watch films at home.   C go shopping.

2 If I won the lottery, I'd give some money to a charity. I'd choose …
A Free Sport for Everyone.   B Save the Children.
C Love Eco Fashion.

3 If I had to describe myself in six words, it would be easy. I'd say …
A I love walking by the sea.   B I want to help other people.
C I like spending time in shops.

4 If I needed money, I'd get a part-time job …
A in a sports centre.   B at home.   C in a shop.

5 If I was super rich, I'd live in a big house …
A near a beach.   B with all my family.   C in the city centre.

What your score means

Mainly As = Your ideal part-time job is outside, possibly something connected with sport, e.g. a lifeguard or a skiing instructor.
Mainly Bs = You would be good at caring for people, e.g. a babysitter or a carer for elderly people.
Mainly Cs = Your ideal part-time job is in retail, e.g. a shop assistant or a beautician.

3 **Read the GRAMMAR FOCUS. Complete the examples using the Second Conditional forms in blue in Exercise 2.**

GRAMMAR FOCUS

Second Conditional

• You use the **Second Conditional** to talk about the present or future result of an imaginary situation.

imaginary situation	→	result
if + Past Simple		**would/wouldn't + verb**

If I ¹_____ a day off tomorrow, I ²_____ the day with a friend.
(but I don't have a day off tomorrow so I won't spend the day with a friend)
If I was super rich, I'd live in a big house.

Note:

• **'d = would**

• **If I/he/she/it were** … is more formal than **If I/he/she/it was** …
If he were rich, he wouldn't work.
If I were you, I'd get a summer job.

4 **Complete the statements with the correct Second Conditional form of the verbs in brackets.**

1 If everybody <u>went</u> (go) to university, nobody <u>would want</u> (want) to do manual jobs.

2 There _____ (not be) so much traffic if more people _____ (work) from home.

3 Family relationships _____ (improve) if parents _____ (take) more time off work.

4 If people _____ (retire) at fifty, there _____ (be) more jobs for young people.

5 The world _____ (be) a better place if everybody _____ (have) a job.

5 SPEAKING **Discuss whether you agree with the statements in Exercise 4.**

6 **Rewrite these real situations as imaginary situations. Begin each sentence with If.**

> If I had a part-time job, I'd earn money.

1 I don't have a part-time job, so I don't earn money.
2 I don't earn money, so I don't go out.
3 I don't go out, so I don't meet new people.
4 I don't meet new people, so my life is boring.
5 My life is boring, so I'm not happy.
6 I'm not happy, so I need a part-time job.

7 **Complete the sentences with the correct form of the verbs in brackets and your own ideas.**

1 If I <u>wanted</u> (want) advice about getting a job, I<u>'d ask my uncle</u>.

2 If I _____ (need) to borrow some money, I _____ .

3 If I _____ (can) work anywhere in the world, I _____ .

4 If I _____ (not have) a phone, I _____ .

5 If I _____ (be) an animal, I _____ .

6 If I _____ (not have to) study, I _____ .

8 SPEAKING **Write questions about the imaginary situations in Exercise 7. Then ask and answer the questions as in the example.**

A: *If you wanted advice about getting a job, who would you ask?*
B: *I'd ask …*

FOCUS VLOG About dream jobs

(▶ 27) **Watch the Focus Vlog. For the worksheet, go to page 127.**

Grammar page 147 ▶

LISTENING

Multiple choice

I can understand the main points of a conversation about a familiar topic.

1 SPEAKING **Look at the photos. What kind of person do you have to be to do these jobs? Tell your partner. Use the adjectives below or your own ideas.**

> ambitious brave caring clever energetic practical responsible sensible serious kind

EXAM FOCUS Multiple choice

2 🔊 **3.5 Listen to three recordings. Choose the correct photo, A, B or C.**

1 What is the woman's job?

Ⓐ Ⓑ  Ⓒ

2 Why did the girl's dad get a new job?

Ⓐ  Ⓑ Ⓒ

3 What do you need to do the woman's job well?

Ⓐ  Ⓑ  Ⓒ

3 🔊 **3.6 Listen to a dialogue between Sophie and her aunt Mary. Are statements 1–5 true (T) or false (F)?**

1 Aunt Mary doesn't want Sophie to become an airline pilot. ⬜

2 Sophie hasn't been to university yet. ⬜

3 Aunt Mary doesn't enjoy her job and wants to change. ⬜

4 Aunt Mary is already a captain. ⬜

5 Aunt Mary doesn't think it's an easy career for women with children. ⬜

4 🔊 **3.7 Complete the collocations with the words in the box. Then listen, check and repeat.**

> degree eyesight home off people training

Airline pilots must …
1 do long and expensive _____ .
2 have a university _____ .
3 get on well with _____ .
4 have excellent _____ .
5 spend a lot of time away from _____ .

Airline pilots can't …
6 choose when they take time _____ .

5 SPEAKING **Discuss whether you would like to be an airline pilot. Use the collocations in Exercise 4 to help you.**

I don't think I'd like to be an airline pilot. I'd have to spend a lot of time away from home and …

PRONUNCIATION FOCUS

6 🔊 **3.8 Listen and repeat the words. Mark the stress.**

1 journalist receptionist specialist
2 beautician electrician musician
3 carpenter instructor interpreter
4 engineer photographer secretary

7 **Choose the word in each group that has one more syllable than the other words.**

WORD STORE 6D Jobs

8 🔊 **3.9 Complete WORD STORE 6D with the words in the box to make job names. Then listen, check and repeat.**

1 **What are you like? Use the adjectives in the box to finish the sentences.**

1 I'm …   2 I'm sometimes …   3 I'm not …

> active   adventurous   caring   friendly   funny
> hard-working   independent   optimistic   quiet
> responsible   sensible   sociable

2 SPEAKING **Follow the instructions to complete the task.**

1 Choose three adjectives in Exercise 1 or your own ideas to describe your partner's personality.
2 Read the article quickly and decide which personality type best describes your partner.
3 Check if your partner agrees.

3 **Read the article and choose the best title.**

1 There's more to a job than a good salary
2 Career choices for your personality type
3 Personality test: what job would make you happiest?

4 **Read the text again. Match the people (1–5) with the personality types from the text (A–G) that best describe them. There are two extra personality types.**

1 Joe is very well-organised. Doing the same thing every day doesn't scare him. People enjoy talking to him – they know he will not disappoint them.
2 Gena believes in herself and her abilities. But she also wants to improve all the time. She loves books because they teach her new things.
3 Kate cares about people and enjoys being with them and having fun. But she also tries to help them grow, to become better, to learn more. She's their motivator.
4 Bo feels best when he's on his own. He doesn't like people telling him how to do things. He loves analysing difficult theoretical problems. And he's definitely not an adventurous type.
5 Vlad is open and friendly with people he likes, but he also needs some alone-time, when he can rest, relax and think. And what he hates the most is when people fight.

1 Joe ☐   2 Gena ☐   3 Kate ☐   4 Bo ☐   5 Vlad ☐

Are you thinking about careers
and what kind of job you'd like in the future?

It will help if you ask yourself the question: 'What am I like?'. Some jobs are more suitable for you than others. We've matched jobs to seven different personality types.

🔊 3.10

Ⓐ The Leader

When you go out with friends, you're the person who decides where to go. You're good at making decisions and people trust you. At work and in your social life, you love organising people and projects.
At work, you're a good problem-solver and you enjoy dealing with challenging jobs. You like to be your own boss.

JOBS: businessperson, judge, politician

Ⓑ The Artist

You love to be creative. You're quiet, easy-going and peaceful. You don't like stressful situations and you avoid arguments. You're friendly and caring, and you like spending time with family and close friends, but you also need your personal space. You're a nature lover and you enjoy being outdoors.
You prefer jobs where you make things.

JOBS: musician, designer, writer

Ⓒ The Doer

You're very sociable and you have a wide circle of friends who think you're funny, friendly and charming. You're very active and good at encouraging other people. You're always optimistic. You stay positive even when you have to deal with difficult situations. You're adventurous and competitive, and you take risks if necessary.

JOBS: police officer, sales representative, ski instructor

5 🔊 **3.11** Complete the definitions with the words in blue in the text. Then listen, check and repeat.

1 solves problems = _____
2 makes decisions = _____
3 develops software = _____
4 loves nature = _____
5 fights the fire = _____
6 works for social services = _____

6 Complete the sentences with the compound nouns in Exercise 5.

1 Claire's mum is the _____ in her family. She's a very quick thinker.
2 Dan isn't a _____ . He gets bored in the country and prefers to be in the city.
3 Edith is a brilliant _____ . No problem is too difficult for her.
4 Fred knows a lot about computers and the Internet. I think he'd be a good _____ .
5 Graham wants to be a _____ . He's a caring person and would be good at it.
6 Helen's ambition is to be a _____ . She's adventurous and practical.

7 Replace the names in Exercise 6 with the names of your classmates. Then compare the sentences with a partner.

8 SPEAKING Make predictions about your future life and career five, ten and twenty years from now. Discuss the questions.

1 Where will you live?
2 Who will you live with?
3 What job will you have?

Ten years from now I think I'll still live where I live today. I think I will work as …
I don't think I'll …

WORD STORE 6E | Word families ⟩

9 🔊 **3.12** Complete WORD STORE 6E with adjectives. Mark the stress. Then listen, check and repeat.

D The Thinker

You're quiet and analytical. You enjoy spending time alone and coming up with solutions to problems. You're successful in careers where you have a lot of independence. Careers in science suit your personality.

JOBS: mathematician, scientist, software developer

E The Mechanic

You're attracted to new experiences. You're the kind of person who goes motorcycling, bungee jumping, surfing. You enjoy having time to think alone, and you're very independent. You're logical and practical and you want to understand how things work. When there's a problem you quickly understand the causes, and solve it.

JOBS: engineer, fire-fighter, pilot

F The Strategist

You are the kind of person who is ambitious and you plan to achieve your goals. You're determined and self-confident. You work well under stress – you're a quick thinker and a good decision-maker. You never stop learning. Reading is your favourite way to learn new knowledge.

JOBS: company director, doctor, military leader

G The Carer

You're reliable, responsible and sensible. You're the person who helps friends when they have a problem, because you're caring and you're a good listener. For this reason, you often work in the healthcare sector. You're very organised, you enjoy planning and you don't mind doing repetitive jobs with long hours and a lot of responsibilities.

JOBS: nurse, social worker, teacher

GRAMMAR

6.5

Modal verbs for obligation and permission

I can express obligation, necessity and absence of obligation.

1 SPEAKING **What is the meaning of the saying? What kind of jobs do you think it describes? Discuss with a partner.**

You don't have to be **crazy** to work here ... **BUT IT HELPS!**

2 🔊 3.13 **Listen to three people talking about their jobs. Choose the correct option.**

1 Jonnie is in *the food industry / IT*.
2 Erica works for *a fashion magazine / a clothes shop*.
3 Sam works *in an office / from home*.

3 🔊 3.13 **Choose the correct option to describe some of the working conditions of Jonnie, Erica and Sam. Then listen again and check.**

- He ¹*has to / doesn't have to* wear the company T-shirt.
- He ²*can / can't* eat at his desk.
- He ³*must / mustn't* take his laptop into the canteen.

1 Jonnie

- She ⁴*has to / doesn't have to* work very long hours.
- She ⁵*needs to / doesn't need to* wear designer clothes or a suit.

2 Erica

- He ⁶*needs to / doesn't need to* get up early.
- He ⁷*can / can't* go for a run when he wants a break.
- He ⁸*must / mustn't* remember to have a shave before his conference call tonight.

3 Sam

4 **Read the GRAMMAR FOCUS. Complete the table using the correct affirmative or negative modal in blue in the text.**

GRAMMAR FOCUS

Modal verbs for obligation and permission

You use **must**, **need to**, **have to** and **can** to talk about obligation and permission.

Necessary	Not necessary	Permitted	Not permitted
• have to/ has to • need to/ ¹_____ • must	• don't have to/ ²_____ • don't need to/ doesn't need to/ needn't	³_____	• can't • ⁴_____

Note: You usually use **have to** (NOT ~~must~~) and **can't** (NOT ~~mustn't~~) to talk about rules or arrangements:
I have to work very long hours. (NOT ~~must~~) but
I must remember to shave. (NOT ~~have to~~)

5 **Complete the sentences with *mustn't* or *needn't*.**

1 a You ___needn't___ rush – you've got plenty of time.
  b You ___mustn't___ rush – it's important to be 100 percent accurate.
2 a You _____ go – you can stay if you want.
  b You _____ go – we haven't finished yet.
3 a You _____ tell her – it's a secret between you and me.
  b You _____ tell her – she already knows everything.
4 a You _____ eat that – you can leave it if you want.
  b You _____ eat that – it's really bad for you.

6 **Use *have to* or *can* with *you* to complete these questions. Then answer the questions.**

1 *Do you have to* wear a uniform?
2 _____ call your teachers by their first name?
3 _____ use your mobile phones in class?
4 _____ take end-of-term tests in each subject?
5 _____ change classrooms for each lesson?
6 _____ leave school before you are eighteen?

7 **Write a sentence with *has to* and a sentence with *doesn't have to* for each job. Use the phrases in the box or your own ideas.**

> be fit   be good at maths   have a degree
> have a driving licence   have good eyesight
> speak English   wear a uniform   work at the weekend

1 A police officer _____ .
2 A secondary school teacher _____ .
3 A bus driver _____ .
4 An airline pilot _____ .
5 An accountant _____ .
6 A tourist guide _____ .

1 A police officer has to wear a uniform.
A police officer doesn't have to be good at maths.

8 SPEAKING **Think of three people you know with different jobs and write similar sentences to those in Exercise 7. Tell your partner about each person.**

Grammar page 148 ▸

USE OF ENGLISH

6.6

Adjectives ending in *-ed* and *-ing*

I can form adjectives from verbs and nouns with -ed and -ing.

1 SPEAKING Read UK TODAY. Discuss the questions.

1 What is work experience and why is it useful?
2 If you could do work experience, what would you do and why?

UK TODAY

Did you know that nearly all 15- or 16-year-old students in the UK do work experience before they leave school?

What is work experience?
- 1–3 weeks off school working full time for a local employer.

What are the benefits of work experience?
- It teaches useful work skills.
- It makes you think about possible careers.
- It develops self-confidence and communication skills.

2 ◀))3.14 Listen to Sharon and Adam talking to their teacher about their work experience. Then complete the table.

Who ...	Sharon	Adam
1 had a disappointing time?		
2 is excited about his/her future career?		
3 was embarrassed because he/she turned up for work in the wrong clothes?		
4 got encouraging feedback when he/she finished something?		
5 thinks you learn things if the work is challenging?		

3 Read the LANGUAGE FOCUS. Complete the adjectives with -ed or -ing in comments 1–7 in the conversation.

LANGUAGE FOCUS

Adjectives ending in *-ed* and *-ing*

- You form pairs of *-ed* and *-ing* adjectives from verbs: confuse → *I was confused. The situation was confusing.*
- *-ed* adjectives describe how people feel. *I'm excited about my future. I was tired all the time.*
- *-ing* adjectives describe the thing (or person) that causes the feeling. *Did you do interesting jobs? He was very encouraging.*

Note: Some *-ed* adjectives do not have *-ing* equivalents. e.g. *ashamed, delighted, relieved*

1 I'm **reliev___** .
2 I had a really **reward___** time.
3 That's **amaz___** !
4 I was really **embarrass___** because everyone else was in jeans.
5 It was very **confus___** .
6 I was **bor___** most of the time.
7 It sounds like you had a very **satisfy___** experience.

4 ◀))3.14 Listen again and check your answers in Exercise 3.

5 USE OF ENGLISH Choose the correct sentence, A, B or C to complete the dialogue.

1 X:Why are you going to bed so early? Y: _____
   A Because it's very tiring.
   B Because I'm very tiring.
   C Because I've had a very tiring day.
2 X:She always turns up late when we meet. Y: _____
   A I know, it's so annoying!
   B Really? I'm so relieved!
   C Oh no, I feel so ashamed!
3 X:Did your mum like her birthday present? Y: _____
   A She was encouraging.
   B She was delighted.
   C She was amazing.
4 X:I can't stand this wet weather. Y: _____
   A Yes, it's really depressing.
   B Yes, it's really depressed.
   C Yes, I'm really depressing.

6 SPEAKING Make questions using beginnings 1 or 2 and an appropriate adjective in the box or your own ideas. Then ask and answer the questions as in the example.

> bored/boring   disgusted/disgusting
> exhausted/exhausting   inspired/inspiring
> moved/moving   shocked/shocking

1 When was the last time you were ...?
2 When was the last time you thought that something (someone) was ...?

A: *When was the last time you were exhausted?*
B: *I think it was after PE yesterday. We did cross-country and I hate running!*

Use of English page 149 ▶

WRITING

6.7

A job application

I can write a basic letter of application.

1 **Read the job advert and answer the questions.**

1 What kind of job is it advertising?
2 Is it a permanent job?
3 Is it a well-paid job?
4 How old do you have to be to apply?
5 What characteristics should the candidate have?
6 What are the working hours?

ARE YOU LOOKING FOR A
SUMMER JOB?

JOHNSON'S BUILDERS REQUIRES
an office helper – €10 per hour

ARE YOU
16 or over? • reliable and hard-working?
friendly and willing to learn?

WE OFFER
excellent conditions • flexible hours
a chance to learn office skills

NO PREVIOUS EXPERIENCE NECESSARY!

---

2 **Imagine you want to apply for the job. Tick five pieces of information you should include in your application letter.**

Say where you saw the advert. ☐
Say what you are doing now. ☐
Say how you intend to spend your salary. ☐
Give reasons why you are interested in the job. ☐
Mention any relevant work experience. ☐
Say why you liked or didn't like previous jobs. ☐
Say when you are available for interview. ☐
Warn them not to call you at certain times. ☐

---

3 **Read the letter of application. Check your ideas in Exercise 2. Cross out the three sentences that are NOT appropriate.**

Dear Sir or Madam,

With **reference to** your advertisement in yesterday's *Devonshire Times*, I would like to **apply for** the position of office helper. **At the moment**, I am in my final year at school, and I will be available to start work from 1st June. I really need this job because I want to earn some money to go on holiday.

I am **particularly interested in** your company because I hope to study architecture at university. I **attach my CV** for your information. As you will see, I worked on a building site last summer. It was a bit hard, but I got a really good suntan.

I do not have much experience of office work, but I am a fast learner. I have good communication skills and I enjoy working as part of a team. **For these reasons**, I feel I would be a suitable candidate for the job you are advertising.

I can be available for interview **at any time**. I have listed my contact details on my CV. Please don't call me before ten o'clock in the morning.

I look forward to hearing from you.

Yours faithfully,

Richard Dawson

---

4 **Read the WRITING FOCUS. Complete the examples with the phrases in purple in the letter in Exercise 3.**

WRITING FOCUS

A job application

1 **Say where you saw the advert**
I am writing in connection with your advertisement in …/ With ¹reference to your advertisement in …

2 **Say why you are writing**
I am writing to express my interest in the position of …/ I would like to ²_____ the position of …

3 **Say what you are doing now**
Currently, I am …/At ³_____ , I am …

4 **Give reasons why you are interested in the job**
I found your advertisement very interesting because …/ I am ⁴_____ your company because …

5 **Mention your CV and any relevant work experience**
I have some experience of …/I worked for … as …/ I ⁵_____ for your information.

6 **Give reasons why you are a suitable candidate for the job**
I would be a suitable candidate for the job because …/ ⁶_____ , I feel I would be a suitable candidate for the job you are advertising.

7 **Say when you are available for interview**
I can be available for interview ⁷_____ .

5 Complete the sentences from a job application with phrases in the WRITING FOCUS.

1 I am writing in _____ with the advertisement on your website.
2 I am writing to express my _____ in the position of waiter.
3 I have some _____ of working in a busy restaurant.
4 I found your _____ interesting because I would like to work outside.
5 I would be a _____ candidate for the job because I learn very quickly.
6 I can be _____ for interview after 17 July or any weekend.

6 Read the advert below and sentences 1–6 from different candidates. Are the people right (R) or wrong (W) for the job? Discuss with a partner.

WILD WEST
SUMMER CAMPS

REQUIRE CAMP SUPERVISORS

Do you love outdoor life and camping?

We need friendly, outgoing young people with lots of energy and some knowledge of English.

You must know how to swim.

Experience with children and knowledge of first aid is an advantage.

HAVE A GREAT SUMMER, IMPROVE YOUR ENGLISH AND EARN SOME MONEY AT THE SAME TIME!

Please apply to Ross Field, ross@wwsc.net

1 <u>At present</u> I'm taking swimming lessons. I take my level 1 test in July. <u>I'm confident</u> that I'll <u>succeed</u>. ◯
2 I believe <u>I possess</u> the right skills for the job because I worked on Wild West Summer Camps last year. ◯
3 My spoken English <u>requires</u> some improvement, but I can sing English pop songs. ◯
4 <u>I have experience of working in</u> summer camps, and I've had <u>many opportunities</u> to practise putting up tents. ◯
5 I think I'm <u>a suitable candidate</u> for the job. I'm <u>available</u> for work from 15th August, after my summer holiday. ◯
6 While I was working as a swimming instructor last summer, <u>I obtained</u> a certificate in first aid. ◯

7 Read the LANGUAGE FOCUS. Complete the examples with the underlined phrases in Exercise 6.

LANGUAGE FOCUS

Formal language in a job application letter

Formal	Informal
[1] I possess	I've got
2 _____	the right person
3 _____	free
4 _____	I've worked on
5 _____	plenty of chances
6 _____	I got
7 _____	At the moment
8 _____	I'm sure
9 _____	do well
10 _____	needs

8 Make the sentences more formal. Then tick the ones that you could truthfully include in a letter of application.

1 I got top marks in my English exams at the end of last term. ◯
2 I hope to have plenty of chances to travel in my future career. ◯
3 At the moment I'm doing part-time work in a restaurant. ◯
4 I believe that I am the right person for a job in sales and marketing. ◯
5 I'm sure that I've got good communication skills and can work well in a team. ◯

SHOW WHAT YOU'VE LEARNT

9 Do the writing task. Use the ideas in the WRITING FOCUS and the LANGUAGE FOCUS to help you.

You've read the advertisement from Exercise 6 in *International Student Times* and you'd like to apply for the job. Write a job application and send it online to Ross Field. Include the following information:

• write where you've seen the advertisement
• explain what you do and why you are interested in the job
• mention your CV and describe your work experience
• write when you can come for an interview.

Dear Mr. Field,

I am a sixteen-year-old Ukrainian student and I am writing …

SPEAKING

6.8

Asking for and giving advice

I can ask for and give advice on jobs and solving problems.

1 SPEAKING Read *Modelling – Some Facts* and discuss the questions.

1 What does it mean to be 'scouted'?
2 How do you know if a model agency is a good one?
3 Are you tall enough to be a model?

MODELLING – *some facts*

- Talent scouts go out in public to look for new models for their agency.
- Famous UK model, Kate Moss, was scouted at JFK airport in New York when she was 14.
- Models aged 16–18 in the UK should work part-time and be in full-time education.
- Good model agencies belong to the AMA (Association of Modelling Agents).
- Female models are usually at least 1.73 m and male models are 1.83 m tall.

2 ◀◎ 3.15 Listen to Zoe asking her friend Luke about doing modelling. Are statements 1–3 true (T) or false (F)?

1 Luke enjoyed doing modelling. ◻
2 He doesn't think Zoe should go to the agency. ◻
3 Zoe is going to take Luke with her to the agency. ◻

3 ◀◎ 3.15 Listen again and tick the expressions you hear.

4 Match the sentence halves to give useful advice to somebody preparing for a job interview.

1 I think you should ◻
2 I don't think you should ◻
3 My best advice would ◻
4 It's a good idea ◻
5 If I were you, ◻

a be nervous.
b do some research.
c be to be on time.
d I'd just be yourself.
e to prepare some questions.

5 ◀◎ 3.16 Listen, check and repeat the advice in Exercise 4.

6 Look at the statements below and think about the advice you would give in each case. Make notes.

1 I want to stay fit.
2 It's my mother's birthday soon.
3 I need some new clothes, but I haven't got any money.
4 I want to watch a good film.
5 I can't wake up in the mornings.

7 SPEAKING Follow the instructions below to make dialogues. Use your notes in Exercise 6 and the SPEAKING FOCUS to help you.

Student A: Choose a problem in Exercise 6 and tell Student B about it.
Student B: Give Student A some advice.

ROLE-PLAY Asking for and giving advice

⊙ 29 Watch the video and practise. Then role-play your dialogue.

6.1 Vocabulary 🔊 4.41

apply for a job /əˌplaɪ fər ə 'dʒɒb/
be badly paid /bi ˌbædli 'peɪd/
be employed/self-employed /ˌbi ɪm'plɔɪd,self ɪm'plɔɪd/
be in charge of /ˌbi ˌɪn 'tʃɑːdʒ əf/
be responsible for /ˌbi rɪ'spɒnsəbəl fə/
be unemployed /ˌbi ˌʌnɪm'plɔɪd/
be well paid /ˌbi ˌwel 'peɪd/
challenging /'tʃælɪndʒɪŋ/
come up with /ˌkʌm 'ʌp wɪð/
creative /kri'eɪtɪv/
demanding /dɪ'mɑːndɪŋ/
do/work long hours /ˌduː/ˌwɜːk lɒŋ 'aʊəz/
do/work night shifts /ˌduː/ˌwɜːk 'naɪt ʃɪfts/
do/work overtime /ˌduː/ˌwɜːk 'əʊvətaɪm/
employ (v) /ɪm'plɔɪ/
employer /ɪm'plɔɪə/
full-time job /ˌfʊl ˌtaɪm 'dʒɒb/
get fired/get the sack /ˌget 'faɪəd/ˌget ðə 'sæk/
get/have/take a day off /ˌget/ˌhæv/ˌteɪk ə deɪ 'ɒf/
get/have/take five weeks' paid holiday /ˌget/ˌhæv/ˌteɪk faɪv wiːks ˌpeɪd 'hɒlədi/
have a job /ˌhæv ə 'dʒɒb/
part-time job /ˌpɑːt taɪm 'dʒɒb/
put sb off sth /ˌpʊt 'sʌmbɒdi 'ɒf 'sʌmθɪŋ/
put up with /ˌpʊt 'ʌp wɪð/
repetitive /rɪ'petətɪv/
resign from a job /rɪˌzaɪn frəm ə 'dʒɒb/
rewarding /rɪ'wɔːdɪŋ/
run a business/company /ˌrʌn ə 'bɪznəs/'kʌmpəni/
stressful /'stresfəl/
take sb on /ˌteɪk ˌsʌmbɒdi 'ɒn/
tiring /'taɪərɪŋ/
turn up /ˌtɜːn 'ʌp/
work experience /'wɜːk ɪkˌspɪəriəns/
work indoors/outdoors /ˌwɜːk ɪn'dɔːz/aʊt'dɔːz/

6.2 Grammar 🔊 4.42

babysitter /'beɪbiˌsɪtə/
carer /'keərə/
lifeguard /'laɪfgɑːd/
retail /'riːteɪl/
retire /rɪ'taɪə/
work from home /ˌwɜːk frəm 'həʊm/
work outside /ˌwɜːk aʊt'saɪd/

6.3 Listening 🔊 4.43

airline pilot /'eəlaɪn ˌpaɪlət/
away from home /əˌweɪ frəm 'həʊm/
beautician /bjuː'tɪʃən/
benefit /'benəfɪt/
brave /breɪv/
bus driver /'bʌs ˌdraɪvə/
carpenter /'kɑːpəntə/
clever /'klevə/
do training /ˌduː 'treɪnɪŋ/

driving instructor /'draɪvɪŋ ɪnˌstrʌktə/
electrician /ɪˌlek'trɪʃən/
energetic /ˌenə'dʒetɪk/
engineer /ˌendʒə'nɪə/
estate agent /ɪ'steɪt ˌeɪdʒənt/
get on well with people /ˌget ˌɒn 'wel ˌwɪθ ˌpiːpəl/
have excellent eyesight /hæv 'eksələnt ˌaɪsaɪt/
interpreter /ɪn'tɜːprətə/
journalist /'dʒɜːnəlɪst/
lifeguard /'laɪfgɑːd/
male-dominated job /ˌmeɪl ˌdɒmɪneɪtɪd 'dʒɒb/
manual job /ˌmænjuəl 'dʒɒb/
musician /mjuː'zɪʃən/
office /'ɒfəs/
office assistant /'ɒfəs əˌsɪstənt/
personal skills /ˌpɜːsənəl 'skɪlz/
practical /'præktɪkəl/
promotion /prə'məʊʃən/
receptionist /rɪ'sepʃənɪst/
salary /'sæləri/
secretary /'sekrətəri/
shop assistant /'ʃɒp əˌsɪstənt/
skiing instructor /'skiːɪŋ ɪnˌstrʌktə/
specialist /'speʃələst/
take time off /ˌteɪk taɪm 'ɒf/
taxi driver /'tæksi ˌdraɪvə/
travel agent /'trævəl ˌeɪdʒənt/
university degree /ˌjuːnə'vɜːsəti dɪ'griː/

6.4 Reading 🔊 4.44

active /'æktɪv/
businessperson /'bɪznəsˌpɜːsən/
charm (n, v) /tʃɑːm/
charming /'tʃɑːmɪŋ/
compete /kəm'piːt/
competition /ˌkɒmpə'tɪʃən/
competitive /kəm'petətɪv/
decision-maker /dɪ'sɪʒən ˌmeɪkə/
designer /dɪ'zaɪnə/
determination /dɪˌtɜːmɪ'neɪʃən/
determined /dɪ'tɜːmɪnd/
director /daɪ'rektə/
fire-fighter /'faɪəˌfaɪtə/
logic /'lɒdʒɪk/
logical /'lɒdʒɪkəl/
mechanic /mɪ'kænɪk/
military leader /ˌmɪlətəri 'liːdə/
nature lover /'neɪtʃə ˌlʌvə/
nurse /nɜːs/
peace /piːs/
peaceful /'piːsfəl/
problem-solver /'prɒbləm ˌsɒlvə/
quiet /'kwaɪət/
reliable /rɪ'laɪəbəl/
reliance /rɪ'laɪəns/
rely (on) /rɪ'laɪ (ɒn)/
sales representative /'seɪlz reprɪˌzentətɪv/
social worker /'səʊʃəl ˌwɜːkə/
software developer /'sɒftweə dɪˌveləpə/

6.5 Grammar 🔊 4.45

accountant /ə'kaʊntənt/
accurate /'ækjərət/
be/work in (IT) /ˌbi/ˌwɜːk ɪn (ˌaɪ'tiː)/
conference call /'kɒnfərəns kɔːl/
fashion magazine /'fæʃən mægəˌziːn/
food industry /'fuːd ˌɪndəstri/
have a shave /ˌhæv ə 'ʃeɪv/

6.6 Use of English 🔊 4.46

ashamed /ə'ʃeɪmd/
be relieved /ˌbi rɪ'liːvd/
bored /bɔːd/
confused /kən'fjuːzd/
confusing /kən'fjuːzɪŋ/
delighted /di'laɪtɪd/
disgusted /dɪs'gʌstɪd/
disgusting /dɪs'gʌstɪŋ/
embarrassed /ɪm'bærəst/
encouraging /ɪn'kʌrɪdʒɪŋ/
exhausting /ɪg'zɔːstɪŋ/
moved /muːvd/

6.7 Writing 🔊 4.47

at any time /ət ˌeni 'taɪm/
at present /ət 'prezənt/
at the moment /ət ðə 'məʊmənt/
attach /ə'tætʃ/
available /ə'veɪləbəl/
be a fast learner /ˌbi ə ˌfɑːst 'lɜːnə/
be confident that /ˌbi 'kɒnfɪdənt 'ðæt/
camp supervisor /'kæmp ˌsuːpəvaɪzə/
flexible hours /ˌfleksəbəl 'aʊəz/
have experience of /ˌhəv ɪk'spɪəriəns əv/
in connection with /ɪn kə'nekʃən wɪð/
interview /'ɪntəvjuː/
job advert /'dʒɒb ˌædvɜːt/
look for a job /ˌlʊk fər ə 'dʒɒb/
obtain /əb'teɪn/
opportunity /ˌɒpə'tjuːnəti/
position /pə'zɪʃən/
possess skills /pə,zes 'skɪlz/
require /rɪ'kwaɪə/
succeed /sək'siːd/
suitable candidate /'suːtəbəl 'kændədət/
with reference to /ˌwɪð 'refərəns tə/

6.8 Speaking 🔊 4.48

association /əˌsəʊsi'eɪʃən/
model /'mɒdl/
scout /skaʊt/

VOCABULARY AND GRAMMAR

1 Complete the sentences with the words about work. The first letters are given.

1 My sister is an o_____ a_____ .
She answers phones and takes messages.
2 Mathew is a t_____ a_____ .
He arranges trips and holidays for customers.
3 My parents usually take two weeks' p_____
h_____ in summer so we can all go
somewhere together.
4 I'd like to be s_____-e_____ and run
my own business in the future.
5 My brother has started a p_____-
t_____ job in the evenings to earn some extra
money.

2 Complete the sentences with the correct form of the words in capitals.

1 Grace finds her new job interesting but _____ .
DEMAND
2 Writing the first job application was quite
_____ for me. **STRESS**
3 The company is offering a job for ambitious and
_____ people. **COMPETE**
4 If Chris was more _____ , he'd find a summer
job. **DETERMINATION**
5 I don't understand why he resigned from his job.
His decision does not seem _____ . **LOGIC**

3 Complete the Second Conditional sentences with the correct form of the verbs in brackets.

1 If Tom _____ (have) a full-time job, he
_____ (not resign) from it.
2 If you _____ (can) work for any company,
which company _____ you _____
(like) to work for?
3 If I _____ (be) you, I _____ (take) this
job.
4 She _____ (give) lots of jobs to young people
if she _____ (be) a successful businessperson.
5 If we often _____ (come) to work late, we
_____ (get) the sack.

4 Complete the second sentence using the word in capitals so that it has a similar meaning to the first. Do not change the word in capitals.

1 I'll let you take an extra day off. **CAN**
You _____ an extra day off.
2 You don't have to wear a suit. There isn't an official
meeting today. **NEEDN'T**
You _____ a suit. There aren't
any formal meetings today.
3 I mustn't forget to call my boss at 11 a.m. **REMEMBER**
I _____ my boss at 11 a.m.
4 I have to get to work on time this morning. **LATE**
I _____ for work this morning.
5 It's not a good idea to work overtime so often.
SHOULDN'T
You _____ overtime so often.

USE OF ENGLISH

5 Choose the correct answer, A, B or C.

1 Alan _____ last week because he didn't get
on well with people.
A got fired
B got employed
C got rid of
2 I'm writing _____ to the advertisement on
your website.
A with reference
B to apply
C to express my interest
3 We could work in the garden now _____ .
A if it was sunny
B if it will be sunny
C if it is sunny
4 My gap year was a very _____ experience.
A satisfy
B satisfying
C satisfied
5 John is a police officer. This summer he is going to
do _____ at a survival camp.
A training
B practise
C teach
6 This is your desk, but you _____ come to
the office every day – it's OK to work from home
sometimes.
A don't have
B needn't
C don't need

6 Read the text and choose the correct answer, A, B or C.

What's my dream job?

I'm a university student, and today it is clear to me
exactly what I would like to do after getting a university
¹___ . But as a little boy I dreamt of becoming a fire-fighter
or a police officer. We used to play 'cops and robbers' with
other boys. Those were really ²___ days. For a few years at
primary school I wanted to become a famous sportsman,
but too much physical training put me ³___ this idea.
I have always loved working with computers, so after high
school I started studying Computer Science at university.
My interests in specific areas of computer technology have
developed and I've come ⁴___ the idea of becoming
a software developer. It is a very responsible and
demanding job. If I worked as a software developer, I ⁵___
spend a lot of time in front of the computer screen, but
I know I would never get ⁶___ with the job.

1 A experience	B study	C degree
2 A amazing	B competitive	C reliable
3 A down	B off	C up
4 A up with	B down with	C in with
5 A would have to	B needn't	C must
6 A bore	B bored	C boring

7 Complete the questions with the words in the box. There are two extra words. Then, in pairs, ask and answer the questions.

> boss   ever   kind   never   office   overtime

1 What _____ of job do you hope to get in the future? Why?

2 Have you _____ worked? Why?/Why not?

3 Would you like to work in an _____ ? Why?/Why not?

4 Do you think you could be a good _____ ? Why?/Why not?

8 The photos show people in situations at work. In pairs, take turns to say what you can see in your photo. Then discuss the questions about each photo.

(A)

1 How is the woman in the photo feeling? Why?

2 What would you do if you were late for an important exam? Why?

3 Tell me about a situation when you or someone you know were late for an important event.

(B)

1 In your opinion, why is the man in the photo sleeping?

2 What would you do if you suddenly felt very tired/sleepy during a lesson?

3 Tell me about a situation when you or someone you know felt bored during an important event.

9 🔊 **3.17** Listen to a conversation between a teenage girl and her uncle. Are the statements true (T) or false (F)?

1 Leia only knows one male nurse. ⬜

2 Jon's friends have always taken his profession seriously. ⬜

3 Jon is satisfied with his salary. ⬜

4 Sometimes Jon starts work at night. ⬜

5 Jon has been promoted to nurse manager. ⬜

10 You have an opportunity to get a holiday job in one of these places (a–c). Think what responsibilities you might have in each of the jobs. Choose the place you'd like to work at. Note down arguments you could use to persuade the business owner to employ you. Look at the example arguments below:

a greengrocer's
b café
c pet hotel

- **SKILLS:** I'm very good with pets because at home we've got three dogs and a cat.
- **WORK EXPERIENCE:** Last summer I worked part-time at my uncle's shop in Valencia, Spain.
- **PERSONALITY:** People who know me say I'm very patient and responsible.

11 Choose one of the places (a–c) in Exercise 10. Do the writing task.

> You're spending your summer holiday with your family in England. You've just found out that a local _____ is looking for a part-time employee. Write a job application to the business owner. Include the following information:
>
> - write how you found out about the job offer
> - introduce yourself and explain why you are interested in the job
> - describe your work experience
> - say you can meet for the interview anytime.

7

Consumer society

Money makes the world go round.

A proverb

BBC

CHEAP SHOPPING

▶30 Watch the BBC video.
For the worksheet, go to page 128.

SHOW WHAT YOU KNOW

1 List all the clothes and accessories you can think of in two minutes.

sunglasses, jeans, …

2 Put the words in Exercise 1 into groups 1–5. Some items can go into more than one group. Compare your lists with a partner.

1 Items you only wear outdoors
2 Items you wear for special occasions
3 Items you wear all the time
4 Items you never wear
5 Items you have bought recently

THE TRUTH ABOUT SHOPPING

▼

BETH

MIA

	1 What do you think about shopping for clothes?	I love it! But I really don't want to look the same as everyone else. So I go to **charity shops** and a second-hand **jeweller's**. I want to <u>look original</u>.	I'm addicted to clothes and shopping. The bad news is that I'm poor! So I can't afford to buy much, except during the sales. But I **go window shopping** – it's still fun to look.
	2 How often do you go clothes shopping?	Probably once a month. Or more often if I need something for a special occasion. Sometimes I shop online too – there are some great online **vintage** shops.	Oh dear, it's bad – I go every weekend. I get bored with my clothes – I can't help it.
	3 When was the last time you picked up a bargain?	I always **pick up a bargain**! Last time I went to my favourite charity shop, I found this <u>gorgeous</u> <u>silk</u> dressing gown.	Last weekend my favourite **high street store** had a sale. I got an amazing <u>leather</u> jacket for half price.

3 Read four people's answers to an online survey about shopping. Answer the questions.

1 Who doesn't have enough money to buy lots of clothes?
2 Who uses the Internet to look for clothes?
3 Who avoids shopping for clothes?
4 Who is willing to pay more for the right kind of clothes?

4 SPEAKING Which person is most like you? Why? Tell your partner.

RYAN

I really enjoy shopping. I love <u>designer clothes</u>. I mean, they're really expensive but I think they're worth it. Anyway, I want to <u>look smart</u> like my favourite celebrities.

I don't need to go shopping often because I buy <u>good quality clothes</u> made from nice natural materials like <u>cotton</u> and <u>wool</u>. They last for ages.

A bargain – hmm. Oh yes, I got a really nice <u>cashmere</u> pullover – it was on special offer.

SAM

My mum buys all my clothes! I don't care what I wear. I don't think you should judge people by the <u>brands</u> they wear. I hate clothes that have logos all over them.

As I said, I never go shopping. I don't even know what <u>suits</u> me. If something <u>fits</u> me and it feels comfortable – like my favourite hoodie – then I'm happy.

You'll have to ask my mum!

Go to **WORD STORE 7** page 15

WORD STORE 7A ⟩ Shops and services ⟩

5 🔊 3.18 Complete WORD STORE 7A with the words in red in the survey. Then listen, check and repeat.

6 SPEAKING Discuss which shops you would go in to buy the items on the shopping list.

Shopping list

- Shoelaces (for trainers)
- A birthday cake
- Printer ink
- A4 paper
- A present for Alfie (cousin aged 6)
- Some aspirin
- Bird food
- Some paint
- Contact lens solution
- Bananas
- A watch battery
- Some stamps

7 SPEAKING Complete the sentences with shops and services in WORD STORE 7A. Compare your sentences with a partner.

I often go into …
I sometimes go into …
I rarely go into …
I never go into …

WORD STORE 7B ⟩ Clothes and appearance ⟩

8 🔊 3.19 Complete WORD STORE 7B with the underlined words in the survey. Then listen, check and repeat.

9 SPEAKING Answer the questions. Then compare your answers with a partner.

Can you name …
1 a brand or logo that you like?
2 a person you know who often wears designer clothes?
3 a colour that doesn't suit you?
4 a natural material you like wearing?
5 a person you know who looks fashionable?
6 a shop where you can buy good quality clothes?
7 an item of clothing that fits you really well?
8 a person you know who never looks scruffy?

I think my favourite brand is Sole Soul. It's a local brand. I always buy their trainers, they're so comfortable. What about you?

WORD STORE 7C ⟩ Collocations ⟩

10 🔊 3.20 Complete WORD STORE 7C with the highlighted phrases in the survey. Then listen, check and repeat.

11 SPEAKING Choose the correct option. Then ask and answer the questions.

1 Do you ever *go / look* window shopping? How often?
2 When do shops usually *offer / have* a sale in your country?
3 When did you last buy something *in / on* special offer?
4 Where can you pick *up / off* a bargain? Name shops.
5 Do you always *keep / stay* your receipts? Why?
6 Have you ever taken something back and *got / asked* a refund? What was it?

The Passive

I can use the Passive in the Present Simple, Present Perfect and Past Simple.

1 SPEAKING Discuss the questions.

1 Who usually does the shopping in your family?
2 What food products do you and your family usually buy?
3 Which of the things in the box are important when you buy these kinds of products?

> the quality   how it is produced
> where it is produced   a fair price

2 Read the text about Fairtrade. Why is it good for farmers?

Many of the products we buy in supermarkets are grown by farmers in developing countries. But farmers aren't paid enough to make a living.

So the idea of 'fair trade' has been around for many years. When you see the FAIRTRADE mark on a product, you know that the farmers have been paid a fair price for their crops. You also know that they have been given extra money – the Fairtrade premium. This can be used by farmers to develop their businesses, invest in their communities or protect the environment.

In 1997, many organisations from different countries came together and one international Fairtrade organisation was formed. So far, the lives of approximately seven million people in developing countries have been improved by Fairtrade.

3 Read the GRAMMAR FOCUS. Then find all the passive verb forms in the text in Exercise 2.

GRAMMAR FOCUS

The Passive

You use passive forms when it isn't important (or you don't know) who performed the action. Passive verbs have the same tenses as active verbs.

The Passive: *be* + Past Participle

+	*Fairtrade products are grown in developing countries.*
–	*Fairtrade products aren't grown in developed countries.*
?	*Where are Fairtrade products grown?*

4 Complete the examples in the table using the passive forms in blue in the text in Exercise 2.

Present Simple

Active

People don't pay farmers enough.

Passive

Farmers ¹_____ enough.

Past Simple

Active

In 1997, somebody formed one international Fairtrade organisation.

Passive

In 1997, one international Fairtrade organisation
² _____ .

Present Perfect

Active

Fairtrade has improved the lives of approximately seven million people in developing countries.

Passive

The lives of approximately seven million people in developing counties ³_____ by Fairtrade.

5 Choose the correct form of the verb, active or passive.

Chocolate & Fairtrade

Last year, more than one billion kilos of chocolate ¹*ate / were eaten* around the world. Chocolate ²*makes / is made* from the cacao plant. However, many cacao farmers ³*don't earn / aren't earned* enough money and ⁴*can't afford / can't be afforded* food, medicine or clean water. In Africa, a typical cacao grower ⁵*pays / is paid* less than a dollar a day. Now Fairtrade is helping farmers to get fair prices. Farming organisations ⁶*have set up / have been set up* in African countries and the extra money ⁷*invests / is invested* in projects such as drinking water.

6 Complete the passive sentences with the Present Simple, Past Simple or Present Perfect form of the verbs in brackets.

1 My house *was built* (build) more than fifty years ago.
2 My name _____ (not pronounce) the same in English.
3 My shoes _____ (make) in Italy.
4 This school _____ (open) in the 1990s.
5 I _____ (never/stop) by the police.
6 Fairtrade products _____ (not sell) in my country.

7 SPEAKING Rewrite the sentences in Exercise 6 to make them true for you. Then make questions and ask your partner.

1 Was your house built more than fifty years ago?

> Grammar page 150

7.3 LISTENING

Matching

I can identify key details in a simple radio interview.

(A) perfume

(B) a tablet

(C) time in a recording studio

(D) a friendship bracelet

(E) a purse

(F) face cream

(G) a bunch of flowers

(H) a game console

1 **SPEAKING Discuss the questions.**

1 Have you ever given or received a present like the ones in the photos?
2 What is the best or worst present you've ever received?

2 **◀)) 3.21 Listen to a radio interview about buying presents. Which presents A–H are suggested for the three people below?**

1 Isabelle's mum: _____
2 Alexander's girlfriend: _____ , _____
3 Charlotte's classmate: _____

3 **Read statements 1–5 in Exercise 4. Match the underlined words and phrases with the words and phrases below.**

can buy
cheer her up ⬜
is a question of ⬜ [2]
classmates ⬜
it isn't the value of the present that matters ⬜

4 **◀)) 3.21 Listen to the radio interview again. Write A (Amy), I (Isabelle) or Ch (Charlotte).**

Who …
1 doesn't think the ability to choose good presents <u>is a matter of</u> personality? ⬜
2 thinks that both men and women <u>are capable of buying</u> good presents? ⬜
3 thinks her mother is upset about being forty, so she wants to <u>make her feel happier</u>? ⬜
4 wants to buy a nice expensive gift for one of her <u>school friends</u>? ⬜
5 concludes that <u>a successful present doesn't have to cost a lot of money</u>? ⬜

5 **Complete the advice with the verbs in the box. Which piece of advice is NOT given in the interview? Which is best?**

Be   Collect   Do   Don't spend   Keep   Spend

1 _____ some research.
2 _____ time thinking about the person.
3 _____ careful when buying women's toiletries.
4 _____ lots of money. It isn't necessary.
5 _____ the receipt so you can take the present back.
6 _____ money from friends to buy something really good.

6 **SPEAKING Tell your partner about the last time you bought a present for somebody.**

1 Who was it for?
2 What was the occasion?
3 What did you buy?
4 Why did you buy it?
5 Where did you buy it?
6 How much did it cost?

7 **◀)) 3.22 Listen to the words and identify the silent letter in each case.**

1 receipt   psychology
2 write   wrong
3 debt   doubt
4 island   aisle
5 know   knife
6 listen   castle

8 **◀)) 3.22 Listen again and repeat the words.**

WORD STORE 7D Word families

9 **◀)) 3.23 Complete WORD STORE 7D. Add verbs or nouns to the table. Then listen, check and repeat.**

1 SPEAKING Discuss the questions.

1 How often do you shop online?

2 Which of the following have you bought online in the last three months?

books   clothes   music   technology   tickets

3 What would you never buy online? Why?

2 ◄)) 3.24 Complete the information about Amazon with the numbers in the box. Then listen and check.

2   5   100   600   45,000   341,000

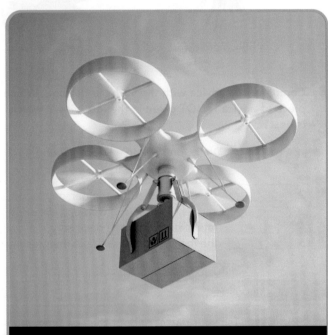

Amazon's logo has a smile that goes from A to Z. It shows that the company is ready to deliver anything to anywhere in the world.

AMAZON IN NUMBERS

■ Amazon employs ¹_____ people and ²_____ robots.

■ Every employee at Amazon has to spend ³_____ days a year dealing with **customers'** complaints (including Jeff Bezos, the Company Director).

■ At Amazon ⁴_____ items are **shipped** every second.

■ One new book is added to Amazon's site every ⁵_____ minutes.

■ Amazon delivery drones fly at up to ⁶_____ metres high and up to 100 kilometres per hour.

3 Complete the headings in the text with the words in the box. Then read the text and check your answers.

biological   company   future   helicopter
space   technology

4 Read the text again. For questions 1–5, choose the correct answer, A, B, C or D.

1 Miguel Bezos adopted Jeff
  A when he was a baby.
  B when he was a teenager.
  C when he was four years old.
  D when he was ten years old.

2 Jeff Bezos started Amazon because
  A he was a university graduate.
  B he wanted to leave New York.
  C he had a well-paid job.
  D he saw that the Internet was growing.

3 The name *Cadabra* wasn't used because
  A it means 'dead body'.
  B it's difficult to pronounce correctly.
  C another online site had a similar name.
  D it didn't go to the top of website lists.

4 Bezos's company Blue Origin
  A is producing drones to deliver orders.
  B is building a human space station.
  C is developing space travel for everyone.
  D is selling space travel on Amazon.

5 At Amazon Go
  A you pay at a checkout desk.
  B you don't have to pay.
  C you use your smartphone to pay.
  D you can only use cash.

WORD STORE 7E   Shopping

5 ◄)) 3.26 Complete WORD STORE 7E with the words or phrases in blue in both texts. Then listen, check and repeat.

6 Read some facts about eBay. Complete the sentences with the words and phrases in WORD STORE 7E. Which is the most interesting fact?

1 The first thing that was _____ from eBay was a broken laser pointer.

2 800 million items are _____ on eBay at any one time.

3 Most eBay _____ do their shopping at weekends, especially Sunday afternoons.

4 On Christmas day, there's always _____ of 300 percent in sales of perfume as people sell their unwanted Christmas presents.

5 There are more _____ on eBay from British customers than any other nationality.

6 The big advantage of online stores like eBay and Amazon is that you never have to _____ at the _____.

THE BRAINS BEHIND AMAZON.COM

🔊 3.25

Amazon.com is a household name, but what do you know about the billionaire entrepreneur, Jeff Bezos, who started it in a garage in 1994?

His ¹_____ father was a unicyclist

Bezos was born in 1964 when both his parents were still teenagers, and his father was a unicyclist in the circus. They divorced after a year. When Bezos was four, his mother remarried and he was adopted by his stepfather, Miguel Bezos, a Cuban immigrant to the United States. Jeff learnt that he was adopted when he was ten.

He showed an early interest in science and ²_____

When he was a schoolboy, Bezos made an electrical alarm to keep his younger brother and sister out of his room. Later, he graduated in electrical engineering and computer science. He was working in a well-paid job in New York when he heard about the rise of Internet use by 2,300% in one year. It was 1994, and he decided to start his own Internet business.

His ³_____ wasn't called Amazon at first

Amazon started as a bookstore in a garage, and grew fast. In its first month of business, orders came in from forty-five countries around the world. At first, the online bookstore was named Cadabra, but it was hard to say, and some people thought it was similar to 'cadaver' (dead body). Instead he chose the name Amazon: firstly, it appeared at the top of lists of website addresses because it begins with 'A'; secondly, Bezos could see the similarity between the world's largest river and the world's largest bookshop.

He survived a ⁴_____ accident

A helicopter Bezos was travelling in crashed. Bezos and the other passengers were not badly hurt, but the accident put him off helicopters. However, flying objects are still a passion for him. Amazon is working on drones that can deliver orders in thirty minutes.

He's passionate about exploring ⁵_____

Bezos has dreamt about space travel since he was a child. At high school he said he wanted '… to build space hotels, amusement parks and colonies for two or three million people.' He started a company, Blue Origin, to make space travel more widely available. With Amazon he made shopping easy, and now he wants to do the same for space travel.

He has big ideas for the ⁶_____ of Amazon

Jeff Bezos is always trying to improve the customer experience. His latest innovation is Amazon Go, or the 'just walk out' store. Amazon Go is a supermarket where you take food off the shelf, put it in your bag and leave. No credit cards, no queues at the checkout desk. All you need is a smartphone and an Amazon account. Bezos sees this as the future of shopping.

---

7 SPEAKING Discuss the questions.

1 How many online shopping stores can you think of?
2 Do you like the idea of Amazon Go? Why?/Why not?
3 What do you think the future is for the following forms of payment: cash; debit/credit card; smartphone?

8 SPEAKING Complete the sentences with the words in the box to make them true for you. Then compare your sentences with a partner.

> billionaire brother businessperson company
> customer director employee entrepreneur
> immigrant passenger schoolboy sister
> stepfather teenager unicyclist wife

1 I was/I am a(n) …
2 I will possibly be a(n) …
3 I will never be a(n) …

Quantifiers

I can use a wide range of quantifiers with countable and uncountable nouns.

1 SPEAKING Discuss the questions.

1 Which of these types of shoes have you got?

> ballet flats   knee-high boots   flip-flops
> high heels   sandals   trainers

2 Where is the best shoe shop in your city?

3 When was the last time you bought a pair of shoes?

2 Read the text. What happens when you buy a pair of TOMS shoes?

Do you have too many pairs of shoes? How many pairs do you need? Most people have a few pairs of trainers, some smart shoes, a pair of boots and some sandals. But can you imagine living without any shoes at all?

Blake Mycoskie was shocked when he found out that a lot of children around the world were growing up without any shoes. So he set up a company called Shoes for Tomorrow (TOMS). Every time he sells a pair, he gives a free pair to a child in need. He doesn't have to do much advertising – when people hear about TOMS, they tell one another. Over the years, he's given away lots of shoes to people in need – more than a million, in fact. TOMS has become the One for One™ company who give eyewear as well as shoes to people around the world. With a little imagination and a lot of hard work, Mycoskie has transformed the lives of a lot of people.

3 Look at the examples of nouns and quantifiers in blue in the text. Which of the underlined nouns are countable and which are uncountable?

4 Read the GRAMMAR FOCUS. Complete the rules using *countable* and *uncountable*.

GRAMMAR FOCUS

Quantifiers

You can use different expressions to talk about quantity:
- With ¹_____ nouns you use:
  very few/a few/too many/How many?
- With ²_____ nouns you use:
  very little/a little/too much/How much?
- With both ³_____ and ⁴_____ nouns you use:
  any/some/a lot of/lots of

Note: Usually, you use **a few**, **a little** or **some** in affirmative sentences and **many**, **much** or **any** in negative sentences and questions.

5 Read the text and choose the correct quantifiers.

FAQ

How did TOMS begin?

When Blake Mycoskie was twenty-nine, he took ¹*a little / a few* time off work to go travelling. He met a charity worker, and she told him how ²*much / many* children in developing countries were without shoes. This gave Mycoskie an idea for a shoe company, and a way to help ³*some / any* of these children.

How ⁴*much / many* difference can a simple pair of shoes make to so ⁵*much / many* children's lives?
A pair of shoes can make ⁶*many / a lot of* difference to a child. Firstly, there are ⁷*lots of / a little* diseases in the soil, and shoes protect children's feet. Secondly, ⁸*very few / very little* schools allow children to attend classes without shoes. So shoes help children to get an education.

6 Complete the sentences with the correct Present Simple form of the verbs in brackets.

1 There <u>are</u> (be) lots of shoe shops near here.
2 A lot of people _____ (do) their shopping online.
3 There _____ (be) a lot of pollution in our city.
4 A lot of fast food _____ (be) bad for you.
5 Lots of department stores _____ (be) closed on Sundays.
6 A lot of people in my country _____ (know) about TOMS.

7 Read REMEMBER THIS. Then rewrite the sentences in Exercise 6, replacing *a lot of/lots* of with *little* or *few*. Which sentences from Exercises 6 and 7 are true?

1 There are few shoe shops near here.

REMEMBER THIS

| little = not much | BUT | a little = some |
| few = not many | | a few = some |

8 Make the sentences negative using *not much* or *not many*. Which sentences are true for you?

1 I eat a lot of bread. → *I don't eat much bread.*
2 I send a lot of texts. → _____ .
3 I drink a lot of water. → _____ .
4 I do a lot of homework. → _____ .
5 I talk to a lot of people. → _____ .

9 SPEAKING What's your typical school day? Use *How much …?* or *How many …?* with the activities in Exercise 8 and the activities in the box. Ask and answer the questions as in the example.

> watch/television   spend/time online   do/exercise
> spend/money   listen to/music   get/sleep

A: *How much bread do you eat?*
B: *Lots. How about you?*
A: *Very little. I don't like bread.*

FOCUS VLOG   About clothes

🅑 33 **Watch the Focus Vlog. For the worksheet, go to page 129.**

1 SPEAKING **Discuss the questions.**

1 Are there any street markets near you?
2 What kind of things can you do and buy there?
3 When was the last time you went to a market and what did you buy?

2 ◀) **3.27** **Listen to two people at Camden Market in London. Number the photos in the order in which they visit the shops. What do they buy?**

3 ◀) **3.27** **Choose the correct option. Then listen again and check.**

1 Are you doing *anything / nothing* tomorrow?
2 Who told you that? *Anybody / Nobody.*
3 How many pairs of Dr Martens have you got? *None / Any.*
4 Everybody *has / have* a pair of Dr Martens!
5 Are you kidding? *No one / None* would wear that!
6 *Nothing / None* of them fit.
7 Let's have *something / anything* to eat first.
8 I haven't eaten *something / anything* since breakfast.

LANGUAGE FOCUS

Indefinite pronouns

- You use indefinite pronouns to talk about people, things or places when you don't know who, what or where they are, or it is not important.

People	Things	Places	Examples
someone/ somebody	something	somewhere	Affirmative sentences: *Let's find somewhere to eat.* Requests/Offers: *Would you like something on your pancake?*
anybody/ anyone	anything	anywhere	Negative sentences or questions: *Is anyone at home?*
no one/ nobody	nothing	nowhere	Affirmative sentences (negative meaning): *Nobody knows.*
everyone/ everybody	everything	everywhere	**All** people/things/ places: *Is everything ready?*

- You use a singular verb: *Everybody has a pair of Dr Martens!*
- You can give extra information with …
  a to + infinitive: *I need something to wear.*
  b an adjective: *We have something similar.*
  c a relative clause: *It's somebody who serves customers.*
- *None* means 0 (zero). NOT ~~nothing~~ or ~~anything~~
  None of my friends. NOT ~~No one of my friends.~~

4 **Read the LANGUAGE FOCUS. Choose an appropriate indefinite pronoun to replace the underlined phrases in sentences 1–7.**

1 I know I put my bag down <u>in a place</u> in this shop.
2 There is <u>not one item of clothes</u> in this shop that fits me!
3 <u>All the things</u> I wanted to buy cost a fortune.
4 <u>Not one</u> of the shop assistants offered to help.
5 My girlfriend says she hasn't got <u>one single thing</u> to wear.
6 <u>Not one of the people</u> knew who I was.
7 <u>Not one place</u> in this town sells TOMS shoes.

5 **USE OF ENGLISH Write a second sentence so that it has a similar meaning to the first. Use the word in brackets.**

1 There is nothing to see here. (anything)
2 There wasn't anybody to talk to. (nobody)
3 I met a person who knows you. (somebody)
4 Is there a quiet place where we can talk? (anywhere)
5 I wanted some flip-flops but there weren't any in stock. (none)
6 We all know what you're thinking. (everyone)
7 Let's go to a hot place for our next holiday. (somewhere)
8 He doesn't have any friends who like window shopping. (none)

6 **Complete the sentences with an appropriate indefinite pronoun. Which sentences are true for you?**

1 There is <u>nothing</u> to do in my town. It's so boring!
2 I didn't go _____ last night. I stayed in.
3 I'd like _____ to eat. I'm really hungry!
4 I can't find my sunglasses. I've looked _____ .
5 I bought my mum _____ expensive for her last birthday.
6 _____ of my old jeans fit me any more.
7 I don't think _____ in the class enjoys doing the shopping.
8 I love vintage shops, but there are _____ in my city.

Use of English page 152

WRITING

7.7

A formal written complaint

I can write a basic email of complaint requesting action.

1 SPEAKING **Tick any problems that you, your family or your friends have had when buying something. Tell your partner.**

1 It was past its sell-by date.
2 It didn't work.
3 It was broken or damaged.
4 Some parts were missing.
5 The service was bad.
6 The delivery was late.
7 It was different from the description.
8 It was the wrong product.

2 **Read Email 1 and answer the questions.**

1 Which problems in Exercise 1 did the customer have?
2 Do you think this is a formal written complaint? Why?/Why not?

3 **Read the tips in the WRITING FOCUS. Which tips does Email 1 NOT follow?**

WRITING FOCUS

A formal written complaint
1 Open and close the email or letter formally.
2 Give a reason for writing.
3 Say what you bought and when.
4 Explain the problem giving details.
5 Tell the reader what you expect them to do.
6 Use formal language with no contractions.

4 **Read Email 2. For WRITING FOCUS tips 1–6, underline examples of formal language in the email.**

②

Dear Sir or Madam,

I am writing to complain about the service provided by your company.

I bought a pair of headphones (Model: SA-DIV-RED) from your website on 3rd March and paid for them online. They arrived the next day, but when I tried them, they did not work, so I returned them to you on 5th March and you exchanged them for a new pair. Unfortunately, the second pair you sent were the wrong model, so I emailed you again and sent them back one more time. I received a pair of headphones from you today, but when I unpacked them, I found they were damaged, and they do not work.

I am very disappointed with your service. I do not want another pair of headphones. I would be grateful if you could send me a full refund for the headphones and the cost of sending them back to you three times.

Yours faithfully,

R. Barker

①

Your company is rubbish.

I got some headphones from you online but they didn't work. So I sent them back and you swapped them for a new pair. They weren't the right ones, so I sent them back again. I got another pair from you today and they're broken and they don't work.

I'm so angry! You can keep the headphones but I want all my money back now, and I'll never use your store again.

Ronnie

5 Read the LANGUAGE FOCUS. Complete the examples with words and phrases in Email 2.

LANGUAGE FOCUS

Formal language

- You can make your language more formal by avoiding contractions and using more formal words and expressions.

Informal – Email 1		Formal – Email 2
they didn't work	→	they ¹ ___did not___ work
I got some headphones	→	I ² _____ some headphones
I sent them back	→	I ³ _____ them to you
You swapped them	→	You ⁴ _____ them
I got another pair	→	I ⁵ _____ another pair
I'm so angry	→	I ⁶ _____
I want all my money back	→	I ⁷ _____ refund

Other common words and phrases

if you need more information	if you require further information
I want the chance to chat about this	I would like the opportunity to discuss this
Call us	Please contact us
We're sorry about the problem	We apologise for the problem

6 Rewrite the following exchange to make it more formal. Use the LANGUAGE FOCUS to help you.

CUSTOMER

I'm so angry. A couple of weeks ago, I got a suit from you to wear to a wedding but it was too small. You swapped it for a bigger size, but it's the wrong colour and the zip doesn't work on the trousers. I've sent them back because it's too late for the wedding. I want all my money back, including the price of postage.

I am very disappointed with …

ONLINE CLOTHES STORE

We're sorry about the problem you've had with this order. We'll give you all your money back but we can't pay the postage. If you want the chance to chat about this, call us on 09000 999 999.

We apologise for …

7 Do the writing task. Use the ideas in the WRITING FOCUS and LANGUAGE FOCUS to help you.

Look at the online music store website and read the customer's comment. Write a formal email of complaint. Include the following information:

- explain the reasons for your complaint
- describe what you bought and when
- explain the problem with the product in detail
- explain how you expect the company to solve the problem.

Contact	Customer Services	Returns	FAQ's

CONTACT US

Select a category: choose from the dropdown menu

Please tell us the type of problem you are experiencing:

- **My download won't complete**
- This is not the music I wanted
- My file won't play
- The quality of sound is low
- I deleted the file by mistake

Comment

I want to complain about your service. I have tried to download Adele's album 21 three times this month but every time the download has not completed. I've contacted you three times on 1st, 8th and 17th April. I've been a loyal customer for two years and I've enjoyed the music I've bought each month from your site. But now I want a refund of my last month's subscription. Please close my account.

 SEND

Dear Sir or Madam,

I am writing to complain about …

97

1 SPEAKING Think about shopping in your city. Discuss which shop is …

1 the cheapest and the most expensive.
2 the most and least fashionable for clothes.
3 the one with the most and least helpful shop assistants.

2 Match customer comments 1–7 with situations a–e.

1 Get it. It really suits you.
2 Oh no! They've sold out.
3 They're on offer – buy one and get one free.
4 I'm just looking, thanks.
5 Look, it's half price!
6 It's not exactly what I'm looking for.
7 It's reduced from £50 to £19.99.

a The item is on special offer. ☐☐☐
b The colour and style are perfect. ☐
c The item is not quite right for you. ☐
d The item is out of stock. ☐
e You don't want the shop assistant to bother you. ☐

3 🔊 3.28 Look at the pictures and listen to two dialogues. Which dialogue are words a–h linked to?

a complain ☐   e ripped ☐
b dress ☐   f size 12 ☐
c receipt ☐☐   g top ☐
d present ☐   h zip ☐

4 Summarise what happens in each dialogue using the words in Exercise 3.

5 🔊 3.28 Complete the SPEAKING FOCUS with the words in the box. Then listen to the dialogues again and check.

> changing ~~help~~ How looking
> receipt refund size fit

SPEAKING FOCUS

Shopping for clothes

Shop assistant
Can I ¹*help* you?
Would you like to try it on?
The ² _____ rooms are over there.
³ _____ would you like to pay?
Make sure you keep your receipt.

Customer
Excuse me, I'm ⁴ _____ for a top.
I'm a ⁵ _____ 10.
Do you have this in a size 12, please?
I'll take it.
Cash, please./By credit card.
If it doesn't ⁶ _____ , can we get a refund?

Making complaints

Shop assistant
What's wrong with it?
Do you have your ⁷ _____ ?
We can exchange it for a new one.

Customer
I bought this dress last week but the zip doesn't work.
I think it's faulty./It shrank./There's a hole in it./The colour ran.
I'd like a ⁸ _____ please.

6 SPEAKING Follow the instructions below to prepare a dialogue. Use the SPEAKING FOCUS to help you.

Student A: You are a customer returning a faulty pair of jeans. Say when you bought the jeans and explain what is wrong with them (colour ran/they shrank).

Student B: You are a shop assistant. Ask Student A if he/she has a receipt. Suggest a solution to the problem (refund/repair/new pair of jeans).

7 SPEAKING Practise your dialogue. Then act it out to the class.

ROLE-PLAY Shopping

🎬 34 🎬 35 Watch the video and practise. Then role-play your dialogue.

7.1 Vocabulary 🔊 4.49

baker's /'beɪkəz/
bank /bæŋk/
be worth it /ˌbi 'wɜːθ ɪt/
brand (n, adj) /brænd/
butcher's /'bʊtʃəz/
cashmere /'kæʃmɪə/
charity shop /'tʃærəti ʃɒp/
chemist's /'kemɪsts/
clothes shop /'kləʊðz ʃɒp/
computer shop /kəm'pjuːtə ˌʃɒp/
contact lens solution /ˌkɒntækt lenz sə'luːʃən/
cotton /'kɒtn/
denim /'denɪm/
department store /dɪ'pɑːtmənt ˌstɔː/
designer clothes /dɪˌzaɪnə 'kləʊðz/
DIY store /ˌdiː aɪ 'waɪ stɔː/
do the shopping /ˌduː ðə 'ʃɒpɪŋ/
estate agent's /ɪ'steɪt ˌeɪdʒənts/
fit /fɪt/
florist's /'flɒrɪsts/
get a refund /ˌget ə 'riːfʌnd/
go shopping /ˌgəʊ 'ʃɒpɪŋ/
go window shopping /ˌgəʊ ˌwɪndəʊ 'ʃɒpɪŋ/
greengrocer's /'griːŋgrəʊsəz/
hairdresser's /'heəˌdresəz/
have a sale /ˌhæv ə 'seɪl/
health centre /'helθ ˌsentə/
high street store /ˌhaɪ ˌstriːt 'stɔː/
jeweller's /'dʒuːələz/
keep the receipt /ˌkiːp ðə rɪ'siːt/
last for ages /ˌlɑːst fər 'eɪdʒɪz/
leather (n, adj) /'leðə/
look fashionable /ˌlʊk 'fæʃənəbəl/
look good /ˌlʊk 'gʊd/
look gorgeous /ˌlʊk 'gɔːdʒəs/
look original /ˌlʊk ə'rɪdʒɪnəl/
look scruffy /ˌlʊk 'skrʌfi/
look smart /ˌlʊk 'smɑːt/
newsagent's /'njuːzˌeɪdʒənts/
on (special) offer /ɒn (ˌspeʃəl) 'ɒfə/
optician's /ɒp'tɪʃənz/
pet shop /'pet ʃɒp/
pick up a bargain /ˌpɪk ʌp ə 'bɑːgən/
post office /'pəʊst ˌɒfəs/
printer ink /'prɪntər ɪŋk/
quality /'kwɒləti/
shoe shop /'ʃuː ʃɒp/
shoelaces /'ʃuːleɪsɪz/
shop online /ˌʃɒp ɒn'laɪn/
silk /sɪlk/
sports shop /'spɔːts ʃɒp/
stationer's /'steɪʃənəz/
store /stɔː/
suit /suːt/
supermarket /'suːpəˌmɑːkət/
toy shop /'tɔɪ ʃɒp/
vintage shop /'vɪntɪdʒ ʃɒp/
wool /wʊl/

7.2 Grammar 🔊 4.50

approximately /ə'prɒksɪmətli/
consumer /kən'suːmə/
crops /krɒps/
drinking water /'drɪŋkɪŋ ˌwɔːtə/

make a living /ˌmeɪk ə 'lɪvɪŋ/
plant /plɑːnt/
protect the environment /prəˌtekt ði ɪn'vaɪrənmənt/
set up /set 'ʌp/

7.3 Listening 🔊 4.51

aisle /aɪl/
be a matter of sth/a question of sth /ˌbi ə 'mætər əv/ə 'kwestʃən əv 'sʌmθɪŋ/
be capable of doing sth /ˌbi ˌkeɪpəbəl əv ˌduːɪŋ 'sʌmθɪŋ/
be in debt /bi ɪn 'det/
cheer up /ˌtʃɪər 'ʌp/
debt /det/
debtor /'detə/
earn /ɜːn/
earner /'ɜːnə/
earnings /'ɜːnɪŋz/
face cream /'feɪs kriːm/
friendship bracelet /'frendʃɪp ˌbreɪslət/
invest in /ɪn'vest ɪn/
investment /ɪn'vestmənt/
investor /ɪn'vestə/
make sb feel happier /ˌmeɪk ˌsʌmbɒdi fiːl 'hæpiə/
pay /peɪ/
payer /'peɪə/
payment /'peɪmənt/
perfume /'pɜːfjuːm/
produce /prə'djuːs/
producer /prə'djuːsə/
product /'prɒdʌkt/
purse /pɜːs/
recording studio /rɪ'kɔːdɪŋ ˌstjuːdiəʊ/
sale /seɪl/
sell /sel/
seller /'selə/
toiletries /'tɔɪlətriz/
trade (n, v) /treɪd/
trader /'treɪdə/
value /'væljuː/

7.4 Reading 🔊 4.52

account /ə'kaʊnt/
available /ə'veɪləbəl/
billionaire /ˌbɪljə'neə/
bookstore /'bʊkstɔː/
checkout desk /'tʃek-aʊt ˌdesk/
complaint /kəm'pleɪnt/
customer /'kʌstəmə/
delivery /dɪ'lɪvəri/
employee /ɪm'plɔɪ-iː/
entrepreneur /ˌɒntrəprə'nɜː/
household name /ˌhaʊshəʊld 'neɪm/
immigrant /'ɪmɪgrənt/
increase /'ɪnkriːs/
order /'ɔːdə/
passenger /'pæsɪndʒə/
passion /'pæʃən/
queue /kjuː/
request /rɪ'kwest/
rise /raɪz/
ship /ʃɪp/
stepfather /'stepˌfɑːðə/
unicyclist /'juːniˌsaɪklɪst/
wait in line /ˌweɪt ɪn 'laɪn/

7.5 Grammar 🔊 4.53

advertising /'ædvətaɪzɪŋ/
ballet flats /'bæleɪ flæts/
boots /buːts/
broken /'brəʊkən/
disease /dɪ'ziːz/
flip-flops /'flɪp flɒps/
high heels /ˌhaɪ 'hiːlz/
imagination /ɪˌmædʒɪ'neɪʃən/
knee-high /ˌniː 'haɪ/
sandals /'sændəlz/
slippers /'slɪpəz/
soil /sɔɪl/
trainers /'treɪnəz/

7.6 Use of English 🔊 4.54

be kidding /bi 'kɪdɪŋ/
cost a fortune /ˌkɒst ə 'fɔːtʃən/
street market /striːt 'mɑːkət/

7.7 Writing 🔊 4.55

apologise /ə'pɒlədʒaɪz/
complain /kəm'pleɪn/
damaged /'dæmɪdʒd/
exchange sth for sth /ɪks'tʃeɪndʒ ˌsʌmθɪŋ fə ˌsʌmθɪŋ/
headphones /'hedfəʊnz/
postage /'pəʊstɪdʒ/
receive /rɪ'siːv/
return /rɪ'tɜːn/
sell-by date /'sel baɪ deɪt/
service /'sɜːvəs/
some parts are missing /səm ˌpɑːts ə 'mɪsɪŋ/
subscription /səb'skrɪpʃən/
swap /swɒp/
wedding /'wedɪŋ/
zip /zɪp/

7.8 Speaking 🔊 4.56

bother /'bɒðə/
cash /kæʃ/
changing room /'tʃeɪndʒɪŋ ruːm/
faulty /'fɔːlti/
out of stock /ˌaʊt əv 'stɒk/
reduced /rɪ'djuːst/
ripped /rɪpt/
sell out /ˌsel 'aʊt/
size /saɪz/
try on /ˌtraɪ 'ɒn/

FOCUS REVIEW 7

VOCABULARY AND GRAMMAR

1 Choose the odd one out in each group.

1 businessperson, employee, company director, entrepreneur
2 trader, entrepreneur, customer, investor
3 scruffy, cotton, cashmere, silk
4 smart, fashionable, original, denim
5 butcher's, stationer's, baker's, greengrocer's

2 Complete the sentences with the correct form of the words in capitals.

1 Stanley has saved half of his _____ for a new computer. **EARN**
2 A modern water park was built last year, which was the best _____ in our city. **INVEST**
3 I don't use any cash. All my _____ are made by credit card. **PAY**
4 What company is the largest _____ of personal computers in the world? **PRODUCE**
5 This shop has had a _____ for two weeks. **SELL**
6 The factory tried to keep some _____ by offering them more money. **EMPLOY**

3 Complete the second sentence so that it has a similar meaning to the first.

1 How much does the factory pay the workers?
How much _____ the factory workers _____ ?
2 Farmers have never grown rice in this field.
Rice _____ never _____ in this field.
3 They have sold over 1,000 bikes so far this year.
Over 1,000 bikes _____ so far this year.
4 They keep their investments secret.
Their investments _____ secret.
5 He painted more than 100 pictures in this studio.
More than 100 pictures _____ in this studio.
6 When did they open their first shop?
When _____ their first shop _____ ?

4 Choose the correct answer, A, B, C or D.

1 'How ___ tablets do you own?' 'Just one.'
A any   B few   C much   D many
2 There are ___ people in the queue. It's too long to wait.
A a lot of   B lots   C a little   D lot
3 'I'm so hungry.' 'I have ___ biscuits in my bag. Would you like one?'
A very little   B a few   C too much   D any
4 I think there is ___ advertising on TV. I can't stand it.
A too many   B lot of   C too much   D a little
5 ___ homework do you get every day?
A How   B How long   C How many   D How much
6 She's got ___ money to buy designer clothes, but she often goes window shopping.
A very little   B too many   C very few   D any

USE OF ENGLISH

5 Choose the correct answer, A, B or C.

1 There _____ supermarkets in my neighbourhood.
A is little
B aren't much
C are few
2 If you haven't got money for an expensive jacket, you should try to _____ .
A pick up a bargain
B have a sale
C be worth it
3 We need to find _____ to buy food.
A somewhere
B anywhere
C everywhere
4 _____ of their debtors have returned the money yet.
A No one
B None
C Anyone
5 The T-shirt didn't fit my brother, so I sent it back and asked for a _____ .
A receipt
B refund
C bonus

6 Read the text and choose the correct answer, A, B or C.

Mystery shopping
– a type of market research

Kara, 19, a university student, has an unusual part-time job. She works as a mystery shopper. What does she do? One day she buys a pair of glasses at **1**___ , another day she has a meal in a restaurant. She looks like an average customer, but after the visit she writes a report about the place and sends it to the company's office. This is how the shops or restaurants get information about their goods or services and whether **2**___ is not satisfied.

'It's the perfect job for me', explains Kara. 'Going shopping has always been my hobby but I don't have **3**___ money to buy what I like. With this job I can have a free meal in an elegant restaurant or get some designer clothes. Mystery shopping also gives me **4**___ interesting to do at weekends and during my lunch hours.'

Market Force, the company which employs people like Kara, says: 'Mystery shoppers **5**___ once a month. To make sure that our employees are honest and reliable, we sometimes send **6**___ shoppers to the same place.'

1 A a jeweller's   B an optician's   C a shoe shop
2 A everybody   B anybody   C nobody
3 A many   B much   C some
4 A something   B nothing   C everything
5 A pay   B paid   C are paid
6 A a few   B a little   C none

7 Read the text and choose the correct answer, A, B, C or D.

THE HIGH STREET

Last summer I visited Britain. On the first day I needed some aspirin for my headache, so I asked the hotel owner where I could get some. She said: 'There's *a chemist's* on the high street.' I soon learned that a chemist's is what British people call *a pharmacy* and *high street* is called *main street* in America. That was a classic illustration of two nations divided by a common language.

The phrase *high street* is hardly ever explained to tourists because it is a part of everyday life in the UK. It means the main commercial street in every British town. What can be surprising is that a town's high street is not always the most important place in town and is not often called *High Street*, but has another official name.

In small villages, the high street has little more than a mail box, a newsagent's and a small supermarket. In a bigger town, you will find a chemist's, a DIY store, a pub and also traditional food shops like a butcher's or greengrocer's. In big cities, pubs, clothes shops, toy shops, banks and estate agents line up on the high street. But there are not many vintage shops or fast food bars, unless they are part of big, multinational companies. This is because high street rents are usually the highest for businesses in the town.

Another surprise is *high street fashion*, which does not refer to the clothes that are sold in the high street shops – it only describes clothes that are not too expensive but are fashionable. They are usually produced from good quality materials and you can find them everywhere, from big department stores to small local shops. Everyone can afford them.

Is the high street going to disappear from the British culture? I don't think so. Every year the competition for The Best High Street is announced. In 2016, there were 900 candidates. The title went to Blackburn, a big town in the north of England and one of my favourites.

1 The writer:
   A is a British tourist to the USA.
   B is an American tourist to the UK.
   C runs a shop in the high street.
   D lives in Blackburn.

2 What did the writer find out about *the high street*?
   A It is the central part of every British town.
   B Every high street looks the same.
   C Most town sellers have their shops there.
   D You can't have a fast food meal there.

3 *High street fashion* refers to:
   A the most popular clothes.
   B clothes on special offer.
   C good quality brands.
   D very expensive clothes.

4 In the text, the writer:
   A gives the reasons for the differences between British and American English.
   B invites people to go shopping in the high street.
   C encourages towns to take part in the competition for the Best High Street.
   D shares his/her discoveries about British culture.

8 Do the task in pairs.

Student A

You are spending the summer with your family in the UK and you have been invited to an 'end of summer' party with your cousins. You go to a clothes shop to buy some new clothes for the special occasion. Student B starts the conversation.
- Explain what you need and what the special occasion is.
- Say what size you are and ask if you can try it on.
- Say there is a problem with an item of clothing and explain what it is.
- Decide to buy an item and ask about payment.

Student B

You have a summer job at a clothes shop. A customer, Student A, enters your shop and wants to buy some clothes. Help him/her. You start the conversation.
- Suggest an item of clothing from the new collection and ask what size he/she needs.
- Say where the changing rooms are. Ask if everything is OK.
- React to the problem and offer help.
- Answer the customer's question and finish the sale.

9 Match the products (1–4) with the possible problems you might have when you buy them (a–d). Then, in pairs, add one more possible problem for each of the products.

PRODUCTS
1 a box of chocolates
2 a book
3 a pair of jeans
4 an MP3 player

PROBLEMS
a Some pages are missing.
b It has bad sound quality.
c They are past their sell-by date.
d They shrank after the first wash.

10 Use one of the products in Exercise 9 and do the writing task.

A few weeks ago you made an online purchase. The shop promised that the parcel will be delivered within two days but you had to wait longer. When you opened the parcel, there was a problem with the product you ordered. Write an email of complaint. Include the following information:
- explain what you bought and when
- complain about the fact that the parcel was delivered late
- describe the problem with the product you received
- explain what you expect the company to do to solve the problem.

8

Well-being

A good laugh and a long sleep are the two best cures for anything.

Irish proverb

BBC

KEEPING FIT

▶ 36 Watch the BBC video.
For the worksheet, go to page 130.

VOCABULARY

8.1

Body parts • symptoms • health • phrasal verbs

I can use language related to wellness and illness.

SHOW WHAT YOU KNOW

1 **Put the body parts in order from head to toe in each set of words.**

1 mouth forehead ear heart → *forehead ear mouth heart*
2 shoulder nose throat eyebrows
3 hip tongue back foot
4 chest lips eyelashes knee
5 tooth finger neck leg

2 **Point to a part of your body and ask your partner to say the word.**

APPS TO KEEP YOU FIT

Feel unhealthy or unfit? Need to lose weight? Stressed out? No worries – just get the right app!

Here are five types of apps that will help to improve your general health and levels of fitness.

1 ☐
You'll find it easier to work out if you have the right tunes. **Fit radio** lets you choose your own playlist, for Zumba®, running or aerobics.

2 ☐
Do you sometimes **feel dizzy** after doing exercise? Get an app that tells you to drink water before you pass out. Apps like **Fooducate** can also help you to make healthy food choices and cut out things that are bad for you. Scan a barcode and get nutritional information like how many calories it contains.

3 ☐
Are those exams stressing you out? Does your **head hurt**? Get a mindfulness app like **Aura** and learn how to be calm. Meditation will reduce anxiety and stress.

4 ☐
Everyone should exercise regularly. If you prefer to do your exercise outdoors, take up cycling. **Strava** can find you a route and track your distances. It can also check your pulse and heart rate.

5 ☐
You've got **a temperature**, **a headache** and you've come out in a rash! Or maybe you've got **a cough**, **a sore throat** and **a pain in your chest**. **Symptomate** will tell you what the problem is and how to get over it. You know you're allergic to nuts, or you suffer from **a runny nose** in spring? Get **Allergy Alert** to keep track of your symptoms.

3 SPEAKING **Discuss the questions.**

1 How many apps do you have on your phone?
2 What are the apps for and which ones do you use most?
3 What apps do you know of that help you keep fit and stay healthy?

4 **Read the article. Match headings A–E with paragraphs 1–5.**

A Feel calmer
B Get the right music
C Stay well
D Keep fit
E Eat and drink the right things

5 SPEAKING **Which apps would you like to use and why? Discuss with a partner.**

WORD STORE 8A | Symptoms

6 🔊 3.29 **Complete WORD STORE 8A with the words in red in the text. Then listen, check and repeat.**

7 SPEAKING **Choose the correct option. Then ask and answer the questions.**

1 When was the last time you felt *ill / runny*?
2 Does your *back / hair* hurt sometimes?
3 Does anything make you feel *allergic / dizzy*?
4 Have you ever had a pain in your *chest / cough*?
5 What do you do if you have a *sore throat / chest*?
6 Did you have a *weight / headache* yesterday?

WORD STORE 8B | Health

8 🔊 3.30 **Complete WORD STORE 8B with the base form of the verb in the underlined collocations in the text. Add a translation. Then listen and repeat.**

9 SPEAKING **Match the sentence halves. Discuss whether you agree with the statements.**

1 The only way to lose ☐
2 Children don't know how to make ☐
3 It's important to keep ☐
4 People usually come out in ☐
5 If you are allergic ☐
6 Most people don't know how to check ☐

a healthy food choices.
b to nuts, you should tell everybody.
c weight is to eat less and exercise more!
d a rash because of something they've eaten.
e their pulse.
f track of the calories you eat in a day.

WORD STORE 8C | Phrasal verbs

10 🔊 3.31 **Complete WORD STORE 8C with the base form of the verb in the highlighted phrasal verbs in the text. Then listen, check and repeat.**

11 **Replace the underlined verb phrases with the phrasal verbs in WORD STORE 8C.**

1 I like doing physical exercise to music.
2 I've decided to start jogging.
3 I don't think I've ever fainted.
4 Fortunately, nobody in my family has asthma.
5 It always takes me a while to recover from a cold.
6 I don't really like meat so I'm going to stop eating it.
7 Exams always make me feel nervous.

12 SPEAKING **Read the sentences in Exercise 11 to each other. Are they true for you or your partner?**

103

GRAMMAR

8.2

Past Perfect

I can use the Past Perfect in a range of common situations.

1 Read Part 1 of a story about a very lucky footballer. What happened to Fabrice Muamba?

Fabrice Muamba

Part 1

Shauna Muamba was watching her fiancé play football on television with her three-year-old son Joshua and her mother when Josh said 'Mummy, Daddy is frozen.'

Bolton footballer, Fabrice Muamba, had fallen down on the pitch. 'He's probably passed out,' Shauna's mother said.

But he hadn't fainted – he had had a heart attack.

Around the world, millions of people were watching the FA Cup match between Tottenham and Bolton. Everyone knew it was serious because he had fallen like a tree – he hadn't put out his arms, he'd just dropped to the ground. By the time the medical people got to him, his heart had stopped.

2 Read the GRAMMAR FOCUS and answer the questions.

1 How do you form the Past Perfect?
2 When do you use the Past Perfect?
3 According to the text, what things had Fabrice Muamba done/not done before the medical people got to him?

GRAMMAR FOCUS

Past Perfect

You use the **Past Perfect** to make it clear that one past action happened before another past action.

By the time the medical team **got** to him,
his heart **had stopped**.

past   present

Note: *By the time* + Past Simple, Past Perfect.

Past Perfect: *had* + Past Participle

+	I had ('d) worked.
–	He had not (hadn't) worked.
?	Had they worked?
	Yes, they had./No, they hadn't.

3 Read Part 2 of the story. Choose the correct option. Who/What saved Fabrice Muamba's life?

Part 2

The Bolton physiotherapist ¹*was* / *had been* the first to notice that Muamba ²*fell down* / *had fallen down*. He screamed, 'Get on the pitch, get on the pitch!' It ³*was* / *had been* obvious that something serious ⁴*happened* / *had happened*. But Muamba was lucky. Tottenham fan Dr Deaner, a consultant cardiologist, was one of the 35,000 spectators at the match that day. When he ⁵*saw* / *had seen* that Muamba ⁶*dropped* / *had dropped* to the ground, he turned to his brothers and said 'I should help!' He ⁷*ran* / *had run* onto the pitch and told the ambulance to take Muamba to the London Chest Hospital. He ⁸*knew* / *had known* that they had specialist equipment. This decision saved Muamba's life. When he finally ⁹*woke up* / *had woken up*, he ¹⁰*was* / *had been* 'dead' for seventy-eight minutes.

4 Compare these sentence pairs. In each sentence, decide what happened first. Which sentences are true for you?

1 a When I got home yesterday, <u>my mum had made dinner</u>.
  b When I got home yesterday, my mum made dinner.
2 a When I got to school this morning, I had breakfast.
  b When I got to school this morning, I'd had breakfast.
3 a This lesson started when I arrived.
  b This lesson had started when I arrived.
4 a When the lesson began, I read about Fabrice Muamba.
  b When the lesson began, I had read about Fabrice Muamba.

5 Write six Past Perfect sentences about yourself. Use *By the age of …* and verb phrases in the box or your own ideas.

> learn how to read/swim/ski
> buy (or get) my first phone/laptop/bike
> go to the capital city/a foreign country/a live concert

By the age of six, I had learnt how to swim.
By the age of …

6 SPEAKING Read your sentences in Exercise 5 to your partner and find out how similar you are.

FOCUS VLOG   About achievements

(▶ 38) Watch the Focus Vlog. For the worksheet, go to page 131.

Grammar page 153

1 **SPEAKING Discuss what you know about Central Park in New York.**

2 **Read US TODAY. Guess the missing numbers using the ones in the box. Which fact is the most interesting?**

21   26   93   9,000

3 🔊 **3.32 Listen to the introduction of a podcast about Central Park and check your ideas in Exercise 2. What other things can you do in Central Park?**

EXAM FOCUS   Multiple choice

4 🔊 **3.33 Listen to the complete podcast. For questions 1–6, choose the correct answer, A, B or C.**

1 The podcast presenter thinks Central Park is
  A the busiest place in the world.
  B like a garden for New Yorkers.
  C a good place to enjoy city life.

2 Central Park is a good place to
  A be alone.
  B go shopping.
  C keep fit.

3 The two French girls the presenter speaks to
  A only have a few hours in New York.
  B both want to spend all day in the park.
  C don't want to do the same things.

4 The 'Team Central Park' runner is
  A training for a marathon.
  B not going to do a marathon.
  C doing a 5K fun run.

5 The group of young people
  A spend a lot of time in the park in summer.
  B always bring a picnic.
  C are not allowed to use skateboards.

6 The group of young people
  A watch people playing Frisbee.
  B ride bikes fast through the park.
  C enjoy a lot of different things in the park.

5 🔊 **3.33 Answer the questions. Then listen to the podcast again and check.**

1 Which sporting activities do New Yorkers do in Central Park?

2 Apart from sport, what other things can you do there?

3 Why did the French girls hire bicycles?

4 Why isn't the 'Team Central Park' runner sure he can complete the marathon?

5 Why do you have to be careful when you skateboard in Central Park?

US TODAY

Central Park ...
- covers 6 percent of Manhattan
- welcomes 40 million visitors a year
- was designed by the winners of a competition in 1858
- took 20,000 workers 15 years to complete
- is six times bigger than Monaco
- has featured in over 350 movies
- includes: ¹_____ kilometres of pathways to walk on, ²_____ benches to sit on, ³_____ playing fields, ⁴_____ playgrounds for children, 275 species of bird, 125 drinking fountains, and 36 bridges and arches

6 **SPEAKING Discuss what the biggest public park near you is.**

1 What activities can you do in the park?

2 What kind of people use the park and when is it busiest?

3 How often do you go to the park and what do you do there?

PRONUNCIATION FOCUS

7 🔊 **3.34 Listen and repeat the diphthongs.**

Diphthong	Example	Diphthong	Example
1 /eə/	_air_	5 /əʊ/	_____
2 /eɪ/	_____	6 /ɪə/	_____
3 /ʊə/	_____	7 /aɪ/	_____
4 /ɔɪ/	_____	8 /aʊ/	_____

8 🔊 **3.35 Complete the examples in Exercise 7 with the words in the box. Then listen, check and repeat.**

~~air~~   climb   hear   low   noise   out   skate   sure

WORD STORE 8D   Places to do sport

9 🔊 **3.36 Complete WORD STORE 8D with the nouns in the box. Then listen, check and repeat.**

Open-ended questions

I can identify specific information in a short article.

1 Look at the graph about air pollution and label the photos: *Los Angeles*, *Stockholm* and *Beijing*.

Annual mean concentration of particulate matter with diameter of 2.5 microns

the World Health Organisation's safe limit

Delhi, Beijing, Moscow, Rio de Janeiro, Los Angeles, London, Melbourne, Stockholm

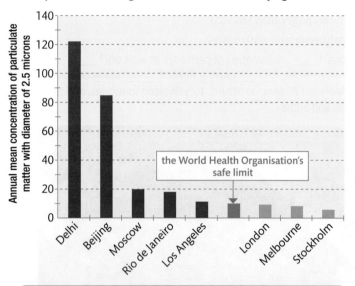

1 _____

2 _____

3 _____

2 SPEAKING **Discuss what you know about:**
1 the causes of air pollution.
2 the health problems caused by air pollution.
3 ways of reducing air pollution.

3 **Read the text and check your ideas in Exercise 2. What do you think about the Smog Free Tower?**

EXAM FOCUS   Open-ended questions

4 **Read the text again and answer the questions.**
1 Who suffers most from air pollution?
2 What do people do to avoid polluted air?
3 How does a Smog Free Tower work?
4 What can you make with smog particles?
5 What motivated the designer to create the Smog Free Tower?
6 How does the Smog Free Tower project develop?

5 **Read the text again and complete the notes.**

Smog Free Tower Project
1 Number of people dying of air pollution: _____ a year
2 Symptoms of health problems caused by air pollution: _____ and _____
3 Name of the Smog Free Tower's inventor: _____
4 The Smog Free Tower's height: _____
5 Type of energy used by the tower: _____
6 Number of towers to be placed in China: _____

6 🔊 3.38 **Complete the collocations with the words in blue in the text. Then listen, check and repeat.**
1 air _____
2 air _____
3 dust _____
4 exhaust _____
5 environmental _____
6 face _____
7 factory _____
8 smog _____
9 vacuum _____

7 **Answer the questions with words in Exercise 6.**
1 What is responsible for over three million deaths every year? *Air pollution*
2 What are the three main causes of smog in Beijing?
3 What do people wear to protect themselves from air pollution?
4 What does the Smog Free Tower look like?
5 The designer says it is the biggest 'what' in the world?
6 What does the tower collect and store?
7 Which Chinese ministry wants to put towers in other cities?

8 SPEAKING **Discuss which of these environmental problems affects the world, your country and you the most.**
1 **air pollution** (smog from exhaust fumes, factory smoke etc.)
2 **ocean and river pollution** (chemicals from factories or plastic)
3 **land pollution** (chemicals used in farming)

9 SPEAKING **List three things that you, your country or the world could do to solve the problem of air, water and land pollution. Discuss as a class.**

You could use public transport more or walk or cycle to places …

The Tower That Sucks in Smog and Spits Out Clean Air

◀) 3.37

The city of Beijing has such a big problem with its air quality that there are days when you can't see the buildings on the other side of the street. According to Nature Magazine, air pollution is responsible for three
5 million deaths per year, and most of these deaths are in Asia. More and more people suffer from chest pain and have difficulty breathing. Children and the elderly are most at risk.

The 'Smog' – a blend of the words 'smoke' and 'fog' – is
10 mainly caused by car exhaust fumes, factory smoke and dust storms from local construction projects. To protect themselves from the unhealthy effects of pollution, people wear face masks and children play sports indoors.

Last week, a Smog Free Tower was erected in the arts
15 district of Beijing. It is part of an air purifying project by Daan Roosegaarde from Holland and is designed to take in smog and release clean air. The seven-metre-high tower resembles the kind of air purifier you may have in your house. Roosegaarde describes it as the largest smog vacuum cleaner in the world.

20 The Smog Free Tower was created by Roosegaarde and a green tech company in the Netherlands. It runs on renewable power. Smog particles that are dangerous to health are collected and stored inside the tower. The tower then blows out cleaner air. Roosegaarde uses the
25 collected smog particles to make jewellery. When you buy a Smog Free Ring or a pair of cufflinks, you buy 1,000 cubic metres of clean air.

Roosegaarde got the idea for the Smog Free Project when he visited Beijing in 2013. One day he looked out
30 of his hotel window and he simply couldn't see anything. The city had disappeared under a thick layer of smog.

Roosegaarde's project has the support of the Chinese Ministry of Environmental Protection, who have requested towers in four other cities. Roosegaarde is
35 planning to set up 800 of his giant air purifiers in parks all over China to raise awareness of the huge problem of pollution. He believes that both citizens and the government need to work together to fight pollution. His dream is that in ten to fifteen years from now, we won't
40 need his towers anymore.

WORD STORE 8E | Word families

10 ◀) 3.39 Complete WORD STORE 8E with the correct noun, verb or adjective in the text. Mark the stress. Then listen, check and repeat.

GRAMMAR

8.5

Reported Speech

I can make tense changes in reported speech.

1 Read the text and answer the questions.

1 What records has he broken?
2 What is his secret for a healthy life?

Stanislaw Kowalski

Stanislaw Kowalski has become the oldest person in Europe to run a 100-metre race. When he crossed the finishing line, the 104-year-old grandfather said that *he felt like a new man*. He said *he wasn't surprised that he had lived to such an old age.* He said *he had always done everything he wanted to do* and *he had never been to the doctor's.* He also said that *he had cycled or walked ten km to work every day* of his working life. He told reporters that *he was looking forward to breaking the world record* for the sixty-metre race, which he actually did half a year later.

2 Compare the Direct Speech 1–6 below with the Reported Speech in blue in the text. What changes are there to the verb forms and pronouns?

1 'I feel like a new man.'
2 'I'm not surprised that I've lived to such an old age.'
3 'I've always done everything I want to do.'
4 'I've never been to the doctor's.'
5 'I cycled or walked 10 km to work every day.'
6 'I am looking forward to breaking the world record.'

3 Read the GRAMMAR FOCUS. Complete the examples using the correct verb form.

GRAMMAR FOCUS

Reported Speech

In Reported Speech verb forms and pronouns change depending on the context.

Direct Speech	Reported Speech
Present Simple	→ **Past Simple**
'I **work**,' she said.	She said she **worked**.
Present Continuous	→ **Past Continuous**
'He's **working**,' we said.	We said he ¹_____ .
Present Perfect	→ **Past Perfect**
'We've **worked**,' he said.	He said they ²_____ .
Past Simple	→ **Past Perfect**
'She **worked**,' they said.	They said she ³_____ .

4 Read the text. Rewrite sentences A–G in Reported Speech and use them to complete the text. Why didn't the officials believe Dharam?

A I am 119 years old. = *He said he was 119 years old.*
B He can't prove his age.
C My secret is cow's milk.
D Singh is lying about his age.
E I am not only the oldest athlete in the world.
F We understand that he has never known his real age.
G I think the people who have accused me of lying are jealous.

Dharam Pal Singh

When Dharam Pal Singh, a farmer from India, entered an Australian Athletics competition, he told the officials that ¹*he was 119 years old*. He said that ²___, but he was also the oldest man in the world. The officials told reporters that ³___. They said that Singh had never had a birth certificate so ⁴___. They said that they liked him, and ⁵___. Singh said that ⁶___ of his health and his running ability. He told reporters that ⁷___, herbal chutney and fruit.

5 Choose the correct verb.

1 My teacher *said / told* me I wasn't concentrating.
2 He *said / told* I looked tired.
3 I *said / told* him that I hadn't slept very well.
4 I *said / told* I had watched a really scary film.
5 I *said / told* him that was why I hadn't done my homework.
6 He *said / told* I'd used that excuse before!

6 Rewrite the sentences in Exercise 5 in Direct Speech.

1 You aren't concentrating.

7 SPEAKING Follow the instructions to complete the task.

1 Tell your partner five true facts about yourself. Use some of the 'facts' in the box or your own ideas.

> I am/am not tired   I can/can't snowboard
> I like/don't like politics
> I've been/haven't been to London
> I'm going out/not going out tonight
> I watched/didn't watch TV last night

2 Your partner then reports back. How many facts can your partner remember correctly?

A: *You said you could snowboard.*
B: *Yes, that's right.*
A: *You said you liked politics.*
B: *No, I said I didn't like politics.*

Grammar page 154

1 SPEAKING **Look at the photo. Jenny and her mum have just moved to a new town. Try to answer the questions.**

  1 Why is Jenny so worried/stressed?

  2 What do you think her mum is telling her?

  3 How would you feel if you had to start a new school now?

2 🔊 3.40 **Listen and check your ideas in Exercise 1. Does the conversation end positively?**

3 🔊 3.40 **Listen again and tick 'Jenny' or 'Mum'.**

Who ...	Jenny	Mum
1 says she has **fallen behind**?		
2 seems negative and **puts** herself **down**?		
3 feels that she doesn't **fit in**?		
4 promises to **figure** things **out** for herself?		
5 thinks it's good to **talk** things **over**?		
6 doesn't like the situation but says she'll **get through** it?		
7 needs to **catch up on** her work?		
8 says they have to **get on with** life?		

4 **Read the LANGUAGE FOCUS. Decide whether the phrasal verbs in blue in Exercise 3 are type 1, type 2 or type 3.**

LANGUAGE FOCUS

Phrasal verbs

A phrasal verb is a verb + particle(s). There are three basic types of phrasal verbs.

1 Verb + particle

*It's difficult to **join in**.*

2 Verb + object + particle

*I can **hand** an essay **in** and I can **hand** it **in**.*

*I can **hand in** an essay but NOT ~~I can hand in it~~*

3 Verb + particle + object

*I want to **go over** some lessons and I want to **go over** them.*

Note: A few phrasal verbs take two particles.

*We just have to **get on with** life.*

5 **Put the words in brackets in the correct order to complete the sentences. Which sentences are true for you?**

  1 I often stayed with my grandparents when I was a child – they *looked after me* (after/looked/me).

  2 I've missed several weeks of my favourite TV series – I need to _____ (it/up/on/catch).

  3 I don't like doing after-school activities – I never _____ (for/up/sign/them).

  4 I guessed all the answers in my last exam – I don't know how I _____ (it/got/through).

  5 I don't like arguing with my friends – I prefer to _____ (talk/over/it).

  6 My parents always encourage me – they never _____ (me/down/put).

6 USE OF ENGLISH **Choose one word, A, B or C to complete both questions.**

  1 How well do you deal ___ difficult problems?
    Are you good at coping ___ extreme pain?
    A with   **B** in   **C** out

  2 How long does it take you to get ___ a cold?
    Do you always go ___ your homework before you hand it in?
    A into   **B** over   **C** through

  3 How do you get ___ with your neighbours?
    If you have a problem, who can you rely ___ ?
    A off   **B** away   **C** on

  4 Do you give ___ easily when things get difficult?
    What time do you normally turn ___ for school?
    A up   **B** after   **C** with

7 SPEAKING **Ask and answer the questions in Exercise 6.**

Use of English page 155 ▶

Newsfocus.com: Daily Discussion

Is social media making you lose sleep?

A new study has found that one in five young people wakes up in the night to send or check messages. **What is more**, research has shown that teenagers need 9.5 hours of sleep each night, but on average they only get 7.5 hours. This means they don't sleep long enough or well enough. A lack of sleep can make them tired, depressed and more likely to catch colds, flu and stomach bugs.

Personally, I don't think that social media is bad in itself. It's a great way to get information and keep in touch with your friends. **However, I believe** there is too much pressure on young people to be available 24/7 on social media. If you think about it, no message is so urgent that it can't wait until morning. **For this reason** I think that young people need to learn the importance of logging off at night. Switch your phone off and get a good night's sleep!

Join the Daily Discussion and tell us what you think in our Reader's Comments section below.

daisy345 says: Thanks for a great post. It made me think about how I use my own phone …

1 SPEAKING Discuss the question on the online forum page. Then read the post and decide whether you agree or disagree with the views expressed.

2 Read the WRITING FOCUS. Complete the examples with the linkers in purple in the article in Exercise 1.

WRITING FOCUS

A reader's comment – linkers

When you give your opinion in a piece of writing such as a reader's comment, use linkers to:

- **give an opinion:** *I think …/*[1] *Personally, I don't think/*
  [2] _____
- **add further points:** *In fact, …/I also agree that …/
  I also think that …/*[3] _____
- **give an opposite opinion:** *On the other hand, I strongly
  disagree …/*[4] _____
- **conclude:** *Therefore …/So …/That's why …/*
  [5] _____

3 Complete the reader's comment on the post in Exercise 1 with appropriate phrases in the WRITING FOCUS.

---

daisy345 says: Thanks for a great post. It made me think about how I use my own phone. [1]P*ersonally*, I b_____ t_____ social media is a fantastic tool for sharing information and staying in touch with friends. I can communicate with my friends when I'm not with them. [2]W_____ i _____ m _____ , I never feel alone. [3]H _____ , sometimes I can't concentrate on my homework. If I get a message, I can't wait – I have to answer it immediately. [4]F_____ t_____ r_____ , I sometimes wake up in the night to answer a message or look at a post. Then I start looking on the Internet and I can't get back to sleep. [5]S_____ I end up feeling really tired and bad-tempered. On the one hand I know I should ignore my phone at night, but [6]o_____ t_____ o_____ h_____ , I don't want my friends to think I'm ignoring them!

---

4 Look at a summary of opinions expressed by both writers. Then answer the questions.

SUMMARY
- Social media is a good thing and has lots of benefits
- Checking your phone at night is not good for you
- It's impossible to ignore your phone

1 Which two opinions do both writers agree on?
2 Which opinion do they disagree about?
3 Who do you agree with and why?

5 Read the LANGUAGE FOCUS. Complete the examples with the sentences underlined in the text in Exercise 1.

LANGUAGE FOCUS

Structures with *make*
Make always takes an object and either the infinitive without *to*, an adjective or a noun.

- *make* + object + infinitive without *to*
  1 _____

- *make* + object + adjective/noun
  2 _____

6 Put the object in brackets in the correct place. Which sentences are true for you?

1 I think smartphones make easier. (everybody's life)
2 I like posting things that make laugh. (my friends)
3 My parents make switch my phone off at night. (me)
4 If I can't check my phone regularly, it makes anxious. (me)
5 Teachers make put our phones on silent in class. (us)
6 I think smartphones make a better place. (the world)

SHOW WHAT YOU'VE LEARNT

7 Read the text. Then do the writing task. Use the WRITING FOCUS and LANGUAGE FOCUS to help you.

Newsfocus.com: Daily Discussion

Does social media make you happy?

The answer is probably not. A recent survey found that one in five people say they feel depressed when they use social media. Academic research suggests that regular use leads to feelings of anxiety, stress and poor sleep. We use social media to present a false picture of our lives – like a movie of the life we'd like to live rather than the one we're actually living. If we post something and don't get enough 'shares' or 'likes', it makes us feel bad or unloved. What is more, teenagers are losing the ability to communicate face-to-face. Social media is addictive, and like all drugs, it is doing us more harm than good. Just say no!

Join the Daily Discussion and tell us what you think in our Reader's Comments section below.

You've read the article above on a news website. Write a reader's comment. Include the following information:

- express your opinion about the article
- write what you agree with and why
- write what you disagree with and why
- describe your conclusions.

1 Complete the sentences with the words in the box.

arm ②	back ☐	chest ☐
a cough ☐	dizzy ☐	foot ☐
ill ☐	indigestion ☐	left leg ☐
neck ☐	a runny nose ☐	shoulder ☐
sick ☐	a sore throat ☐	a temperature ☐
thumb ☐	very well ☐	

1 I've got …
2 I've got a pain in my …/My … hurts.
3 I feel …

2 ◀) 3.41 Read the dialogue and choose the correct option. Then listen and check.

Doctor: Hello, Andrew. What's the problem?

Andrew: I've got a ¹*pain / sore* in my chest.

Doctor: I see. And when did it start?

Andrew: A few days ago.

Doctor: Do you have any other ²*sicknesses / symptoms*?

Andrew: Yes, sometimes my stomach ³*hurts / is dizzy*.

Doctor: And how are you feeling now? Have you got a headache? Do you ⁴*have / feel* dizzy?

Andrew: No, I feel okay. But when I have a stomachache I feel a bit ⁵*sick / hurt*.

Doctor: I see. And do you have this ⁶*illness / pain* all the time?

Andrew: No, I get it in the evening after dinner, and sometimes after lunch.

Doctor: Aha. Okay, I'm going to examine you.

3 ◀) 3.42 Read and listen to Part 2 of the dialogue and answer the questions.

1 What does Andrew think the problem is?
2 What does the doctor think the problem is?
3 What does the doctor suggest?

Doctor: Now … Breathe in and out for me. Good, thank you. Now, open wide – hmm, that looks fine. Right, I'm just going to take your temperature … Okay, that seems normal. Now lie down, please. If I push here, does it hurt?

Andrew: Ow. A little bit. Do you think it's my heart, doctor?

Doctor: Your heart! Why would it be your heart? You're sixteen years old.

Andrew: My mum says I eat the wrong things and I eat too quickly and she thinks I'll have a heart attack before I'm twenty.

Doctor: I see. Well, your heart is fine. We don't need to operate just yet. I think you've got indigestion. But your mother's right – you need to eat more slowly, and you should drink more water. I'm going to give you a prescription – take one tablet after each meal. Make another appointment to see me in a month.

Andrew: Aren't you going to do a blood test?

Doctor: No, I don't think that's necessary.

Andrew: Oh good, thank you very much.

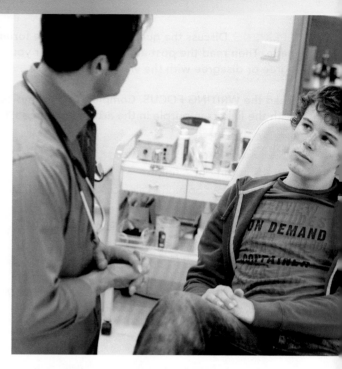

4 Complete the SPEAKING FOCUS with verbs in Part 2 of the dialogue.

SPEAKING FOCUS

Diagnosis

When did the pain start?
I'm going to examine you./¹*take your temperature*.
I'm going to ² _____ a blood test …
Breathe in and out.
³ _____ wide.
Lie down, please.
If I press here, does it hurt?
I think you've got indigestion/flu/an infection/a virus …
You're probably allergic to …

Treatment

You should eat more slowly/go on a diet.
You need to drink more water.
I'm going to ⁴ _____ you a prescription.
I'm going to ⁵ _____ an appointment for you (e.g. to see the specialist).
⁶ _____ one tablet after each meal.

5 SPEAKING Follow the instructions below to prepare a dialogue. Use the SPEAKING FOCUS to help you.

Student A: You're a student. You are doing a language course in the UK. You fall ill and go to see a doctor. Tell the doctor your symptoms and answer any questions.

Student B: You're a doctor. Your patient is a foreign student. Find out about his/her symptoms, ask questions and give advice.

6 SPEAKING Practise your dialogue. Then act it out to the class.

ROLE-PLAY A doctor's appointment

▶ 40 ▶ 41 **Watch the video and practise. Then role-play your dialogue.**

8.1 Vocabulary 🔊 4.57

barcode /ˈbɑː ˌkəʊd/
be allergic to /ˌbi əˈlɜːdʒɪk tə/
be asthmatic /ˌbi æsˈmætɪk/
check your pulse/heart rate /ˌtʃek jɔː ˈpʌls/ˈhɑːt reɪt/
come out in a rash/in spots /ˌkʌm ˌaʊt ɪn ə ˈræʃ/ ɪn ˈspɒts/
cough /kɒf/
cut sth out /ˌkʌt ˌsʌmθɪŋ ˈaʊt/
feel dizzy /ˌfiːl ˈdɪzi/
feel ill /ˌfiːl ˈɪl/
feel sick /ˌfiːl ˈsɪk/
headache /ˈhedeɪk/
healthy choices/decisions /ˌhelθi ˈtʃɔɪsɪz/dɪˈsɪʒənz/
hurt /hɜːt/
keep fit /ˌkiːp ˈfɪt/
keep track of /ˌkiːp ˈtræk əv/
lose appetite /ˌluːz ˈæpətaɪt/
lose weight /ˌluːz ˈweɪt/
make choices /ˌmeɪk ˈtʃɔɪsɪz/
my back/head/thumb hurts /maɪ ˌbæk/ˌhed/ˌθʌm ˈhɜːts/
pain in the chest/leg/shoulder /ˌpeɪn ɪn ðə ˈtʃest/ˈleg/ˈʃəʊldə/
pass out, faint /ˌpɑːs ˈaʊt, feɪnt/
recover from / get over an illness /rɪˈkʌvə frəm / ˌget ˌəʊvər ən ˈɪlnəs/
reduce anxiety/stress /rɪˌdjuːs æŋˈzaɪəti/ˈstres/
runny nose /ˌrʌni ˈnəʊz/
sore throat /ˌsɔː ˈθrəʊt/
stomachache /ˈstʌmək-eɪk/
stress out /ˌstres ˈaʊt/
suffer from /ˈsʌfə ˌfrəm/
take sth up /ˌteɪk ˌsʌmθɪŋ ˈʌp/
temperature /ˈtemprətʃə/
work out /ˌwɜːk ˈaʊt/

8.2 Grammar 🔊 4.58

ambulance /ˈæmbjələns/
capital city /ˌkæpətl ˈsɪti/
cardiologist /ˌkɑːdiˈɒlədʒɪst/
drop /drɒp/
equipment /ɪˈkwɪpmənt/
fiancé /fiˈɒnseɪ/
frozen /ˈfrəʊzən/
heart attack /ˈhɑːt əˌtæk/
physiotherapist /ˌfɪziəʊˈθerəpɪst/
pitch /pɪtʃ/
put out your arms /ˌpʊt ˌaʊt jɔːr ˈɑːmz/
spectator /spekˈteɪtə/

8.3 Listening 🔊 4.59

arch /ɑːtʃ/
badminton court /ˈbædmɪntən kɔːt/
basketball court /ˈbɑːskɪtbɔːl kɔːt/
bench /bentʃ/
boxing ring /ˈbɒksɪŋ rɪŋ/
bridge /brɪdʒ/
climbing /ˈklaɪmɪŋ/
cycling /ˈsaɪklɪŋ/
football pitch /ˈfʊtbɔːl pɪtʃ/
fountain /ˈfaʊntɪn/
handball court /ˈhændbɔːl kɔːt/

hockey pitch /ˈhɒki pɪtʃ/
horse riding /ˈhɔːs ˌraɪdɪŋ/
ice rink /ˈaɪs ˌrɪŋk/
marathon /ˈmærəθən/
motor racing track /ˈməʊtə ˈreɪsɪŋ træk/
pathway /ˈpɑːθweɪ/
playground /ˈpleɪgraʊnd/
rugby pitch /ˈrʌgbi pɪtʃ/
running track /ˈrʌnɪŋ træk/
sailing /ˈseɪlɪŋ/
skateboard /ˈskeɪtbɔːd/
skating rink /ˈskeɪtɪŋ ˌrɪŋk/
species /ˈspiːʃiːz/
swimming pool /ˈswɪmɪŋ puːl/
tennis court /ˈtenɪs kɔːt/
volleyball court /ˈvɒlibɔːl kɔːt/

8.4 Reading 🔊 4.60

(air) pollution /ˈeə pəˌluːʃən/
air purifier /ˈeə ˌpjʊərəfaɪə/
at risk /ət rɪsk/
blanket /ˈblæŋkɪt/
blow out /ˌbləʊ ˈaʊt/
citizen /ˈsɪtɪzən/
construct /kənˈstrʌkt/
construction /kənˈstrʌkʃən/
constructive /kənˈstrʌktɪv/
create /kriˈeɪt/
creation /kriˈeɪʃən/
cufflinks /ˈkʌf lɪŋks/
dust storm /ˈdʌst ˌstɔːm/
environmental protection /ɪnˌvaɪrənˌmentl prəˈtekʃən/
exhaust fumes /ɪgˈzɔːst fjuːmz/
face mask /ˈfeɪs mɑːsk/
factory smoke /ˈfæktəri sməʊk/
fight /faɪt/
government /ˈgʌvənmənt/
pollute /pəˈluːt/
pure /pjʊə/
purification /ˌpjʊərɪfəˈkeɪʃən/
purify /ˈpjʊərɪfaɪ/
smog particle /smɒg pɑːtɪkəl/
support (n, v) /səˈpɔːt/
supportive /səˈpɔːtɪv/
tower /ˈtaʊə/
vacuum cleaner /ˈvækjuəm ˌkliːnə/

8.5 Grammar 🔊 4.61

birth certificate /ˈbɜːθ səˌtɪfɪkət/
break a record /ˌbreɪk ə ˈrekɔːd/
chutney /ˈtʃʌtni/
herbal /ˈhɜːbəl/
old age /ˌəʊld ˈeɪdʒ/

8.6 Use of English 🔊 4.62

catch up on /ˌkætʃ ˈʌp ɒn/
cope with /ˈkəʊp wɪð/
fall behind /ˌfɔːl bɪˈhaɪnd/
figure out /ˌfɪgər ˈaʊt/
fit in /ˌfɪt ˈɪn/
get on with /ˌget ˈɒn wɪð/
get through /ˌget ˈθruː/
go over /ˌgəʊ ˈəʊvə/
join in /ˌdʒɔɪn ˈɪn/
put sb down /ˌpʊt ˌsʌmbɒdi ˈdaʊn/

sign up /ˌsaɪn ˈʌp/
talk sth over /ˌtɔːk ˌsʌmθɪŋ ˈəʊvə/

8.7 Writing 🔊 4.63

addictive /əˈdɪktɪv/
bad-tempered /ˌbæd ˈtempəd/
do harm /ˌduː ˈhɑːm/
importance /ɪmˈpɔːtəns/
pressure /ˈpreʃə/
stay in touch /ˌsteɪ ɪn ˈtʌtʃ/
switch off /ˌswɪtʃ ˈɒf/
therefore /ˈðeəfɔː/
urgent /ˈɜːdʒənt/
what is more /ˌwɒt ɪz ˈmɔː/

8.8 Speaking 🔊 4.64

blood test /ˈblʌd ˌtest/
breathe in /ˌbriːð ˈɪn/
breathe out /ˌbriːð ˈaʊt/
examine /ɪgˈzæmɪn/
flu /fluː/
go on a diet /ˌgəʊ ɒn ə ˈdaɪət/
indigestion /ˌɪndɪˈdʒestʃən/
lie down /ˌlaɪ ˈdaʊn/
make an appointment /ˌmeɪk ən əˈpɔɪntmənt/
meal /miːl/
prescription /prɪˈskrɪpʃən/
press /pres/
tablet /ˈtæblət/
take sb's temperature /ˌteɪk ˌsʌmbɒdiz ˈtemprətʃə/
virus /ˈvaɪərəs/

VOCABULARY AND GRAMMAR

1 Choose the correct options.

1 I've never been *allergic / ill / dizzy* to dust.
2 Tim's had an awful *sick / chest / cough* for two weeks.
3 An indoor skating *ring / rink / pool* has been built in our town.
4 When they saw Sarah *pass / hang / find* out during the match, they called an ambulance.
5 By the time Mark *suffered from / worked out / got over* the indigestion, he hadn't eaten anything.

2 Complete the sentences with the correct form of the words in capitals.

1 We should use public transport to reduce air _____ . **POLLUTE**
2 Centuries ago people could drink _____ water from streams and rivers. **PURIFY**
3 There are a lot of _____ about too much noise in the city centre. **COMPLAIN**
4 My doctor has got a lot of patients because she is really _____ . **SUPPORT**
5 Chris has to make an important _____ about which team he wants to play for. **CHOOSE**

3 Complete the second sentence so that it has a similar meaning to the first. Use the correct forms of past tenses.

1 I had a fast heart rate for three days, so I went to see my doctor.
Before I _____ to see my doctor, I _____ a fast heart rate for three days.
2 The doctor advised Helen to lose weight, so she started to work out in the gym.
Helen _____ to work out in the gym after the doctor _____ her to lose weight.
3 The teacher figured the problem out and then everybody arrived.
By the time everybody _____ , the teacher _____ the problem out.
4 Josh ate a piece of nut cake and came out in spots.
After Josh _____ a piece of nut cake, he _____ in spots.
5 Gustave Eiffel created hundreds of metal constructions all around the world. He died in 1923.
Before Gustave Eiffel _____ in 1923, he _____ hundreds of metal constructions all around the world.

4 Complete the second sentence so that it has a similar meaning to the first. Use Reported Speech.

1 'I feel ill,' said Eva. Eva said _____ .
2 'Every visit to the dentist makes me feel stressed', said Ann. Ann said that _____ .
3 'Steve joined in the race', said Jo.
Jo told me that _____ .
4 'People in the capital city are wearing face masks today', said the minister.
The minister said that _____ that day.
5 'I didn't go out last night', she said.
She said _____ .

USE OF ENGLISH

5 Choose the correct answer, A, B or C.

1 X: My left knee hurts and I can't walk fast.
Y: When ___ ?
A the knee hurt you
B you had a pain
C did the pain start
2 X: Dr Willson's surgery. What can I do for you?
Y: I'd like to ___ for tomorrow morning.
A make an appointment
B see a doctor
C have a meeting
3 X: Mum, can I stay at home today? I don't feel well.
Y: OK. But you'll have to ___ the schoolwork.
A fall behind
B catch up on
C get on with
4 X: Jeff, do you remember that we need to make some decisions about the project?
Y: Can we ___ tomorrow? I'm in a hurry.
A talk it over
B give it up
C hand it in
5 X: I'd like to know your opinion about social media.
Y: ___ social media is very powerful in influencing people's opinions.
A On the other hand
B Personally, I believe that
C Therefore
6 X: Carl can't play basketball since the injury.
Y: I've heard he's going to ___ swimming. It's safe for him.
A take up
B pass out
C turn up

6 Choose the answer, A, B or C that is closest in meaning to the underlined words.

1 I don't have much time to <u>hang out</u> with my friends.
A spend time   B do sports
C discover new places
2 Daria's been in our group for two weeks and <u>she's fitted in</u> already.
A she's made new friends   B she's been accepted
C she's become the group leader
3 The government <u>figured out</u> why there was so much air pollution.
A discussed   B understood   C reported
4 Doing some aerobic activities will help you reduce <u>anxiety</u>.
A body weight   B allergy   C nervousness
5 <u>Exhaust fumes</u> from vehicle engines cause great damage to the environment.
A dust storms   B smog particles   C waste gases

7 ◀)) **3.43** Listen to six speakers. For questions 1–6 choose the correct answers A–C. Listen to the recording twice.

1 The conversation takes place:
  A at a health centre reception
  B in a hospital corridor
  C in a doctor's surgery

2 The speaker is:
  A the Town Mayor
  B a doctor
  C a radio presenter

3 How will the boy get home?
  A by bus
  B by car
  C on foot

4 The woman is:
  A explaining something
  B supporting someone
  C asking people to do something

5 How much time do young people spend on social networking sites?
  A three hours a day or more
  B fifteen hours a day
  C all day long

6 The text <u>does not</u> mention:
  A where the place is located
  B where the visitors can stay
  C how the temperature is kept constant inside

SPEAKING

8 Match the two halves of the questions. Then, in pairs, ask and answer the questions.

1 Would you like to be
2 Do you use
3 What qualities do you need
4 What would you do

a to be a doctor?
b food apps? Why?/Why not?
c if you wanted to lose weight?
d a professional sportsperson? Why?/Why not?

9 Do the task in pairs.

Look at Posters A and B.
You are on a scholarship in a school in England for a few months. The authorities of the city you're staying in want to organise a campaign promoting a healthy lifestyle to accompany World Health Day. You are taking part in a survey to decide which poster is better for the campaign.

• Choose the poster which you think is more suitable for the campaign and explain why.
• Explain why you rejected the other poster.

10 Ask and answer the questions.

1 Does social media help its users have an active lifestyle? Why?/Why not?
2 Why are food apps so popular?
3 What could you do to make your diet healthier?
4 What could we do to make the air less polluted?

WRITING

11 Read the writing task. In what order should the information be presented?

> You've read an article in an English-language magazine in which the author criticises young people's eating habits. Write a reader's comment on an Internet forum. Include the following information:
>
> • present your opinion and arguments behind it ☐
> • explain what article you are referring to ☐
> • encourage other readers to join in the discussion ☐
> • present the article writer's views ☐

12 Do the writing task in Exercise 11.

⟳ BBC   Student Accommodation

BEFORE YOU WATCH

1 **In pairs, match the collocation parts. Use your dictionary if necessary.**

1 wave	☐	a rent
2 miss out	☐	b in a project
3 be involved	☐	c in a nursing home
4 live	☐	d on the fun of student life
5 pay	☐	e somebody goodbye
6 develop	☐	f friendships

2 SPEAKING **Discuss what typical student accommodation is like in your country.**

3 SPEAKING **You are going to watch a video about student accommodation. Discuss which words and phrases in the box you think you will hear.**

books   dining room   deaf   elderly people
isolation   loud music   loud television   parties
peaceful   posters   save money

WHILE YOU WATCH

4 ⟳ 1 **Watch the video and check your ideas in Exercise 3. What is unusual about student accommodation at Humanitas?**

5 ⟳ 1 **Complete the sentences with the numbers in the box. Then watch the video again and check your answers.**

5 18 30 80 160 30,000

1 Most of the residents are over _____ .
2 The accommodation is free for Jurrien and _____ other students.
3 Jurrien must spend _____ hours each month with the elderly residents.
4 Jurrien can save _____ euros while he's studying.
5 One of the students lived in a student house when he was _____ .
6 Jurrien likes having _____ grandparents waving him goodbye when he goes to college every day.

6 ⟳ 1 **Complete the sentences. Watch the video and check your answers.**

1 Jurrien is involved in a project to _____ young and older people and _____ the elderly with feelings of loneliness and isolation.
2 He wanted to have the _____ of connecting with elderly people.
3 'What I've learnt here is to _____ the older residents, the older people in our society.'
4 Both _____ have a lot to learn from each other.
5 The friendships that _____ are important for both young and old.

AFTER YOU WATCH

7 SPEAKING **Discuss the advantages and disadvantages of living in this kind of student accommodation. Use the KEY PHRASES to express your ideas.**

The good thing about living in this kind of accommodation is that you don't have to pay rent.

┌─ KEY PHRASES ─────────────────────┐

The (only) good/bad thing is that it is/about it is …
I would/wouldn't like to live there because …

└───────────────────────────────────┘

⊙ Focus Vlog   About happiness

What makes you happy?

1   SPEAKING **Which three things in the box are likely to make young people happiest? Discuss.**

family   food   fresh air   friends   money
shopping   sport   sunshine

2   ⊙3 **Watch the interviews where people talk about what makes them happy. Complete the table.**

	What makes him/her happy?	Why?
Jake		
Laura		
Lola		

3   ⊙3 **Complete the quotes. Then watch again and check your answers.**

Jake: 'You can get ¹_____ into the countryside and ²_____ air.'

Laura: 'Money makes me happy because I've ³_____ it, it's well-earned and then I get to spend it on ⁴_____ I want to spend it on.'

Lola: 'Life without friends is just ⁵_____ and sad.'

4   SPEAKING **Discuss what makes you happy and why.**

FOCUS ON LIFE SKILLS
Communication

5   **Complete the profile information. Give at least one piece of information which is not true. Share your profile with your partner and guess what is not true about him/her.**

I'm crazy about _____ . I also like _____ and _____ . I find _____ very relaxing. I think _____ can be fun, but I don't like _____ and I really hate _____ .

6   SPEAKING **Ask and answer the questions. Use the adjectives in the box. Explain why you feel these emotions in these situations.**

How do you feel when …
- you are meeting a friend and he/she is really late?
- you work really hard for something and you succeed?
- your team loses a game?
- a teacher appreciates your work?
- you do poorly in a test?
- your best friend doesn't want to help you with your homework?
- you have a house to yourself for the weekend?

angry   bored   excited   happy   irritated
lonely   proud   relaxed   sad   stressed   worried

When I'm meeting a friend who is really late I usually feel irritated. I don't like when people waste my time.

◔ BBC Urban legends

Urban legend: A modern myth, imaginary information that many people believe to be true.

BEFORE YOU WATCH

1 SPEAKING **Only one of sentences 1–5 is a fact, the others are urban legends. Which sentence do you think is true? Discuss.**

   1 You can see the Great Wall of China from space with the naked eye.
   2 People only use 10 percent of their brains.
   3 An earthquake can change the length of a day.
   4 Chewing gum stays in your body for seven years.
   5 Elvis Presley is alive.

2 **Choose the correct option.**

   1 You measure an earthquake on the *Richter / Weighing / Global* scale.
   2 A crowd is a *small / large / young* group of people.
   3 When you want to test a theory, you *make / carry / do* an experiment.

WHILE YOU WATCH

3 **Complete the presenter's introduction to the video with the correct words in the box. There are two extra words.**

   all billion entire exactly move stop

   Imagine in five minutes' time, everyone on the
   ¹_____ planet was going to jump at
   ²_____ the same time. From London to
   Sydney, Delhi to New York, 6.9 ³_____ people
   leap in the air. Could they make the earth
   ⁴_____ ?

4 (◔6) **Watch the first part of the video (up to 0:53) and check your answers. What do you think is the answer to the question in Exercise 3?**

5 (◔6) **Look at the photo. What kind of event is it? Why did Greg choose this place to do the experiment? Watch the next part of the video (00:53 – 01:30) and check your ideas.**

6 (◔6) **Watch the rest of the video (01:30 – 03:13). Put the events in chronological order.**

   a Greg tests Paul Denton's machine.
   b Greg arrives at Reading Festival.
   c Everybody jumps.
   d So the urban legend is completely untrue.
   e The jump measures 0.6 on the Richter Scale.
   f You can see the jump on Paul's machine.
   g Greg tells the crowd about his experiment.
   h But you need 8 on the Richter scale to move the planet.

AFTER YOU WATCH

7 SPEAKING **Greg Foot has done a series of videos like this one. Which of the following would you be most interested in? Tick three and then compare your ideas with a partner.**

   1 Why is fire hot?
   2 Can I escape from quicksand?
   3 If a coin falls off the top of the Empire State Building and hits someone on the pavement, will it kill them?
   4 Why does a boomerang come back?
   5 Can you survive in a falling lift?

▶ Focus Vlog About technology

> When was the last time you had a problem with technology?

Callum

1 SPEAKING **Ask and answer the questions.**

1 What kind of technology do you usually use …
   • for school?
   • in your free time?
   • to keep in touch with people?
2 What do you use the Internet for?
3 What do you use your mobile phone for?

2 ▶8 **Watch the interviews where people talk about problems they've had with technology. Put a tick in the correct boxes. There is one extra problem.**

	a mobile phone	music loudspeakers	a desktop computer
Laura			
Callum			
Jake			

3 ▶8 **Are sentences 1–6 true (T) or false (F)? Discuss with a partner. Then watch again and check.**

1 Laura couldn't get on the Internet in the car. ☐
2 Callum had problems listening to music on his phone. ☐
3 Jake's speakers were making a strange sound. ☐
4 Laura needed to get Wi-Fi to book a flight. ☐
5 Callum was trying to contact his friends while he was at school. ☐
6 Jake was chilling out at home when the speakers started popping. ☐

4 SPEAKING **Have you ever had any of the problems in Exercise 3? Tell your partner about the last time you had a problem with technology.**

FOCUS ON LIFE SKILLS
Communication • Critical thinking

5 SPEAKING **Discuss the questions. Use the phrases below to ask your partner to explain their opinion.**

1 Do you think technology is making the world a better place to live in?
2 Would you say teenagers spend too much time on their mobile phones?
3 Are social media sites important in our lives?
4 Do you agree that technology is improving the way we communicate?

Use the following as examples:
• What evidence is there that …?
• Why do you think that …?
• How do you know that …?
• When did people start believing that …?
• Where did you read that …?

A: *Do you think technology is making the world a better place to live in?*
B: *Yes, I do.*
A: *Why do you think that?*

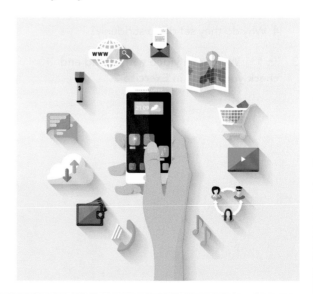

◉ BBC The Musketeers

BEFORE YOU WATCH

1 **What do you know about the Four Musketeers? Discuss. Read the sentences and choose the correct option.**

1 They are *French / Spanish* characters in a book by Alexandre Dumas.
2 Dumas' book is a historical adventure story set in *nineteenth / seventeenth*-century Paris.
3 The Musketeers work for the royal court and their job is to *protect / capture* Queen Anne.

WHILE YOU WATCH

2 ◉ 11 SPEAKING **Watch the video without sound. What is happening? Guess the answers to the questions and compare your ideas with a partner.**

1 Why do they stop at this place?
2 What does Queen Anne do?
3 How do the Musketeers feel about the food?
4 Why do they set off so suddenly?

3 ◉ 11 **Watch the video with sound and check your ideas in Exercise 2.**

4 ◉ 11 **Complete the dialogues. Then watch the video again and check your answers.**

1 M: There's been no sign of them for an hour now. We're safe for a while.
   M: The Queen needs to ¹_____ .
2 Q: Can I help?
   M: Rest while you can, Your Majesty.
   Q: No, I'd like to be ²_____ . Really.
   M: In that case, can you gut a fish?
3 M: Delicious, Your Majesty.
   Q: It's the first time I've ever cooked.
   M: That's hard to ³_____ .
   Q: Would you like ⁴_____ ?
   M: Thank you but I'm full.
4 M: I'm tired of ⁵_____ away. Perhaps we should be the ones doing the chasing.
5 M: The Queen's ⁶_____ is paramount. We can't risk it by making a stand.

5 **Complete a summary of the scene using words from Exercise 4 in the correct form.**

Queen Anne's ¹_____ is at risk. The Musketeers must take her back to the royal palace in Paris. In this scene, they stop so that the Queen can ²_____ . The Queen wants to be ³_____ and so she cooks fish for the Musketeers. However, the food is disgusting and the men politely refuse to eat ⁴_____ portion after they tasted it. Suddenly Athos hears horses in the distance and they prepare to leave. Athos and Porthos have a disagreement – Porthos doesn't want to ⁵_____ away but Athos ⁶_____ that the Queen's life is more important than fighting.

AFTER YOU WATCH

6 SPEAKING **Discuss the questions.**

1 Would you like to watch more episodes of *The Musketeers*? Why?/Why not?
2 What kind of TV series do you like watching?
3 What is the best TV series you've ever watched?

 Focus Vlog   London attractions

Have you done anything interesting recently?

Chelsea

1 SPEAKING Imagine you can have a day out in London. Discuss the activities you would and wouldn't like to do.

> visit the Science Museum   see a musical
> go to Notting Hill Carnival   go shopping
> go on a boat trip   visit Buckingham Palace
> go on the London Eye

2 ▶14 Watch Oliver, Ella and Chelsea answering the questions below. Which of the things in Exercise 1 do they mention?

1 Have you done anything interesting in London recently?
2 What did you like about it?

3 ▶14 Watch again and answer questions 1–3.

1 Who enjoyed a massive party with different kinds of people?
2 Who loved the general atmosphere in the theatre?
3 Who thought the costumes and songs in the show were good?

4 SPEAKING Have you done anything interesting in your city recently? What did you do and what did you like about it?

FOCUS ON LIFE SKILLS
Creativity • Teamwork • Communication

5 Ask questions to find someone who fits each description below and write their names in the first column. Collect some more information about him/her by asking further questions.

A: *Have you recently been to a concert?*
B: *Yes, I have.*
A: *What concert was it?*
B: *A famous Italian pop singer came to my city to give a concert.*

Find someone who ...	Name	Extra information
performs music in a band or solo		
likes painting and crafts		
attends drama classes		
has never watched a musical		
binge watches TV series		
likes theatre better than cinema		
has been in a play		

6 In groups, write a survey question about students' film and TV preferences beginning with *Who ...* and giving three options. (e.g *Who prefers watching sci-fi/comedy/documentary series on TV?*) Each group asks the class the question and notes down the answers. Then presents their findings using a pie chart.

> **What is a pie chart?**
> A pie chart uses 'slices' to show the proportion of things with a number or a percentage. The whole 'pie' is the total number and each segment is a part of the 'pie'.

3.5 GRAMMAR

⏵ BBC   Cave houses

BEFORE YOU WATCH

1   Label the photos with the words and phrases in the box. There is one extra word.

> hot air balloon   cave   volcanic rock
> conical rock formations   basement

1 _____

2 _____

3 _____

4 _____

2   SPEAKING   Which adjectives in the box are appropriate to describe the landscape? Discuss. Add more adjectives to your list.

> amazing   crowded   lonely   incredible   magical
> modern   prehistoric   strange   quiet   unique

WHILE YOU WATCH

3   ⏵15   Watch the video and check whether you can hear any of the adjectives in Exercise 2.

4   ⏵15   SPEAKING   Are sentences 1–5 true (T) or false (F)? Discuss with a partner. Then watch the first part of the video again (up to 2:00) and check your answers.

1   Every evening people visit the incredible landscape in hot air balloons.
2   The rock formations are called fairy chimneys.
3   Humans started living here hundreds of years ago.
4   Rafik owns a local restaurant.
5   His grandparents live in a cave.

5   ⏵15   SPEAKING   Watch the rest of the video (02:00 – 03:13). Then discuss the questions with a partner.

1   Why do Rafik and his wife live in a house now?
2   Does Rafik miss living in a cave? Why?/Why not?
3   Have you ever seen a landscape like this? Would you like to visit it by hot air balloon?

AFTER YOU WATCH

6   SPEAKING   Discuss the questions. Use the KEY PHRASES to express your ideas.

1   Do your parents and grandparents still live in the place where they grew up?
2   Do you think you'll stay in the place where you grew up or do you think you'll move away? Why?

I think one of the disadvantages of moving away is that you are far away from the family.

> **KEY PHRASES**
>
> I think the advantage/disadvantage of (moving away) is that … One of the good/bad points of (moving away) is that …

▶ Focus Vlog   Where people live

Where do people live?

1 Put the words in the box under an appropriate heading.

> bedroom   bathroom   drive   flat   garden   kitchen
> floors/storeys   in London   opposite a park
> terraced house

Type of house
Location
Inside
Outside

2 (▶ 17) Watch the interviews where people talk about the places they live. Complete the sentences with the names of the speakers.

Oliver

Esme

Amber

Millie

1 _____ lives in a house which is opposite a park.
2 _____ lives in a small house in London.
3 _____ shares his house with other university students.
4 _____ has chickens in the garden.
5 _____ lives in a four-bedroom flat.
6 _____ has a house full of colours.

3 (▶ 17) Watch the video again. How long have they lived there?

Oliver _____
Esme _____
Amber _____
Millie _____

4 SPEAKING What do you like about your house or flat? How long have you lived there? Tell your partner.

FOCUS ON LIFE SKILLS
Critical thinking • Teamwork • Communication

5 Would you consider living in a different house from the one you are living in now? In groups, discuss which are the most important things to consider when renting or buying a house.
- location (in the centre or in the suburbs)
- type of house (a detached house, a flat etc.)
- price
- neighbourhood
- age (old/modern)
- pets (allowed/not allowed)
- size (number of rooms)
- distance (from school and other important places, e.g. the railway station, the hospital etc.)
- garden
- garage

6 In pairs, decide on the top three things to consider when looking for a house. Present your opinion to the class.

In my opinion the most important thing to consider while looking for a house or flat is the neighbourhood it's in because ...

◔ BBC   South Korean schools

BEFORE YOU WATCH

1 **Tick the boxes next to the words or phrases you associate with school and learning.**

- test and exams ☐
- scores ☐
- creativity ☐
- long hours of study ☐
- pressure ☐
- hard work ☐
- extra lessons ☐
- time to relax ☐

2 SPEAKING **List the three things that are most important to you at school. Then compare your answers with a partner.**

WHILE YOU WATCH

3 ◔20 **Watch the first part of the video (up to 1:38) and answer the questions.**

1 How does Hye-Min feel about her school day?
2 How many hours does she study every day?
3 What time does she have dinner, go to bed and get up in the morning?
4 What does her mother think about Hye-Min's daily routine?

4 SPEAKING **Discuss the advantages and disadvantages of the South Korean education system. Think about:**

- the standard of education
- young people's health

5 ◔20 **Watch the second part of the video (01:38 – 03:11). Does anybody mention the ideas you discussed in Exercise 4?**

6 **Match 1–8 with a–h to make collocations.**

1 education ☐
2 extra ☐
3 achieve ☐
4 huge ☐
5 suicide ☐
6 test ☐
7 under ☐
8 pay ☐

a her dreams
b investment
c system
d a high price
e lessons
f scores
g rate
h a lot of stress

7 **Complete the sentences with the collocations in Exercise 6 in the correct form.**

1 When they finish their regular classes they go to private school in the evening for _____ .
2 This _____ has transformed Korea.
3 It's the only thing she can do to _____ .
4 The _____ is the highest in developed countries.
5 _____ may be important in the age of industrialisation but not any more.
6 But people have been _____ and young people have _____ .
7 The South Korean _____ is one of the best in the world.

8 ◔20 **Watch the whole video again. Who says the sentences in Exercise 7: Hye Min's mother, Professor Lee or the presenter?**

AFTER YOU WATCH

9 SPEAKING **Discuss the questions in small groups.**

1 What do you think you can learn from South Korea's education system?
2 How would a South Korean student manage in your school?

I think a South Korean student would do great in my school because ...

▶ Focus Vlog   About education

> Can you describe a perfect student?

Lewis

1 SPEAKING Choose the qualities you would use to describe a perfect student. Discuss with a partner.

A perfect student is someone who …
- sets goals and works hard to achieve them
- is disciplined and well-organised
- is not afraid of asking questions and making mistakes
- likes sharing his/her knowledge with others
- knows his/her strong and weak points
- can keep stress and emotions under control
- spends long hours studying.

2 (▶ 23) Watch the interviews where people describe a perfect student and a perfect place to study. Match the statements with the speakers: Callum, Oliver, Millie or Lewis.

Who says the perfect student …
1 enjoys reading? _____ , _____
2 is a sociable person? _____
3 makes lots of effort to learn? _____
4 has the right balance between work and play? _____
5 is a happy person? _____
6 likes spending time in a library? _____

Who thinks the perfect place to study is …
1 a library? _____
2 a place with food and drink? _____ , _____
3 somewhere you can also relax? _____
4 somewhere you feel comfortable? _____

3 SPEAKING Are you a perfect student? Discuss.

FOCUS ON LIFE SKILLS
Collaboration • Communication • Digital skills

4 In pairs, answer the questions about your study habits.

- Do you like listening to music or having the TV on when you study? Why?/Why not?
- Do you study best with low or bright lighting? Why?
- Do you prefer sitting upright in a chair when you study or lying down on the sofa? Why?
- Do you have a regular schedule or time of day when you study? If you do, what time?
- Do you study best alone, or in a group? Explain why.
- Do you ever take breaks to get up and move around while you study? How does this help you?

I love listening to music when I study because …

5 Now organise a survey to collect data about your classmates. Use an online survey builder to organise an online survey with eight multiple-choice questions. Give out the link and collect the data over a period of time. Then present the results to the class.

Making a survey:
Surveys are a method of gathering information from individuals. They have a variety of purposes, and can be conducted in many ways, through a printed questionnaire, over the telephone, by email, in person, or on the web. Every participant is asked the same questions in the same way.

⏵ BBC   Window cleaning

BEFORE YOU WATCH

1   SPEAKING   Discuss the questions.

1   What's the highest building or structure you've ever been to the top of? How did you feel then?

2   What could you see when you looked down?

2   Decide whether the adjectives are positive (P), negative (N) or can be both (B).

complex   disappointing   excellent   fascinating
good   iconic   intense   lovely   nervous   nice
terrified   scared

WHILE YOU WATCH

3   ⏵25   Watch the video. Which words from Exercise 2 can you hear? Which words does Dallas use most?

4   SPEAKING   Discuss the questions.

1   What is Dallas's job for the day?

2   How does Dallas feel before he starts working and after he has finished?

5   ⏵25   Complete quotes 1–5. Then watch the video again and check your answers.

1   I was secretly hoping that it was going to be too windy today and it would all be _____ and we could all just go home and somehow the windows would just clean themselves.

2   I'm absolutely _____ right now. I've never been so scared in my life.

3   I haven't _____ down yet. Now I've _____ down.

4   It's hard to believe how _____ these windows are.

5   If Dallas dropped something it could do a lot of _____ .

6   ⏵25   Complete the email to Dallas. If necessary, watch the video again and check your answers.

Hi Dallas,
Welcome to Dubai. Please come to the Burj Khalifa – we're proud of it because it's the ¹_____ building in the world. When you get here, take the lift to Floor ²_____ . Ask for the ³_____-cleaning team. We need to prepare you for your day's work. When you begin your window-cleaning, try not to ⁴_____ down – you will be more than ⁵_____ metres above the ground – that's higher than the world's ⁶_____ tallest building.
Don't worry about the ⁷_____ . The Burj Khalifa has an aerodynamic design and it is not a problem. Don't ⁸_____ anything – you could do a lot of damage. There are ⁹_____ windows to clean. It takes three ¹⁰_____ to clean them all. Then we start cleaning them again!
See you soon,
The Burj Khalifa window-cleaning team.

AFTER YOU WATCH

7   SPEAKING   Discuss the most dangerous jobs in the world. Which would be the worst job for you? Why?

- Snake charmer
- Gold miner
- Deep sea fisher
- Fire-fighter
- Racing driver
- Underwater construction worker

For me, the most dangerous job is fire-fighter, because fire is uncontrollable.

▶ Focus Vlog About dream jobs

> If you could have any job in the world, what would you want to be?

Freya

1 SPEAKING Discuss the questions.

1 When people talk about a dream job, what do they mean?
2 What was your dream job when you were a child?
3 If you could do any job in the world, what would you like to be?
4 Would you refuse a job that isn't 'perfect' for you?

2 ▶ 27 Watch the interviews where people talk about the jobs they'd like to have. Match the statements with the speakers: Oliver, Ethan, Esme or Freya.

Who would like to …
1 help others? _____
2 do something creative? _____
3 be wealthy? _____
4 become a composer? _____
5 work abroad? _____ , _____
6 work in Oxford? _____
7 stay in London? _____

3 ▶ 27 Are sentences 1–5 true (T) or false (F)? Discuss with a partner. Then watch again and check.

1 Oliver is a teacher. ☐
2 Ethan wants to have access to the latest technology. ☐
3 Freya wants to be her own boss. ☐
4 Oliver thinks Oxford is too big. ☐
5 Ethan wants to work in Austria. ☐

FOCUS ON LIFE SKILLS
Communication • Critical thinking

4 What three things would you consider important in a job?

- Working with your hands (e.g. in construction, with animals, doing the gardening etc.)
- Meeting people and making connections
- Travelling abroad
- Working creatively with words and images
- Working in a team
- Inventing something new or coming up with new ideas
- Achieving concrete results
- Listening and responding to people's needs
- Spending time outdoors rather than sitting in front of a screen
- Other (explain _____)

I think that achieving concrete results is important when you work, because that shows that you make progress.

5 Read the list in Exercise 4 again and decide which things you …

- are able to do (skills)
- like doing (passions)
- dream of doing (ambitions)

6 Read about Europass CV. Start filling in your CV online. You can update it when you have new information to add, for example about a course or an exam you have taken.

> **Europass curriculum vitae:**
> What is Europass CV?
> Europass is a service started by the European Union to help people communicate their skills, qualifications and experience through a collection of documents.
> In particular, the Curriculum Vitae helps you present your skills and qualifications. You can create your CV online using tutorials or download the template, examples and instructions.
> If you want to learn more:
> https://europass.cedefop.europa.eu

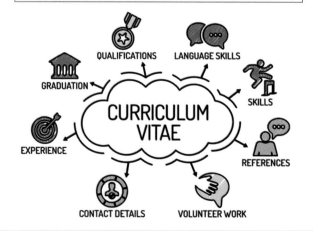

ⓑ BBC Cheap shopping

BEFORE YOU WATCH

1 SPEAKING **Do the mini-questionnaire. Then compare your answers with a partner. What do your answers say about you?**

What kind of shopper are you?

1 Do you think shopping is …
   a a necessity?   b a leisure activity?   c a hardship?

2 Do you prefer shopping for clothes in …
   a small shops?   b designer shops?   c a shopping mall?

3 When you go shopping for clothes, do you look for …
   a bargain?   b good quality?   c designer style?

WHILE YOU WATCH

2 **Try to match the prices in the box with the items 1–6 below.**

62p 75p £7.99 £15.99 £19.99 £21

1 _____   4 _____

2 _____   5 _____

3 _____   6 _____

3 ⓑ30 **Watch the first part of the video (up to 0:33) and check your answers in Exercise 2. What is 'weird' about the price of things?**

4 ⓑ30 **Read the leaflet about the Mall of America. Then watch the next part of the video (00:33 – 01:42) and complete the sentences.**

★ The MALL OF AMERICA ★
THE WORLD'S BUSIEST SHOPPING MALL

It's enormous! You could put [1] _____ jumbo jets inside.
Shopping at the Mall of America is a [2] _____ activity!
It opened in [3] _____ and since then more than half a [4] _____ people have visited. It's [5] _____ in Bloomington, Minnesota.
There are 520 [6] _____ and 40 million [7] _____ every year.
That's more than Graceland, the Grand Canyon and Disneyland combined.
There's no [8] _____ on apparel (clothes)!
It's a great place to shop!

5 ⓑ30 **Watch the next part of the video (01:42 – 03:33) and answer the questions.**

1 What did people in the video buy?
2 Why did they buy these items?
3 What is fast fashion?

6 ⓑ30 SPEAKING **Discuss the possible disadvantages of fast fashion. Then watch the last part of the video (03:33 – 03:55) and compare with your ideas.**

AFTER YOU WATCH

7 SPEAKING **Work in two groups. Discuss the statement 'Fast fashion is a good thing'.**

Group 1: Agree with the statement. Think of arguments to support your case.
Group 2: Disagree with the statement. Think of arguments to support your case.

⟲ Focus Vlog   About clothes

How many pairs of jeans
do you have?

Oliver

1   SPEAKING **Answer the questions.**

1 How many people in your class are wearing jeans
   today? Count the percentage.
2 How many pairs of jeans do you have
   in your wardrobe?
3 How many pairs of jeans have you thrown
   away in the past year?
4 How much did your last pair of jeans cost?

2   ⟲ 33 **Watch the interviews where people talk
about how many pairs of jeans they've got and
how much they usually spend on them. Choose the
correct option.**

1 Ethan has *many / two / only a few* pairs of black
   jeans.
2 *Rachel / Freya / Oliver* is the one who has the most
   pairs of jeans of all.
3 Rachel has a *black / white / blue* pair of jeans
   with rips in them.

3   ⟲ 33 **Watch the interviews again and answer the
questions.**

1 How much do Ethan and Freya usually spend
   on a pair of jeans?
2 What does Rachel consider when buying a pair
   of jeans?
3 How much does Oliver usually spend on a pair
   of jeans?
4 Why is Oliver ready to spend that much on a pair
   of jeans?

FOCUS ON LIFE SKILLS
Collaboration • Communication • Digital skills

4 **In pairs, prepare a list of five questions about
fashion. For example:**

• How important is fashion to you?
• How many pairs of jeans have you got?
• How much do you spend on clothes every
  month?

**Ask the questions to other students, collect the
answers and prepare an infographic with the
results. Then present your findings using graphs
and charts in a survey infographic. You can draw
the infographics or use an online tool to create
them.**

Survey infographic:
What is a survey infographic?
Survey infographics present survey data using
a combination of graphs, charts and text.
Visual graphics are a powerful way to show survey
results.
A well-designed infographic will capture the attention
of your audience and engage them.

BBC Keeping fit

BEFORE YOU WATCH

1 SPEAKING **Discuss your preferred ways of keeping fit. Refer to the activities in the box or your own ideas.**

> cycling   going to the gym   running   swimming

2 **Match the activities in the box with pictures 1–8. Which of these activities uses the most and which the least energy in your opinion?**

> cleaning windows   dusting   gardening   ironing
> mopping   mowing the lawn   vacuuming
> washing a car

WHILE YOU WATCH

3 🕒 36 **Complete the doctor's recommendation. Then watch the first part of the video (up to 0:32) and check your answer.**

> Adults should try to get at least ___ minutes of 'moderate intensity physical exercise' per week.

4 🕒 36 **Watch the next part of the video (00:32 – 01:50). Complete the sentences.**

1 Eight _____ are going to do some household jobs indoors and outdoors.
2 Activity monitors will measure the _____ they use.
3 Dr Andy Blannin is an _____ .
4 He will give each activity a MET (Metabolic Equivalent of Task) _____ .
5 A score of more than _____ shows that the activity is good enough to call it exercise.

5 🕒 36 SPEAKING **Tick the activities which are 'exercise' in your opinion. Then watch the next part of the video (01:50 – 03:07) and check your answers.**

ironing	☐	washing the car	☐
dusting	☐	washing the window	☐
mopping	☐	mowing the lawn	☐
planting flowers	☐	vacuuming	☐

6 🕒 36 **Match 1–5 with a–e to make collocations. Which activity do you think uses the most/the least energy? Watch the last part of the video (03:07 – 03:34) and check.**

1 Walking ☐   a trolley
2 Going ☐   b up a shopping basket
3 Picking ☐   c shopping bags
4 Using a ☐   d briskly
5 Carrying ☐   e cycling

AFTER YOU WATCH

7 SPEAKING **Make a list of activities you can do to keep fit without going to the gym. Discuss your ideas.**

Instead of going to the gym, you can take the stairs every day to keep fit.

> **What had you learnt by the time you left school?**

1 SPEAKING **Think of a victory (in sports, school, personal life) and answer the questions.**

1 What did you achieve?
2 How did you prepare?
3 Who helped you? How?

2 ⏺ 38 **Watch the interviews where people talk about what they had learnt by the time they left school or turned eighteen. Match the statements with the speakers.**

Tristan Jeffrey Anna Jenny

What had they learnt by the time they left school?

1 _____ had realised how important education is.
2 _____ had understood the importance of family and friends.
3 _____ had learnt how to be independent.
4 _____ had acquired the skills for cooperating with others.
5 _____ had experienced the joy of learning languages.

What had they achieved by their eighteenth birthday?

1 _____ had learnt to play a musical instrument.
2 _____ had run several marathons.
3 _____ had started to study a foreign language.
4 _____ had had a platinum CD.
5 _____ and _____ had been abroad.

3 SPEAKING **What had you learnt by the time you left primary school? Discuss with a partner.**

FOCUS ON LIFE SKILLS
Communication

4 **Ask three adults the following questions.**

1 What had you learnt by the time you left school?
2 What had you achieved by your 18th birthday?
3 Who/What had helped you to achieve these goals?

5 **Prepare a short presentation about the people you have interviewed.**

For each of them:
• give some personal information (who they are, what they do, how you are related to each of them)
• go through the answers you have collected and explain their achievements
• say if they are a model for you and what lessons you have learnt from their examples.

GRAMMAR AND USE OF ENGLISH

1.2 Present tenses – question forms

We form *yes/no* questions, *wh-* questions and subject questions in different ways. Look at the tables below for questions in the Present Simple, the Present Continuous and the Present Perfect.

Present Simple

Yes/No questions

| Do | I/you/we/they | speak English? |
| Does | he/she/it | |

Wh- questions

| What languages | do | I/you/we/they | speak? |
| | does | he/she/it | |

Subject questions

| Who | speaks | English? |

Present Continuous

Yes/No questions

Am	I	
Are	you/we/they	working now?
Is	he/she/it	

Wh- questions

What	am	I	doing?
	is	he/she/it	
	are	you/we/they	

Subject questions

| Who | is working | now? |

Present Perfect

Yes/No questions

| Have | I/you/we/they | swum in a river? |
| Has | he/she/it | |

Wh- questions

| What | have | I/you/we/they | done? |
| | has | he/she/it | |

Subject questions

| Who | has swum | in a river? |

Notice the position of the preposition in *wh-* questions with verbs followed by a preposition, e.g. *listen to music*.

What does Emily listen **to**?

In subject questions in the Present Simple, we do not use an auxiliary verb (*do/does*).

Julia gives money to charity.

Who gives money to charity?

What does Julia give to charity?

---

1 Choose the correct option.

1 Who *sits / does sit* next to you in class?
2 Where *does your best friend live / lives your best friend*?
3 Which capital cities *has visited your best friend / has your best friend visited*?
4 *You are watching / Are you watching* the news now?
5 Why *Jamie and Toni have been / have Jamie and Toni been* so quiet today?
6 What *you do / do you do* at the weekends?

2 Write questions about the underlined information.

1 My grandparents give money to <u>a charity</u>.
_____
2 <u>Tina</u> has tried Japanese food.
_____
3 I'm dreaming about <u>my winter holiday in Austria</u>.
_____
4 My best friend lives <u>in Frankfurt</u>.
_____
5 Jo has visited <u>Poland, Russia and Slovakia</u>.
_____
6 <u>Jim</u> is watching a comedy at the moment.
_____

3 Ask questions for the following answers.

1 No, I haven't. I've never met an important person.
_____?
2 No, she hasn't. She has never worked in an office.
_____?
3 My Dad usually cooks dinner in our family.
_____?
4 Yes, I am. I am studying at the moment.
_____?
5 I love reading books in my free time.
_____?

4 Complete the questions with the correct forms of the auxiliary verbs *do, be* or *have*. One question does not need an auxiliary verb.

1 What music _____ you like, Sebastian? I like hip-hop.
2 Who _____ your parents talking to in the kitchen?
3 _____ you seen my laptop? I can't find it anywhere.
4 Why _____ Asha always so serious? She never looks happy.
5 What _____ Martin eaten this afternoon?
6 _____ Jane looking for her glasses? They're over here.
7 Who _____ wants to help me bake dad's birthday cake?
8 _____ you like apples? These ones are really juicy.

1.5 Verb + -ing or verb + to + infinitive

English sentence clauses often contain two consecutive verbs. After some verbs we use the -ing form, after others to + infinitive.

We use the -ing form after:

* verbs expressing emotions, e.g. *enjoy, hate, like, love, (not) mind*
  I **hate wearing** a suit and a tie.
* particular verbs and verb phrases: *avoid, consider, can't stand, prefer, spend time*
  Laura **prefers texting** to sending emails.

We use the *to + infinitive* after:

* most verbs expressing plans, decisions, intentions and willingness, e.g. *hope, want, decide, choose*
  Tim **wants to study** Law.
* verbs such as: *agree, can't afford, manage, need, pretend, refuse*
  Why do you **refuse to lend** me your shoes?
* verbs expressing preferences: *would like, would love, would prefer*
  I like going out with my friends, but today I **would like to stay** at home.

1 Complete the sentences with the correct forms of the verbs in brackets.

1 I don't mind _____ (get up) early.
2 Karen spends a lot of time _____ (chat) online.
3 I refuse _____ (wear) this skirt – it is too short!
4 I always agree _____ (help) my brother at home.
5 They hope _____ (meet) Sting after the concert.
6 I can't stand _____ (shop). It's so boring!
7 Peter wants _____ (be) like Steve Jobs.
8 Sue has decided _____ (lend) me her new dress.
9 Does Angela enjoy _____ (work) as a volunteer?
10 Ben prefers _____ (swim) to running.

2 Choose the correct option.

1 Karen really enjoys *reading / to read* poetry.
2 Would you like *going / to go* to the cinema?
3 Pete can't stand *wearing / to wear* formal clothes.
4 We can't avoid *telling / to tell* him.
5 I've decided *going / to go* abroad.
6 He would like *spending / to spend* more time with me.
7 I really hate *getting / to get* up early in the winter.
8 Did she manage *completing / to complete* her work?
9 We don't mind *waiting / to wait* for you.
10 I can't afford *buying / to buy* a new computer.

3 Complete the sentences using the prompts in brackets. Add any necessary words. Do not change the order of the words given.

1 I can't _____ (stand/spend) the holidays at home. I'd like to go somewhere exotic!
2 Why does Peter _____ (pretend/worry) Sarah? He clearly doesn't like her.
3 It's a good idea to _____ (avoid/depend) people that you don't know very well.
4 I finally _____ (manage/focus) my homework.
5 We _____ (hope/see) you both at the party.
6 Roger _____ (not/mind/talk) his ex-girlfriend. They're still very good friends.
7 I _____ (miss/spend/time) my best friend from primary school.
8 Edgar _____ (hate/listen) heavy metal music. He prefers hip-hop.

4 Complete the second sentence so that it means the same as the first. Use no more than five words including the word in capitals.

1 I don't want to wear the same clothes every day. **REFUSE**
  I _____ the same clothes every day.
2 It's not a problem for me to get up early in the morning. **MIND**
  I _____ early in the morning.
3 He didn't want to see me, so he stayed at home. **AVOID**
  He stayed at home to _____ me.
4 It's my choice to study Art at university next year. **CHOSEN**
  I _____ Art at university next year.
5 Karen doesn't want to go to the theatre, she wants to go to the cinema. **PREFERS**
  Karen doesn't want to go to the theatre, she _____ cinema.
6 It is really fun for me to play football with my team. **ENJOY**
  I really _____ with my team.

5 Complete the text with the correct form of the verbs in the box.

> change do go join play practise
> spend tell win

Last month I decided [1]_____ my lifestyle. Why? Well, I don't mind [2]_____ you that I was a bit worried about my size and my weight. I spent too much time [3]_____ computer games and I refused [4]_____ any kind of exercise as well.
Firstly, I considered [5]_____ to the gym. But this is expensive and I can't afford [6]_____ much money. Plus, it's a little boring and unsociable, I think. So, I chose [7]_____ a badminton club, instead. I wasn't very good at first, but I managed [8]_____ my first game yesterday so I'm really happy. Of course, I need [9]_____ more, but I'm really passionate about my new hobby.

1.6 so and such

We use the pronouns **so** and **such** when we want to stress the noun they precede.

We use **so** before:

- adjectives without nouns:

  *I love talking with my aunt Tanya. She is **so inspiring**.*

- quantifying expressions (e.g. **many/much**) followed by a noun:

  *I'm very happy that **so many friends** are coming to the party.*

  *Teenagers don't spend **so much time** watching TV these days.*

We use **such** before:

- adjectives followed by nouns:

  *Greg has got **such a comfortable sofa** in his bedroom.*

- nouns:

  ***Such people** will always help you in need.*

  *Angela always has **such luck** – she is always in the right place, at the right time.*

Notice that with **such**:

- we use the indefinite article **a/an,** if it precedes a countable singular noun:

  *Moving to the UK was **such a good decision** because we live closer to my family now.*

  *Uncle Tom has **such an interesting life** – he travels a lot.*

- we do not use any article if it precedes a plural or uncountable noun:

  *Bob works as a police officer and he often gives people **such bad news** that they feel upset.*

  *Every morning Josh goes for **such long walks** with his dogs.*

So and *such* may be also used in expressions **such ... that** and **so ... that**, when we want to stress an adjective or noun and focus on the consequences of events described in the main sentence clause:

*Luckily, my parents bought **such a cheap house** that we've got some money for new furniture.*

*My younger sister has got **so many toys** that my parents want to give some away.*

1 Choose the correct option.

1 He's *so / such* adventurous and loves extreme sports.

2 That was *so / such an* irresponsible thing to do!

3 There were *so / such* many people at the restaurant – we couldn't get a table.

4 They're never at home because they're *so / such* busy people.

5 The book was *so / such an* interesting – I read it in one day.

6 It's *so / such* a lovely day today – let's go to the park.

7 I had *so / such* much work to do yesterday.

8 Becky made *so / such a* good impression when she met my parents.

2 Complete the sentences with *so, such,* or *such a(n)*.

1 You really shouldn't spend _____ much time playing games.

2 My sister is _____ friendly and caring person!

3 My neighbours are _____ outgoing people and love having garden parties.

4 You've got _____ many clothes that you must have something I can borrow.

5 It was _____ amazing idea to have a family picnic in the park.

6 I won't ask Ann because she gave me _____ irresponsible advice last time.

3 Join the two sentences to make one. Use *so, such* and *that*.

1 My brother is a cheerful person. He says hello to everybody.

_____

2 It was a wonderful holiday. We want to go back next year.

_____

3 My father was inexperienced at cooking. He burned our breakfast.

_____

4 It was a comfortable armchair. I fell asleep.

_____

5 The shirt was inexpensive. I bought one for you too.

_____

6 The weather was bad. We decided to stay at home.

_____

4 UNIT REVIEW Choose the correct answer, A, B or C to complete the text.

My favourite cousin is the son of my dad's brother. His name is Jack and he's the same age as me. We don't have any brothers or sisters but we spend **1**___ time together that we are like brothers. We have **2**___ fun together and do all kinds of adventurous things like going climbing and visiting new places. We are different in many ways, however. For example, I think that Jack is **3**___ hard-working person. He always gets good grades at school and is able to really focus **4**___ one thing and does the best he can at everything. I can be rather lazy, to be honest. On the other hand, Jack can be rather shy – not like me. I also think he's a little too **5**___ because sometimes I have to tell him not to worry **6**___ what other people think or say. Despite these differences, he's still my best friend.

1	A so much	B so many	C such a
2	A so	B such	C such an
3	A such	B such a	C so
4	A at	B with	C on
5	A sensible	B selfish	C sensitive
6	A on	B about	C at

2.2 Past Continuous and Past Simple

We use the Past Continuous:

- to describe a longer background scene in a story, during which other main events (described in the Past Simple) took place:

  *At 7 p.m. Doug **was working** on his computer. He **was sitting** at his desk and **downloading** some photos when the lights **went out**.*

- to talk about an action that was in progress when another action took place (for the shorter action, which happened while the longer one was in progress, we use the Past Simple):

  *While Meg **was texting** a message to her friend, she **dropped** her phone.*

- to talk about actions in progress at the same time:

  *While Ann **was doing** some experiments, Terry **was taking** some measurements.*

Affirmative			Negative		
I/He/She/It	was	watching TV.	I/He/She/It	wasn't (was not)	watching TV.
You/We/They	were		You/We/They	weren't (were not)	

Yes/No questions			Short answers
Was	I/he/she/it	watching TV?	Yes, I/he/she/it was. No, I/he/she/it wasn't.
Were	you/we/they		Yes, you/we/they were. No, you/we/they weren't.

Wh- questions				Subject questions		
What	was	I/he/she/it	watching?	Who	was	watching TV?
	were	you/we/they				

1 Choose the correct option.

1 I *lay / was lying* on the beach when suddenly it *started / was starting* raining.

2 I *read / was reading* a book when you *called me / were calling me* at 4 o'clock yesterday.

3 The first time I *was seeing / saw* my boyfriend, he *danced / was dancing* at a party.

4 We *were having / had* lunch when the door opened.

5 It was a sunny day. I *left / was leaving* home. Suddenly the postman *was knocking / knocked* on the door.

6 When my mum *drove / was driving* to work yesterday, she *saw / was seeing* her old friend from school.

7 Molly *was breaking / broke* her leg when she *climbed / was climbing* a tree.

8 *Was Ben studying / Did Ben study* yesterday at 8 p.m.?

2 Write questions for the following answers.

1 Sally was doing her homework when the phone rang.
(What) _____ ?

2 Clare was wearing a fantastic dress at the party.
(What) _____ ?

3 We played tennis from five to eight.
(How long) _____ ?

4 At 7:30 yesterday morning, Sophie was driving to the airport.
(Where) _____ ?

5 They were having dinner at seven.
(When) _____ ?

6 We saw Mark at the café.
(Who) _____ ?

7 Alice was crying during the film because it was a drama.
(Why) _____ ?

8 Chris bought a sandwich for lunch.
(What) _____ ?

3 Complete the sentences with the correct form of the verbs in brackets. Use the Past Simple or the Past Continuous.

1 Mum _____ (work) on her laptop while dad _____ (listen) to music on his new MP3 player.

2 Margaret _____ (talk) on her smartphone when she _____ (start) crying.

3 Adam _____ (not/watch) the film so I _____ (change) TV channels.

4 Tony _____ (not/take) any photos with his phone at the party because he _____ (send) text messages to Jessica all the time.

5 I _____ (drop) my memory stick when I _____ (run) for the tram.

6 Alan and I _____ (play) on the games console when my dad _____ (come) home.

4 Write sentences from the prompts.

1 I / run / in the park / when / Joanna / telephone / me.
_____

2 while / Gareth / update / social media profile / his wife / do / yoga.
_____

3 what / you / eat / when / I / get / back home?
_____

4 you / sleep / when / the teacher / explain / the task to us?
_____

5 Jo / use / computer / when / it / crash.
_____

6 I / cook / dinner / then / visit / favourite website.
_____

7 while / Jane / study / Dan / play / video games.
_____

8 Jim / get up / and then / get ready / for school.
_____

2.5 used to

We use **used to** to talk about past states or actions which happened regularly in the past but do not happen anymore.
I **used to play** tennis a lot. (I don't play anymore or I don't play very often.)
He **didn't use to be** so unkind. (But he's different now.)
Did you **use to study** astronomy? (You don't study anymore.)

When we talk about single actions that happened only once or that did not happen regularly, we use the Past Simple, <u>not</u> used to.
In high school we **went** to the mountains two or three times.
Kim **bought** a new mobile phone yesterday.

Affirmative			Negative		
I/You/ He/She/ It/We/ They	used to	swim.	I/You/ He/She/ It/ We/ They	didn't (did not) use to	swim.

Yes/No questions				Short answers
Did	I/you/ he/she/ it/we/ they	use to	swim?	Yes, I/you/he/she/it/we/they did. No, I/you/he/she/it/we/they didn't.

Wh- questions					Subject questions		
Where	did	I/you/ he/ she/ it/we/ they	use to	swim?	Who	used to	swim?

1 Complete the sentences with *used to* and the verbs in brackets.

1 Kim _____ (be) much more confident about herself.
2 _____ (our neighbours/live) abroad before they moved here?
3 My boyfriend's friends _____ (not like) me.
4 Who _____ (cook) you dinner when you were ten years old?
5 _____ (you/have) a mobile phone when you were very little?

2 Write sentences from the prompts. Use *used to* where possible. If not, use the Past Simple.

1 I / go to the cinema / with my grandparents / every week
_____
2 we / not have / mobile phones or computers
_____
3 my family / move / to San Francisco
_____
4 I / get / a digital watch / for my seventh birthday
_____
5 he / eat / sweets / every day
_____

3 Complete the sentences with *used to* or *didn't use to* and the verbs in brackets.

1 Ten years ago I _____ (love) cycling in the park. Now I don't even have a bike.
2 I _____ (use) my old phone much, but then I got a smartphone and I use it all the time now.
3 My grandfather _____ (be) an astronomer, but now he's stopped working.
4 We _____ (take) measurements using a really big computer. Now we use an app on a tablet.
5 Paula got an MP3 player for her birthday. Before then, she _____ (listen) to music very often.
6 Did Ali really _____ (have) the same password for everything? How silly!

4 Complete the dialogue between Ben and his dad with *used to* or *didn't use to* and the verbs in the box.

[do find go meet use write]

B: Dad, where did you **1**_____ information before somebody invented the Internet?
D: Good question. I **2**_____ to the library, of course. I know this might sound strange to you but some people still use libraries.
B: Really? Nooo. Only joking. And what about your schoolwork? Probably you **3**_____ everything with a pen.
D: In school, yes. But at home I **4**_____ a pen or a pencil very much. In fact, I **5**_____ everything on a typewriter. You know, it has a keyboard like a desktop computer but you put paper in the top of it.
B: Yes, dad. I know what a typewriter is. And where did you **6**_____ your friends before they invented coffee shops?
D: Very funny. Haven't you got any homework to do?

5 Write positive sentences (✓), negative sentences (✗) and questions (?) from the prompts. Use the correct forms of *used to*.

When I was a child …
1 mobile phones / be really big. (✓)
_____
2 people / use phones as alarm clocks. (✗)
_____
3 children / play on the streets. (✓)
_____
4 people / need passwords (?)
_____
5 Richard / like me, but now we're very good friends. (✗)
_____
6 people / drive electric cars (✗)
_____
7 you / live in a big house (?)
_____
8 teenagers / spend much time online (?)
_____

2.6 Linkers and time expressions

Linkers and time expressions are followed by full sentences (i.e. linker + subject + main verb).

While and *when* are used to link two sentences describing events taking place at the same time:
While the astronauts were collecting specimens on the Moon, they found some interesting rocks.
David became interested in psychology when he was in high school.

After, as soon as, before and *when* are used to link two sentences describing events taking place one after another:
After Mark spent hours observing the work of archaeologists, he realised how important their job is.
I checked the price of the new smartphone before I bought it.
As soon as Ann published the photos of her new experiments on social media, she got a lot of positive comments.
When Sarah received text messages asking for the password to her account, she deleted them straight away.

Linkers and time expressions are followed by nouns or noun phrases: *during the holidays, for twenty-two days, until (till) late evening, by the end of the century.*

During refers to a period of time:
The linguist explored several languages during his stay in India.

Until and *till* refer to a point in time:
We didn't do many experiments in Chemistry classes until (till) last year.

By, when used with a noun, refers to an event which is happening or which happened before a particular point in time:
By the time we got home, we were tired and hungry.

1 Choose the correct option.

1 Bill Gates became interested in computers *when / during* he was a kid.
2 My sister always buys the latest gadget *until / as soon as* it is available.
3 Computers had smaller memories than smartphones *during / while* my childhood.
4 We completed all of the chemistry reports *by / till* twelve o'clock.
5 I learned how to analyse data *during / while* I was working in Silicon Valley.
6 Text me *after / until* you get home tonight, OK?
7 You need to enter a password *until / before* you can use the computer.
8 I didn't know how to use the printer *as soon as / till* you showed me.

2 Complete the second sentence so that it means the same as the first. Use no more than five words including the word in capitals. Do not change the word given.

1 The chemist developed a theory at the same time she analysed the data. **WHILE**
_____ the data, she developed a theory.
2 We finished the biology class and then immediately went home. **SOON**
We _____ we finished the biology class.
3 I collected the evidence and then started writing this report. **AFTER**
I started writing this report _____ the evidence.
4 I became an optician last year, in December. **UNTIL**
I didn't _____ December last year.
5 When David was doing the experiment, he discovered something interesting. **DURING**
David _____ the experiment.
6 He washed his hands and then he prepared lunch. **BEFORE**
_____, he washed his hands.
7 Everyone was in the classroom when I arrived. **BY**
_____, everyone was in the classroom.
8 Lisa began to panic when she saw the Maths test. **AS**
_____ the Maths test, she began to panic.

3 UNIT REVIEW Choose the correct answer, A, B or C to complete the text.

Steven Jobs (1955–2011) was an American businessman and **1**___ who changed the world. He grew up with an adoptive family **2**___ his biological parents decided not to keep him. As a child, he helped his father fix things in their garage, and in this way, he developed an early love for engineering. At college he studied Physics, literature and poetry, but after some time he quit and decided to travel through India instead. **3**___ he was there, he became interested in Zen Buddhism. Perhaps he was inspired by this Eastern philosophy, because Jobs later became famous for producing simple and minimalist devices. What's more, he did not **4**___ research on these gadgets but designed them by using only his intuition. Many of these products **5**___ a big effect on modern life and Jobs' company became successful and iconic.

1	**A** invention		**4**	**A** have
	B inventor			**B** make
	C invented			**C** do
2	**A** while		**5**	**A** used to have
	B by			**B** were having
	C after			**C** had
3	**A** While			
	B Till			
	C During			

GRAMMAR AND USE OF ENGLISH

3.2 Comparative and superlative adjectives

- We use the comparative form of adjectives and the word *than* to compare two people or things:
  *Daniel Craig is **taller than** Zac Efron.*

- To compare two people or things, we can also use the structure: (*not*) *as* + adjective + *as*:
  *Rupert Grint is **not as famous as** Daniel Radcliffe.*

- We use the superlative form of adjectives to show that a person or thing has the higest degree of a certain quality (compared to at least two other people or things):
  *Sean Connery is **the tallest** of the three James Bond actors.*

Adjectives		Comparative	Superlative
one-syllable	young	younger	the youngest
	nice	nicer	the nicest
	hot	hotter	the hottest
one- and two-syllable ending in -y	pretty	prettier	the prettiest
	dry	drier	the driest
two-syllable or longer	attractive	more attractive	the most attractive
	difficult	more difficult	the most difficult
irregular	good	better	the best
	bad	worse	the worst
	far	further	the furthest

To compare two people or things, we can also use the following structures:

- **(just) as** + adjective + **as**, when two things or people are the same:
  *The plot of Angela's latest novel is **as complex as** her previous one.*

- **not as** + adjective + **as**, when two things or people are different:
  *For me, talent shows **aren't as interesting as** game shows.*

Comparative adjectives may also be used with *a bit* or *much/far*:

- **a bit**: *Reading an e-book is **a bit easier**.*

- **much/far**: *This television is **much more expensive** because it has a better screen.*

1 Choose the correct option.

1 This is the *longer / longest* film I've ever seen.
2 He's not as clever *than / as* his sister.
3 The Po is *more short / shorter* than the Nile.
4 The *taller / tallest* building in the world is in Dubai.
5 Is this car *more cheap / cheaper* than that one?
6 Which is the *worse / worst* play you've ever seen?
7 Can I use your smartphone camera? It's *better / best* than mine.
8 A restaurant is usually *more expensive / most expensive* than a pub.
9 My school friends are *more friendly / friendlier* than my cousins.
10 Jane is the *prettier / prettiest* girl in the class.

2 Complete the sentences with *as*, *more* or *than*.

1 E-books are often a bit cheaper _____ paper books.
2 Watching documentaries is _____ engaging than watching sitcoms.
3 The soundtrack to this movie is just as moving _____ the script.
4 This romantic comedy is much funnier _____ I expected.
5 Reality TV shows aren't as imaginative today _____ they used to be.
6 The plots of thrillers are usually far _____ complex than the plots in horrors.
7 A wide-screen TV is better _____ one with a small screen.
8 Classical music isn't _____ popular as hip hop with teenagers.
9 Do you think poems are _____ difficult to write than stories?
10 This film is worse _____ the first one in the series.

3 Complete the second sentence so that it has the same meaning as the first.

1 *The Hunger Games* series was more popular than *the Maze Runner* films.
  The Maze Runner films weren't _____ as *The Hunger Games* series.
2 In my opinion, no actor is funnier than Will Ferrell.
  In my opinion, Will Ferrell is _____ actor of all.
3 Reading an e-book isn't as enjoyable as reading a paper book.
  Reading a paper book is _____ reading an e-book.
4 Gaming computers used to be more expensive.
  Gaming computers aren't as _____ they used to be.
5 She doesn't think any writer is as good as J.K. Rowling.
  She thinks J.K. Rowling is _____ writer in the world.
6 Ariana Grande isn't as old as Katy Perry.
  Katy Perry is _____ Ariana Grande.

4 Complete the text with the adjectives in brackets in the comparative or superlative form.

The first *Maze Runner* film, based on a series of books by James Dashner, came out in 2014. It wasn't [1] _____ (popular) as other teen series like *The Hunger Games*, but the producers decided to make more. There have been three films up to now, and for me [2] _____ (interesting) of them is the second one, *The Scorch Trials*. The plot is [3] _____ (crazy) than I expected. There are so many different things happening that I sometimes thought it was a bit [4] _____ (complicated) than it needed to be. But the action scenes and the sets are so amazing that in the end I decided I enjoyed watching this movie. The last film, *The Death Cure*, is definitely [5] _____ (long) of the three, probably because it included so many details from the book. Still, there are good things in all three films, so give them a try!

3.5 Present Perfect with *just*, *already*, *(not) yet* and Past Simple

We use the Present Perfect:

- to talk about actions which happened and finished in the past, but we do not know when exactly or it is not important:
  I have read a lot of biographies and autobiographies.

- to talk about actions which happened in the past and the result is visible in the present:
  Eddie has painted his first portrait.

Common time expressions used with the Present Perfect:

- *ever* – used in questions:
  Have you ever been to an art gallery?

- *never* – used in negative sentences:
  My grandparents have never left England.

- *since then*:
  She won The X Factor in 2006. Since then she has sold millions of albums.

- *already* and *just* – used mainly in affirmative sentences between *have* and the Past Participle verb form:
  I have already seen it.
  They have just left.

- *yet* – used in negative sentences and questions and always at the end of the sentence:
  I haven't seen her yet.
  Has she written any songs yet?

If we want to say when something happened, we use the Past Simple. We also use the Past Simple in questions with *when*.
She won a Grammy in 2016.
When did you see Blur play live?

1 Write questions, positive (✓) and negative (✗) answers from the prompts. Use the Present Perfect and *already* or *yet*.

1 Leonardo DiCaprio / win / an Oscar _____ ?
  (✓) _____ .

2 Katy Perry / write / her autobiography _____ ?
  (✗) _____ .

3 Madonna / play concerts / in Poland _____ ?
  (✓) _____ .

4 E-books / replace / paper books _____ ?
  (✗) _____ .

5 Harry / buy / his concert ticket _____ ?
  (✓) _____ .

6 the play / start _____ ?
  (✗) _____ .

7 Rihanna / release / a new album _____ ?
  (✓) _____ .

8 the shops / open _____ ?
  (✗) _____ .

2 Complete the sentences with the words in brackets in the correct tense.

1 A: _____ (you/ever/be) to the opera?
  B: Yes. I _____ (go) to the opera last month. I _____ (see) *Madame Butterfly* by Puccini.

2 Camilla Läckberg _____ (write) a lot of crime stories. She _____ (write) *The Witch* in 2017.

3 Look, Pierre _____ (just/upload) some videos.

4 My favourite singer _____ (release) his new single last week, but I _____ (not hear it/yet).

5 Emily _____ (already/buy) a birthday present for her mum.

3 Choose the correct option.

AN OPERA TO REMEMBER

I [1]*just came / have just come* back from the opera house where I watched a new production of *The Magic Flute* and I have to say it is one of the best operas I [2]*have ever seen / ever saw*! It is a famous opera which Wolfgang Amadeus Mozart [3]*wrote / has written* around 1790. It is a magical romantic comedy. The audiences in the eighteenth century [4]*thought / have thought* it was a bit silly, but the music and the characters are so interesting that it is still popular three centuries later. The latest film version of the opera [5]*has come / came* out in 2006, but it [6]*didn't receive / hasn't received* very good reviews at the time. In my opinion, you can't really understand the beauty of *The Magic Flute* if you [7]*haven't had / didn't have* a chance to see it in one of the great opera houses, where all of its magic comes to life.

4 Choose the best option from the brackets and add it to the sentence in the correct position.

1 I haven't seen the new *Star Wars* film. (yet / just)

2 James has been to a rock concert, so he's got a bit of a headache at the moment. (just / already)

3 You can have your book back now because I've finished it. (already / yet)

4 Oliver hasn't been in a film, but he acted in a TV show last year. (already / yet)

5 I've been to Hollywood, but I've never been to Miami. (already / yet)

6 Hannah is tired because she has got home from the theatre and the play was over four hours long. (just / already)

3.6 *too and not enough*

We use **too** and **(not) enough** to make comparisons and talk about a degree of a quality. **Too** means 'more than you need or want'. **Enough** means 'the amount you need'. **Not enough** means 'less than you need or want'.

We use **too**:
- before adjectives:
  *The painting is **too dark** and I can't see what's in it.*
  Too has a negative meaning when used in an affirmative sentence. When used with negation, it has a positive meaning:
  *The plot **is too complex** – I can't understand it.*
  *The plot **isn't too complex** – it's easy to follow it.*
- with nouns, in expressions **too many/much**:
  *There are **too many horror films** at the cinema these days.*
  *The artist didn't give **too much advice** to the kids so they painted how they liked.*

We use **(not) enough**:
- after adjectives:
  *The special effects weren't **realistic enough** so the film wasn't very popular.*
- before nouns:
  *I think there are **enough cooking programmes** on TV nowadays.*

Enough has a positive meaning when used in an affirmative sentence. When used with negation, it has a negative meaning:
*We had **enough photos** to prepare the exhibition.*
*We **didn't have enough** photos to prepare the exhibition.*

---

1 **Complete the sentences with *too* or *enough* and the adjectives in the box.**

> chilly complex dishonest embarrassing
> generous good imaginative outgoing

1 I think Angela is _____ to trust with the money for our concert tickets.
2 Do you think Adam is _____ to write a fantasy novel?
3 Sarah isn't _____ to take part in a live TV show.
4 It's much _____ to go painting outside, so we'll stay in the art studio today.
5 John thinks it's _____ to walk through the streets in his Batman costume.
6 Do you think the company is _____ to buy us new cameras?
7 Tom's grades aren't _____ to get into a better school.
8 I didn't enjoy that thriller – the plot was _____ for me.

2 **Complete the dialogues with *too* or *enough* and the word(s) in brackets.**

1 **A:** Are you going to watch the new *Star Wars* film at the cinema?
  B: The tickets are _____, so I'll wait for the DVD. (expensive)
2 **A:** Why was the exhibition cancelled?
  B: In the end, there weren't _____. (paintings)
3 **A:** Do you still want to learn how to play the guitar?
  B: No. I think there are _____, so I'll learn the drums. (guitar players)
4 **A:** Do you want to watch this new science fiction series?
  B: No. TV series are _____ and a waste of time. (addictive)
5 **A:** This thriller isn't very good, is it?
  B: Yes, it isn't _____ to continue watching. (gripping)
6 **A:** I don't know what's happening in this period drama.
  B: Yeah, the plot is much _____ to understand. (complex)

3 **UNIT REVIEW Choose the answer, A, B or C, that is closest in meaning to the words in bold.**

1 I think **the concert won't be too popular**.
  A a lot of people will go to the concert
  B not many people will go to the concert
  C nobody will go to the concert
2 There **shouldn't be more** game shows on TV.
  A are enough
  B aren't enough
  C aren't many
3 I think **there should be more** art in public spaces.
  A there is enough
  B there isn't enough
  C there is too much
4 At the end of this film, the bad character **shows his support for** the hero.
  A takes on
  B gives up
  C stands up for
5 This sculpture is **smaller than** I thought it would be.
  A as big as
  B as small as
  C not as big as
6 I love **books with creative plots set in famous periods in the past**.
  A fantasy novels
  B historical fiction books
  C biographies

4.2 Present Perfect with *for* and *since*

We use the Present Perfect to talk about states and actions that started in the past and still continue. We often use the words *since* and *for* when we use the Present Perfect in this way.

- **Since** refers to a moment or point in time when the activity started:
  since 2000 / Monday / last summer / my birthday / I was born
- **For** refers to a time period between a time in the past and now:
  for five minutes / two weeks / a long time / ages

Notice the example sentences:
*My parents **have had** this house **since** 1990.*
*I **have known** Carol **for** ten years.*

Questions about duration are formed using *How long ...?*
***How long** have you lived in this house?*

1 Look at today's date and time and complete the table with the correct time expressions.

since		for
1 since December	=	
2 since Saturday	=	
3	=	for 45 minutes
4 since breakfast	=	
5	=	for 27 years
6	=	for five weeks
7 since I started school	=	

2 Write questions with *How long ...?* Then write two answers to each question with *since* and *for*.

1 you / live in your house or flat?
_____ ?
_____
_____

2 you / know your best friend?
_____ ?
_____
_____

3 you / be at this school?
_____ ?
_____
_____

4 you / have a mobile phone?
_____ ?
_____
_____

3 Complete the sentences with the Present Perfect form of the verbs in brackets. Then choose *for* or *since*.

1 We _____ (live) in this house *for / since* 2005.
2 I _____ (not/see) Rob *for / since* my birthday six weeks ago.
3 Birgit _____ (work) in Paris *for / since* ages.
4 We _____ (not/visit) grandma *for / since* last winter.
5 It looks like you _____ (not/clean) this kitchen *for / since* several weeks.
6 My family _____ (stay) in this holiday villa in Spain every year *for / since* I was born.
7 John and Magda _____ (not/speak) to each other *for / since* five days.
8 Karen _____ (not/be) near the sea *for / since* a long time.

4 Correct the mistakes.

1 How long has Ravi and Sibel owned this cottage?
2 I have lived in the suburbs since three weeks.
3 I love the countryside. How long you have been here?
4 Charlie, have you did the ironing?
5 Bob, look! Monica has came round to visit us.
6 I haven't spent Christmas with my family for 2015.
7 I have known her from ten years.
8 Sarah hasn't got any money left because she has buy a new flat.

5 Complete the second sentence so that it means the same as the first. Use no more than five words including the word in capitals.

1 We moved to Ankara two years ago. **FOR**
We _____ two years.
2 I last saw Mark in February. **SINCE**
I _____ February.
3 Annette bought the cooker last week. **HAD**
Annette _____ last week.
4 Dad stopped making furniture about five years ago. **NOT**
Dad _____ about 2015.
5 I met my neighbour a long time ago. **KNOWN**
I _____ ages.

6 Complete the text with the correct form of the verbs in the box. There are two extra gaps. Use *for* or *since* in the extra gaps.

invite   make   move   plan   promise   show

I'm really happy because my family has just **1**_____ near the sea. In fact, we've lived here **2**_____ one month. Of course, I was sad to leave my friends back in Manchester, but I've **3**_____ them to stay with me next summer and I've **4**_____ to write to them often. I've been at my new school **5**_____ last Monday and I have already **6**_____ some new friends. They're really nice and have **7**_____ me the best places to see. I'm sure they've **8**_____ something interesting for this weekend too. I think I'm going to really enjoy living here.

4.5 Future forms: Present Continuous, *be going to* and *will*

- We use the Present Continuous for fixed future arrangements, which have already been planned and prepared:

  I can't go shopping tomorrow at five. I'm playing tennis with Joy. (I've already made an arrangement with Joy.)

- We use *be going to* + infinitive to talk about future intentions or plans, which may still be changed:

  Are you going to invite your aunt to the party?

- We use *will* + infinitive for spontaneous decisions made at the moment of speaking, often in reaction to a new situation. We often use *will* with:

  I think I'll …, I'll probably …, Don't worry, I'll …

  I think I'll ask Luke for help.

Affirmative			Negative		
I	am ('m)		I	am not ('m not)	
You/We/They	are ('re)	going to sleep.	You/We/They	are not (aren't)	going to study.
He/She/It	is ('s)		He/She/It	is not (isn't)	

Yes/No questions			Short answers
Am	I		Yes, I am. No, I am not ('m not).
Are	you/we/they	going to study?	Yes, you/we/they are. No you/we/they are not (aren't).
Is	he/she/it		Yes, he/she/it is. No, he/she/it is not (isn't).

Wh- questions			
	am	I	
When	are	you/we/they	going to study?
	is	he/she/it	

Subject questions		
Who	is	going to study?

Affirmative			Negative		
I/You/He/She/It/We/They	will	drop biology.	I/You/He/She/It/We/They	will not (won't)	drop biology.

Yes/No questions			Short answers
Will	I/you/he/she/it/we/they	drop biology?	Yes, I/you/he/she/it/we/they will. No, I/you/he/she/it/we/they will not (won't).

Wh- questions			
What	will	I/you/he/she/it/we/they	drop?

Subject questions		
Who	will	drop biology?

1 Choose the correct option.

1 We had a discussion and we've decided we *are not going to / will not* attend the meeting next week.
2 Don't worry. *I'll phone / I'm phoning* you to tell you the news.
3 What time *are you meeting / will you meet* Dr Stevens tomorrow?
4 Who do you think *will / is going to* win the next World Cup?

2 Complete the sentences with the appropriate future forms of the verbs in brackets.

1 Mum _____ (see) the dentist at four o'clock this afternoon.
2 It's my birthday next month but I _____ (not have) a party.
3 Brrr, it's cold in here. I think I _____ (turn) the heating on.
4 What _____ (you / do) later? Do you want to go for a coffee?
5 My cousin _____ (get married) in May.
6 Sorry, I can't talk now. I _____ (call) you back later.
7 These bags are so heavy, I _____ (carry) them for you.

3 What will these people say in the following situations? Choose the best option.

1 A customer at a café:
   I'll have / I'm going to have / I'm having a big glass of orange juice, please.
2 Someone who's just heard about his uncle's problem:
   What? Uncle Bob *will paint / is going to paint* his house all by himself on Saturday? *I'm going to help / I'll help* him!
3 A businesswoman talking about her plans for the new year:
   I'm going to help / I'll help / I'm helping some African charities this year.
4 Someone talking to his/her friend on the phone:
   I'm having / I'll have / I'm going to have a house party on Saturday. I've already bought the food and drink but can you bring the music?
5 Someone talking to his/her friend:
   I'll buy / I'm going to buy / I'm buying Matt a desk lamp for his birthday. Do you think that's a good idea?

4 Complete the text with the appropriate future forms of the verbs in brackets.

Next weekend we ¹_____ (have) a school disco in the main hall. I ²_____ (wear) my favourite shirt with my new jeans and brown shoes.

I ³_____ (work) in the afternoon in my mum's shop, but after that I ⁴_____ (return) home to have a shower and get dressed. I'm quite excited. But who do I invite? I know! I ⁵_____ (ask) Sarah in my Maths class. She's really nice.

4.6 Adverbs

We use adverbs with:
- verbs:
  *Are you **sitting comfortably**?*
- adjectives:
  *The living room is **really beautiful**.*
- other adverbs:
  *We drove **incredibly slowly** because of the traffic jams.*

Adverbs are usually formed by adding **-ly** to an adjective (*soft – softly*).
In other cases:
- for adjectives ending in **-le**: the **-e** changes into **-y** (*possible – possibly*),
- for adjectives ending in a consonant + **-y**: **-y** changes into **-i** and we add **-ly** (*happy – happily*).

Some adverbs take the same form as adjectives:
hard – hard, fast – fast, late – late, early – early.

We use adverbs to define verbs:
- directly after the verb:
  *She **dances beautifully**.*
- after an object, if it is directly after the verb:
  *We **ate our breakfast quickly** and left for our holidays.*

We form the comparative for most adverbs with **more** and the superlative with **the most**:
beautifully – more beautifully – the most beautifully.

Adverbs with the same form as adjectives take the same comparative and superlative forms as the adjectives:
low – lower – the lowest.

Some adverbs take irregular comparative and superlative forms:
- *well – better – the best*
- *badly – worse – the worst*

We can use **adverbs of degree** before both adjectives and adverbs to modify their meaning:
- *a little/a bit/slightly*:
  *Sue says that living in the suburbs is **slightly better** now because there are more shops.*
- *quite/rather/pretty*:
  *Since we redecorated the room, it looks **pretty good**.*
- *really/extremely/completely*:
  *You need to move this chest of drawers **extremely carefully** because it is an antique.*

1 Choose the correct option.

1 This town is *well / extremely* crowded in the summer.
2 You've looked after your garden *good / well*.
3 The dates in this book are *historic / historically* incorrect.
4 Nick works *hard / hardly* to make his home beautiful.
5 The men painted the outside of the house *bad / badly*.
6 He got up *late / lately* this morning and missed the bus.
7 It's *completely / a bit* too dark to read in here.
8 The children are playing surprisingly *quiet / quietly* in the garden.

2 Put the words in the correct order to make sentences.

1 father / the / my / cleans / rather / house / quickly

_____

2 you've / beautifully / your / decorated / room

_____

3 pancakes / makes / pretty / good / Janice

_____

4 your / mine / bigger / is / slightly / wardrobe / than

_____

5 the / carefully / door / close / extremely / front

_____

6 loudly / Laura / the / housework / does / really

_____

3 Make adverbs from the adjectives in the box. Then complete the sentences with the correct adverbs.

> careful easy fast good lucky slow

1 You can _____ have a party in this cosy cottage.
2 How _____ do you play the piano, Bjorn?
3 Please do the washing-up _____ . I don't want you to break my expensive plates.
4 Never drive _____ in a small village – even when you are in a hurry.
5 I love walking _____ through the city centre when I have lots of time.
6 I missed the bus, but _____ there was another one in twenty minutes.

4 UNIT REVIEW Choose the correct answer, A, B or C, to complete the text.

Moving from the city centre and living in the countryside was very strange for me at the beginning. To start with, it is **1**___ quiet compared to living in the city as there is almost no traffic on the roads. We live in a small village and there aren't too many terraced or semi-detached houses. There are beautiful, **2**___ designed stone cottages – most of them with only one or two floors. We live in a bungalow which is **3**___ spacious.
My room, however, is small – but it is very cosy. It's not very entertaining here – there aren't many shops or cafés but there are some amazing **4**___ monuments nearby.
I especially like the ruins of the old castle. We walk there sometimes at the weekends and it's such a fascinating place with lots of gripping stories about it from the past. There are **5**___ views there too, and this Sunday my family and I **6**___ a picnic there. I don't miss life in the city at all!

	A	B	C
1	a bit	extremely	the most
2	tradition	traditional	traditionally
3	pretty	a little	slightly
4	history	historic	historical
5	lush	scorching	breathtaking
6	will have	are having	am going to have

5.2 First Conditional

We use First Conditional sentences to talk about the possible results of an action. First Conditional sentences refer to the future:

If I **tell** them the truth, they **won't believe** me.
He **won't pass** his exams if he **doesn't work** hard.
Will he **pass** his exams **if** he **works** hard?

We use the Present Simple in the if-clause, which describes the condition. We use will/won't in the clause describing the result. Either clause may come first in the sentence. We put a comma at the end of the if-clause if it comes first in the sentence.

If Vicky pays attention in **class, she** will do her homework well.
Vicky will do her homework **well if** she pays attention in class.

If + Present Simple (condition),	will/won't + infinitive (result)
If he **works** hard, **If** George **is** late again,	he **will pass his** exams. the teacher **will send** him to the head teacher.

will/won't + infinitve (result)	if + Present Simple (condition)
He **will pass** his exams The teacher **will send** George to the head teacher	**if** he **works** hard. **if** he **is** late again.

1 Choose the correct option.

1 If Joe *passes / will pass* all his exams, his parents *buy / will buy* him a car.
2 My teacher *doesn't / won't* mind if I *finish / will finish* my essay tomorrow.
3 If Ella *doesn't / won't* find a paid job this year, she *does / will do* voluntary work to get experience.
4 They *miss / will miss* all their friends if they *choose / will choose* to go abroad.
5 If the school uniform *is / will be* compulsory next year, we *have / will have* to wear it.
6 If John *drops / will drop* PE and Art, he *has / will have* more time for academic subjects.
7 *Will you help / Do you help* me with my homework if I *will have / have* a problem?
8 Sandra *doesn't do / won't do* a gap year if she *doesn't save / won't save* some money.

2 Complete the sentences to make them true for you.

1 I will get a place at university if _____
2 If I don't get a place at university, I _____
3 If my timetable is very demanding next year, _____
4 I won't get good marks if _____
5 If I don't get a good job, _____
6 I will move house if _____
7 I will travel round the world if _____
8 If I get stressed about my exams, I _____
9 I will do voluntary work if _____
10 If I have more free time, I _____

3 Put the words in the correct order to make beginnings of sentences. Then match the beginnings (1–5) with the endings (a–e).

1 Andy / carry / will / bag / if / it's / your ☐
_____
2 If / show / watch / you / carefully, / I'll ☐
_____
3 I / you / don't / won't / understand / you / if ☐
_____
4 If / we'll / now, / don't / we / be / leave ☐
_____
5 I / you / help / if / don't / you / won't ☐
_____

a you what to do.
b speak more slowly.
c help me.
d too heavy.
e late for the exam.

4 Write sentences from the prompts. Use the First Conditional.

1 You / not / make friends / if / not speak / new people
_____
2 If / Adam / study / London / improve / English
_____
3 If / I / not / fall asleep / I / finish / my homework
_____
4 We / take / Sociology / next year / if / on the timetable
_____
5 Mum / not happy / if / not pass / my exams
_____

5 Complete the First Conditional sentences with the correct form of the verbs in brackets.

1 If you _____ (not go) abroad, you _____ (not learn) a foreign language.
2 If you _____ (not take) it easy, you _____ (get) sick.
3 Sue _____ (waste) her time if she _____ (go) travelling.
4 _____ (you/phone) me if you _____ (have) time?
5 If it _____ (cost) too much, I _____ (buy) a smaller one.
6 If he _____ (go) backpacking, he _____ (spend) less.
7 She _____ (do) voluntary work if she _____ (go) to Africa.
8 You _____ (miss) the train if you _____ (get up) late.

5.5 Defining relative clauses

In defining relative clauses (which give essential information about a person, thing or place) we use the following relative pronouns:

* **who** and **that** to talk about people:
  *This is the teacher **who/that** teaches my class.*
  *Do you know the girls **who/that** are talking to the PE teacher?*

* **which** and **that** to talk about things:
  *Is this the laptop **which/that** you ordered?*
  *I'll visit you during the term break **which/that** begins next week.*

* **where** to talk about places:
  *We're going to visit the school **where** my mum taught for twenty years.*
  *Ella went to a school **where** most pupils were girls.*

The relative pronouns *who*, *which* and *that* usually come after the noun (i.e. the people, thing or place) they refer to. We can omit the relative pronouns *who*, *which* and *that* if they are followed by a personal pronoun or noun.
*We have a timetable **(which/that) we** can change.*

We **cannot** omit the relative pronoun if it is **not followed** by a personal pronoun or noun.
*We have a gym **which** has a lot of modern equipment.*

1 **Join the pairs of sentences using relative pronouns.**

1 There is a nice café. We can go there.

_____ .

2 I know a boy. He speaks perfect Chinese.

_____ .

3 McDonald's is a restaurant. It sells hamburgers and chips.

_____ .

4 I'm sure you'll find a job. You're going to love it.

_____ .

5 My son knows lots of websites. You can play online games there.

_____ .

6 Tina is a great sportswoman. She never gives up.

_____ .

7 *Titanic* is a film. I've seen it about ten times.

_____ .

8 This is the man. I saw him in front of the jeweller's.

_____ .

2 **Complete the sentences with relative pronouns *who*, *where* or *which* where necessary.**

1 We live in a town doesn't have a university.
2 Do you know the boy is dancing with Molly?
3 Sam used to live in a country the schools are free.
4 This is the teacher teaches my sister.
5 Bath is a small town has many historic sites.
6 What is the school subject you like best?
7 I go to a school uniforms are compulsory.
8 Is this the girl lives in the house opposite yours?
9 France is the country Susan loves the most.

3 **Choose the correct option. More than one answer may be correct.**

1 She's the teacher *who / which* lost my homework.
2 That's the library *where / which* has lots of good DVDs.
3 That's the dog *who / which* stole my bag.
4 There's the staffroom *where / which* the teachers go after class.
5 Is this the biography *who / which* you wanted to borrow from me?
6 There's Jim. He's the person *who / that* can help you.

4 **Complete the sentences with *who, which, where*. Use no pronoun where possible.**

1 Can you tell me _____ Mr Smith is? I can't find him anywhere.
2 PE is the subject _____ Adrian loves the most.
3 She's the professor of Maths _____ Anna admires a lot.
4 Does Jon know _____ room we need to go to next?
5 I can't show you _____ Brian is because I've never seen him.
6 That's the school _____ got the best exam results.

5 **Correct the mistakes.**

1 Ms Armstrong is the teacher which teaches French.
2 Do you know the boys which are waiting in the hall?
3 This is the lab we do science experiments.
4 The playground where is behind the school is the biggest one.
5 That's the girl isn't keeping up with her studies.
6 I know a shop you can get cheap books.
7 Amanda is a girl which never makes mistakes.
8 It's the elementary school where my sister goes to.

6 **Rewrite the sentences without using *who, which, that*.**

1 The book is very interesting. I bought it yesterday.

_____

2 The school is very well organised. We visited it last week.

_____

3 The library didn't have the book. I wanted the book.

_____

4 You've spoken to the man just now. Is the man a friend of yours?

_____

5 The exam was difficult. We did it yesterday.

_____

6 You borrowed a book from me. Can I have the book?

_____

5.6 Future time and conditional clauses

Conditional clauses are introduced with:

- **if**: **If** Mark doesn't hand in his homework today, his Maths teacher will get really angry.
- **unless**: Amy will not make any progress **unless** she works systematically.

Time clauses are introduced with:

- **when**: **When** the new term starts, the teachers will attend a conference.
- **before**: **Before** I take Chemistry and Physics for my A levels, I will talk to my teachers.
- **after**: **After** you mark your students' homework, you will know where they tend to make most mistakes.
- **as soon as**: The kids will feel better **as soon as** the school breaks up for holiday.

We use the Present Simple in future time and conditional clauses.

Subordinate clause		Main clause
if **unless** **when** **before** **after** **as soon as**	**+ Present Simple,**	**will/won't + verb**

My sister will never succeed **unless she learns** from her mistakes.

Either clause may come first in the sentence. We put a comma at the end of the subordinate clause if it comes first in the sentence, but we don't use a comma if the main clause comes first:

I will let you know about the time of our meeting **as soon as I get** my new timetable.
As soon as I get my new timetable, I will let you know about the time of our meeting.

1 Choose the correct option.

1 I like to take it easy *after / unless* I finish football training.
2 Sarah gets into trouble *when / unless* she skips lessons.
3 I'll pay for your tuition fees *if / before* you promise to work hard.
4 *As soon as / Unless* I pass this exam, I'm going to start revising for the next one.
5 Jan won't get good grades *if / unless* he learns how to cope with exam stress.
6 You should always arrive at least fifteen minutes *before / when* an important exam.
7 *If / Unless* you work hard, I'm sure you'll succeed.
8 You should check your homework *while / before* you hand it in.

2 Complete the text with the correct form of the verbs in brackets. Use the First Conditional.

As soon as I [1]_____ (finish) school today, I [2]_____ (go) home and have something to eat. If my mother [3]_____ (be) still at work, I [4]_____ (eat) a cheese and onion sandwich. Before I [5]_____ (watch) my favourite TV series, I [6]_____ (do) my Physics homework.

3 UNIT REVIEW Choose the correct answer, A, B or C to complete the sentences.

1 When the new term starts next month, we _____ such a busy timetable.
   A aren't having
   B don't have
   C won't have
2 We will have more free time _____ our Biology projects.
   A before we complete
   B as soon as we'll finish
   C as soon as we hand in
3 Robert won't keep up with other students _____ in class.
   A unless he pays attention
   B if he won't pay attention
   C if he pays attention
4 You won't fail your exam _____ everything by heart.
   A if you will learn
   B if you learn
   C if you learned
5 As soon as I see my Science teacher today, I _____ her about our next project.
   A ask
   B am asking
   C will ask
6 He'll go to the cinema tomorrow _____ he has too much homework to do.
   A if
   B unless
   C when
7 _____ of other people is very immature.
   A Having fun
   B Laughing
   C Making fun
8 You should _____ these old notebooks. You don't need them.
   A get rid of
   B break up
   C struggle with

6.2 Second Conditional

We use Second Conditional sentences to talk about:
- imaginary situations in the present:
  *If I **were** rich, I **would live** in a huge house.*
  *If Kate **didn't leave** home before rush hour, she **wouldn't arrive** at the office on time.*
- improbable events in the future:
  *If he **left** home earlier, he **would never be** late for work.*
  *If I **weren't** so tall, I **would become** a figure skater.*

We use the Past Simple in the *if*-clause and *would/wouldn't* in the clause describing the result.

As in First Conditional sentences, the clauses can be in either order. We put a comma at the end of the *if*-clause if it comes first in the sentence.

If + Past Simple (condition),	would / wouldn't + infinitive (result).
If Sue knew Italian,	she'd apply for this job.

would / wouldn't + infinitive (result)	if + Past Simple (condition).
Sue would apply for this job	if she knew Italian.

In Second Conditional sentences we use *was* or *were* after *I*, *he*, *she* and *it*. *Were* is more formal.

Remember to use *were* in **If I were you**:

***If I were you**, I would tell him the truth.*

1 Match the sentence halves.

1 If I were a bit taller,
2 Would your uncle know what to do
3 They'd get access to your computer
4 Of course I would take a car to work
5 If we didn't have to look for a summer job,

a if they knew the password.
b we would be on a sunny beach now.
c I could be a fashion model.
d if I had one.
e if he lost his job?

2 Choose the correct option.

What would you do if you ¹*are / were / be* me? I'm a shop assistant, but if I ²*hadn't / wouldn't have / didn't have* a job, I ³*like / liked / would like* to go travelling all year round. But of course, no work means no money. If somebody ⁴*offered / would offer / did offer* me a job in which I could earn money and travel, however, I ⁵*would take / took / had taken* it without thinking! Maybe I should apply for a job as a flight attendant?

3 Choose three to five words from each set to complete the sentence below it.

1 were, would, for, a, be, apply, she, applied
If she were older, she _____ a job in a clothes shop.
2 brother, did, would, I, when, a, have, had
I would never be lonely if _____ or sister.
3 afford, afforded, will, could, house, a, can, big
If we _____ , we'd have lots of parties.
4 time, didn't, she, have, hadn't, any, wouldn't
If Sue worked long hours, _____ to go out with friends.

4 Complete the sentences with the correct form of the verbs in brackets. Use the Second Conditional.

1 If everybody _____ (go) to university, nobody _____ (want) to do hard physical work.
2 Buses _____ (not be) so crowded if more people _____ (work) from home.
3 If people _____ (not apply) for low-paid jobs, salaries _____ (go) up.
4 Family relationships _____ (improve) if parents _____ (spend) more time with their children.
5 You _____ (be) happier if you _____ (have) an interesting and well-paid job.
6 You _____ (get) the sack if you _____ (go) to work late every day.
7 If he _____ (not have) a full-time job, he _____ (spend) more time on his hobbies.
8 If I _____ (work) overtime, I _____ (earn) more money.

5 Rewrite the sentences using the Second Conditional.

1 I don't earn money because I am unemployed.
_____
2 Sue doesn't have a boss because she's self-employed.
_____
3 Ian sleeps during the day because he works night shifts.
_____
4 We have to work outdoors because we're builders.
_____
5 Jim isn't happy because he is badly paid.
_____
6 Abigail has eight weeks of holiday because she is a teacher.
_____
7 Max comes up with good ideas because he's creative.
_____
8 I won't apply for the job because I don't have enough experience.
_____

6.5 Modal verbs for obligation and permission

To express obligation or necessity, we use:

- **must**, especially when we refer to something the speaker feels is necessary:

  I **must** talk to her right now. (I feel this is necessary.)

- **have to**, especially when we refer to something that is necessary because of a rule or law:

  My brother **has to** wear a suit to work. (These are the rules.)

- **need to**:

  Neil often **needs to** do overtime.

To express lack of obligation or necessity, we use:

- **don't have to**:

  A tourist guide **doesn't have to** do physical work.

- **don't need to/needn't**:

  You **needn't** come to the office. You can work from home.
  You **don't need to** write the essay again.

To say what is allowed, we use **can**:

Journalists **can** work flexible hours.

To say what is not allowed, we use:

- **can't**, especially when the speaker feels something is not allowed:

  I **can't** leave the office during office hours.

- **mustn't**, if we want to express strong prohibition:

  You **mustn't** check your private email at work.

Obligation/necessity	Lack of obligation	Allowed	Not allowed/forbidden
have to / has to need to / needs to must	don't have to / doesn't have to don't need to / doesn't need to / needn't	can	can't mustn't

1 Choose the correct answer, a, b or c.

1 You ___ be physically fit to be a fire-fighter.
   a can   b have to   c need

2 A doctor ___ often work long hours and night shifts.
   a must   b can   c can't

3 A teacher ___ look smart or wear a suit to work.
   a mustn't   b doesn't need to   c can't

4 Self-employed people ___ take a holiday any time they choose.
   a need to   b have to   c can

5 A journalist ___ write things which are not true.
   a needn't   b doesn't have to   c mustn't

6 Office workers usually ___ take many breaks during the day.
   a can't   b don't have to   c needn't

7 You ___ take a taxi. I can drive you to work.
   a can't   b needn't   c mustn't

8 Airline pilots ___ have excellent eyesight.
   a must   b need   c can

2 Choose the correct option.

1 **A:** Is it a formal meeting?
   B: No, you *must / don't need to / can* wear a tie.

2 **A:** Can I smoke in here?
   B: I'm afraid not. You *need to / needn't / mustn't* smoke anywhere inside this building.

3 **A:** What's wrong? You look stressed.
   B: I am. I *can / needn't / have to* finish all this work before the end of the week. There's so much of it!

4 **A:** Mr Long, I'd like to take a day off tomorrow.
   B: Sorry, I'm afraid you *don't need to / must / can't*.

5 **A:** You look worried. What's wrong?
   B: I have a meeting with my boss today. I *needn't / need to / don't need to* get to work on time. Otherwise, I'll lose my job.

6 **A:** Why can't Sarah come with us?
   B: She *mustn't / has to / can* prepare a presentation for her boss.

7 **A:** *Do I have to / Must I* pay in cash?
   B: No, you *needn't / mustn't* pay in cash. Your credit card will be enough.

3 Complete the second sentence so that it has the same meaning as the first. Use no more than five words including the word in capitals.

1 The company expects you to wear a uniform at work. **HAVE**
   You _____ a uniform at work.

2 It's not necessary for you to work long hours. **NEED**
   You _____ long hours.

3 It's forbidden to bring dogs into the laboratory. **MUST**
   You _____ into the laboratory.

4 It isn't necessary for Mike to bring his laptop today. **HAVE**
   Mike _____ bring his laptop today.

5 It's not OK for you to be smoking cigarettes in the office. **CAN'T**
   You _____ in the office.

4 Rewrite the parts of sentences in italics with *mustn't* or *don't have to*.

1 You *are not obliged* to work on Sundays.
   _____

2 *It's forbidden to* smoke in here.
   _____

3 You*'re not allowed to* wait here.
   _____

4 *It's unnecessary for you* to wait here.
   _____

5 *It's forbidden to* walk on the lawn.
   _____

6 *It isn't necessary* for them to work on Sunday.
   _____

6.6 Adjectives ending in -ed and -ing

Pairs of **-ed/-ing** adjectives are formed from the same verb:

amuse – amus**ing** – amus**ed**

motivate – motivat**ing** – motivat**ed**

terrify – terrif**ying** – terrif**ied**

Some **-ed** adjectives do not have an **-ing** equivalent: ashamed, delighted, relieved.

We use **-ing** adjectives to describe:

• people: A **growing child** needs to eat a lot.

• objects/places: **My new office** is rather **depressing.** It's very small and dark.

• events: **The first job interview** is usually **challenging,** especially if the candidates aren't very well prepared.

We use **-ed** adjectives to describe:

• states (of people or objects): **The instructor** was a **determined** person, who wanted to teach us some new skiing techniques.

• emotions and feelings: **Maria** looked rather **confused** when she first arrived in our office.

1 Choose the correct option.

1 It's *disappointing / disappointed* that my first job is so badly paid.

2 Working and studying at the same time is often quite *challenged / challenging*.

3 Kate is quite *excited / exciting* about the idea of being self-employed.

4 Getting the sack can be *depressed / depressing* and stressful.

5 It's *disgusted / disgusting* that Elizabeth had to resign from her job after twenty-five years.

6 I'm really *encouraging / encouraged* by the fact that I won the competition.

2 Complete the sentences with the correct form of the words in the box. Use -ed or -ing endings to make adjectives.

confuse demand encourage move relieve reward

1 The documentary film about social workers was so _____ that I almost cried.

2 I had trouble finding the keys for the office, so I was _____ when I finally found them in my car.

3 Working for a foreign company is sometimes _____ because they do things differently.

4 The job of a ski instructor is quite _____ – it's not all fun in the snow!

5 Margot felt _____ after she read her boss's positive report on her work.

6 Teachers have a really hard but _____ job. Would you like to be a teacher?

3 UNIT REVIEW Choose the correct answer, A, B or C, to complete the dialogue.

1 **X:** How did your job interview go?

  Y: They asked me a lot of personal questions and it wasn't very nice.

  X: ___

  A How embarrassing!   **B** I'm so relieved!

  C It sounds like a satisfying experience.

2 **X:** I'm determined to become a police officer.

  Y: ___

  X: I know. But I don't want to do anything too easy or repetitive.

  A It's a charming job.   **B** It's a rewarding job.

  C It's a challenging job.

3 **X:** The financial situation at Paul's company does not look good.

  Y: ___

  A Yes, it is worrying.   **B** Yes, it is worried.

  C Yes, they worried.

4 **X:** What does your dad do?

  Y: He drives a taxi all day. When he gets home, ___ .

  A it's exhausted

  B he's exhausting

  C he's exhausted

5 **X:** I don't understand these instructions. They're terrible!

  Y: I agree. ___

  A They're confusing.

  B I'm confusing.

  C They're confused.

6 **X:** There's a lot of competition in advertising.

  Y: ___

  X: Then you should be fine.

  A Well, I like to compete.

  B Well, it is a good competition.

  C Well, I'm not very competitive.

7 **X:** You never have any free time.

  Y: ___

  A I know. I work night shifts.

  B I know. I work long hours.

  C I know. I work part-time.

8 **X:** Why do you want to be a taxi driver?

  Y: ___

  X: That's not a very good reason!

  A Because I have to wear a uniform.

  B Because I mustn't wear a uniform.

  C Because I needn't wear a uniform.

7.2 The Passive

We use the Passive when the action is more important than the person who performs it. If we want to add information about the person (the agent), we use the word **by**:

*This shopping mall **is visited by** about 50,000 people every day.*

*How many languages **are spoken** in the USA?*

We form the Passive for different tenses with the correct form of *be* and the Past Participle. In modal clauses, we use a modal verb before *be*.

*Designer clothes **can be found** in high street shops.*

Present Simple Passive	Tea **is grown** in India. Cars **are** not **repaired** here. Where **are** the tickets **sold**?
Past Simple Passive	I **was offered** a job. These tablets **were** not **produced** in China. Where **was** our car **made**?
Present Perfect Passive	The house in Green Street **has been sold**. We **have** not **been informed** about the change. **Has** he **been invited** to Emma's wedding?
Modal verbs	Conditions **must be improved**. Parcels **can be sent** at the post office. Do the rooms **need to be cleaned** every day?

1 Put the words in the correct order to make sentences.

1 be / music / iTunes store / downloaded / from / can / the

_____

2 organically / plants / farm / on / are / our / grown

_____

3 uniforms / are / by / England / all schoolchildren / worn / in ?

_____

4 have / since 1988 / been / these shoes / produced

_____

5 son / month / is / given / presents / their / every

_____

2 Choose the correct option.

1 Movie stars *pay / are paid* a lot of money to advertise products.

2 The factory *mustn't sell / mustn't be sold* to an American company because people will lose their jobs.

3 Francis *taught / was taught* English in Thailand for two years and he really loved the job.

4 The play *has performed / has been performed* in over 200 theatres worldwide.

5 Fairtrade food *has produced / has been produced* for many years now in developing countries.

6 The musicians *gave / were given* their money from the concert to charity.

7 England's prestige football matches *played / have been played* at Wembley since 1923.

8 Jenny *surprised / was surprised* I bought her some flowers.

3 Complete the second sentence so that it has the same meaning as the first. Use the passive.

1 We must protect the environment.
The environment _____ .

2 Department stores sell many different things.
Many different things _____ in department stores.

3 These days, you can do all your shopping online.
These days, all your shopping _____ .

4 You mustn't eat food in the clothes shop.
Food _____ in the clothes shop.

5 Martin didn't set up the company.
The company _____ Martin.

6 Does your aunt own that shop?
_____ your aunt?

7 We can't refund your money.
Your money _____ .

8 They don't make these shoes in England.
These shoes _____ in England.

4 Complete the text with the correct form (active or passive) of the verbs in brackets.

Post offices [1]_____ (use) to deliver letters and packages for over 300 years. In fact, the term 'post office' [2]_____ (exist) even in the 1650s in the UK. Early mail [3]_____ (deliver) on horses, and 'post houses' [4]_____ (build) every few miles between major cities. Here, postmen could feed their horses and rest for a while. These post houses, or 'post stations' in the US, [5]_____ (disappear) when trains and trucks [6]_____ (become) a more popular way of transporting mail.

Today, post offices are very different. Of course, they still [7]_____ (send) our mail. But other services like banking [8]_____ (offer) there too. Since the invention of the Internet, however, the post office has become less important in our lives and, because of modern technology, the transfer of information is now quicker and cheaper than ever before.

5 Correct the mistakes.

1 My car has stolen from the shopping centre car park.

2 Was that email send this morning?

3 Is it true that Aston Martin cars made by hand?

4 We have repaired your computer and it can collect this afternoon.

5 The new greengrocer's on the corner run by my mum.

6 Some great clothes can find at vintage shops.

7 The book I ordered online wasn't delivered yet.

8 Did you give a refund by the shop manager?

7.5 Quantifiers

To talk or ask about quantities, we use the following quantifiers:

Countable nouns	Uncountable nouns
How many? **How many** friends have you got?	How much? **How much** money have you got?
(very) few I've got **(very) few** friends.	(very) little I've got **(very) little** money.
a few I've got **a few** friends.	a little I've got **a little** money.
some I've got **some** friends. I've got **some** money.	
many Have you got **many** friends? I haven't got **many** friends.	much Have you got **much** money? I haven't got **much** money.
a lot of / lots of I've got **a lot of/lots of** friends. I've got **a lot of/lots of** money.	
too many I've got **too many** friends.	too much I've got **too much** money.
any Have you got **any** friends? Have you got **any** money?	
any I haven't got **any** friends. I haven't got **any** money.	

1 Complete the dialogue with quantifiers in the box.

> any (x2)   how many   little   lot of   some   too much

Pia: Thanks for inviting me to your party, Sam. You've got a **1**_____ presents! **2**_____ do you think you've got?

Sam: Maybe ten or twelve. And my parents gave me **3**_____ money. Have you had **4**_____ birthday cake? It's really delicious. Here, try some.

Pia: Oh, thanks, I'll have just a **5**_____ , please. I've already eaten quite a lot. Have you got **6**_____ orange juice?

Sam: Yes, I bought twenty litres. I think we have **7**_____ .

2 Complete the sentences with *few*, *little*, a *few* or a *little*.

1 'Have you read any books by Stevenson?' 'Yes, I've read .'

2 He's got very friends.

3 There were very people at the party.

4 The teacher gave us extra time for the exercise, so I could complete it.

5 The teacher gave us time for the exercise. I couldn't complete it.

6 He had soup for supper.

7 He always has very sugar in his coffee.

8 Buy bananas when you go to the supermarket, please.

3 Complete the sentences with *a*, *an*, *some*, *any*, *how much* or *how many*.

1 'Have you got orange juice?' 'There's in the fridge.'

2 'Did you buy milk?' 'No, I forgot. But there is carton left in the fridge.'

3 Would you like apple? There are in the fruit bowl.

4 'Would you like water?' 'Yes, please. I'll have glass.'

5 'cola do we need?' 'I don't know. There'll be twenty people at the party.' 'Will can each be enough?'

6 Would you like chocolate? There's bar on the table. Have some!

7 pieces of cake have you eaten? Didn't you say you were on a diet?

8 I'd like egg and some toast for breakfast, but there aren't eggs.

9 'cola do you want?' 'I don't want.'

10 'bottles of water do we need for the picnic?'…'Just one. Our friends are bringing too.'

4 Choose the correct answer, A, B or C.

1 There are a _____ shopping centres in this town.
   A lots   **B** lots of   **C** lot of

2 I don't like this shop because there are _____ products to choose from.
   A very few   **B** very little   **C** a few

3 In tourist areas, there are _____ many of exactly the same shops.
   A a bit   **B** too   **C** far

4 Ellen got _____ money for her birthday, so she's going shopping.
   A a little   **B** a few   **C** little

5 I haven't bought _____ new clothes this year.
   A much   **B** some   **C** any

6 Julie, _____ online shopping sites do you use?
   A any   **B** how many   **C** how much

7.6 Indefinite pronouns

We use indefinite pronouns to talk about non-specific people, objects or places.

All indefinite pronouns are used with singular verb forms.
Everybody is fashionable in their own way.

People	Things	Places
someone/somebody	*something*	*somewhere*
anyone/anybody	*anything*	*anywhere*
no one/nobody	*nothing*	*nowhere*
everyone/everybody	*everything*	*everywhere*

We use **someone/somebody, something, somewhere** in affirmative sentences and requests/offers:
Somebody has left their receipt on the counter.

We use **anybody/anyone, anything, anywhere** in negative sentences and questions:
*I haven't bought **anything** made of leather for a long time.*

We use **no one/nobody, nothing, nowhere** in affirmative sentences with a negative meaning:
*I'm not going to the shopping centre today. There will be **nowhere** to park.*

We do not use another negative in a clause with *nobody, no one, nothing, nowhere*.

We use **none (of)** when we talk about three or more objects or people. We don't use nouns after **none**:
*I was looking for some comfortable high heels but I found **none**.*

We use an article + noun after **none of** (*the people*),
a possessive adjective (*my friends*) or a personal pronoun (*us*).
Plural nouns are followed by singular or plural verb forms:
None of her children **is/are** into trade.

We can modify indefinite pronouns with:
- to infinitve:
  *There is **nobody to go** window shopping with me.*
- an adjective:
  *Joan needs to go **somewhere quiet** to rest after work.*
- a relative pronoun (*who, which, that*):
  *A debtor is **somebody who** has spent more money than he or she has got.*

1 **Choose the correct option.**

1 There isn't a post office *everywhere / anywhere* near here.
2 He was looking for some T-shirts for his holiday, but he found *none / some*.
3 I don't think the shop is closed. I can see *someone / anyone* in there.
4 There's *anything / nothing* to buy here. Let's go to another shop.
5 Gyms have become very popular – they're *somewhere / everywhere*.
6 When I can't find *something / anything* I want in the shops, I go online.
7 I'm sure there's a florist's here *somewhere / anywhere*.
8 I never go to that newsagent's. *Someone / Everyone* there is so rude!

2 **Complete the sentences with the correct word in the box.**

anybody anywhere everything nothing
somebody somewhere

1 Do you know _____ that is a billionaire?
2 It's sunny today, but I think I saw _____ wearing wellington boots.
3 I'm not saying I like _____ in the jeweller's, but there are a lot of nice things.
4 Honestly, there was _____ in the clothes shop that suited me.
5 Oh, no! I've lost my ballet flats. They could be _____ .
6 I know they make green Dr Martens so they have to sell them _____ .

3 **Complete the text with appropriate indefinite pronouns.**

It's a fact that [1]_____ I know wears designer clothes or has a special look which makes them cool. But no matter what I wear I always look unfashionable or scruffy. Maybe it's [2]_____ to do with my hairstyle – who knows? Last week, for example, I tried to buy a new pair of glasses. I looked [3]_____ for a pair that suited me and went to every optician I could find. And, surprise surprise, I didn't buy [4]_____ . Is there [5]_____ in this whole town that sells the things I want to make me look good? Maybe there is [6]_____ that looks like me and I have to find an original and unique style all of my own.

4 **UNIT REVIEW Choose the answer, A, B or C, that is closest in meaning to the words in bold.**

1 **There isn't anything tasty** in my local baker's.
   A There is nothing tasty
   B Not everything is tasty
   C There is nothing as tasty
2 **Is it possible for a person to walk** in such high heels?
   A Can nobody walk
   B Can everybody walk
   C Can anybody walk
3 **None of the people I know like** to buy clothes in a vintage shop.
   A No one I know likes
   B Not everybody I know likes
   C Somebody I know likes
4 These trainers are **cheaper than usual**.
   A on offer   B not worth it
   C an investment
5 **There are some** schoolboys at the checkout desk.
   A There are few   B There are a few
   C There are very little
6 Professional footballers **earn too much**, in my opinion.
   A pay too much
   B are paid too much
   C paid too much

8.2 Past Perfect

We use the Past Perfect to talk about the earliest of two or more events in the past. The action expressed in the Past Perfect happened before the action usually expressed in the Past Simple:

*When Alex got to hospital, he **had** already **come** out in a rash.* (The rash appeared before he got to the hospital.)

Notice how the Past Perfect changes the meaning of these sentences:

*The children **went** to sleep when we came.* (First we came and then the children went to sleep.)
*The children **had gone** to sleep when we came.* (The children were asleep when we came.)

We often use **by** with the Past Perfect, e.g. *by the age of six, by the time I was six, by 1978*:

By *the time I was six, I had learnt to read.*

Affirmative			Negative		
I/You/He/She/It/We/They	had	watched TV.	I/You/He/She/It/We/They	hadn't (had not)	watched TV.

Yes/No questions			Short answers
Had	I/you/he/she/it/we/they	watched TV?	Yes, I/you/he/she/it/we/they had. No, I/you/he/she/it/we/they hadn't.

Wh- questions				Subject questions		
What	had	I/you/he/she/it/we/they	watched?	Who	had	watched TV?

1 **Complete the sentences with the correct form of the verbs in brackets.**

1 Betty _____ (feel) nervous because she _____ (not be) in hospital before.
2 Sue _____ (wait) nearly an hour before the doctor _____ (see) her.
3 I _____ (forget) to take my medicine so I _____ (begin) to feel dizzy.
4 By the time Mandy _____ (fall) asleep she _____ (finish) reading her book on acupuncture.
5 Tony _____ (come out) in a rash, probably because he _____ (eat) nuts.
6 Before I _____ (buy) a new pair of glasses I _____ (had) my eyes tested at the optician's.
7 He _____ (see) the dentist because he _____ (break) a tooth playing football.
8 By the time the ambulance _____ (arrive), Jane _____ (begin) to feel much better.

2 **Choose the correct explanation, a or b, for each sentence.**

1 The patient had left the health centre when the receptionist arrived.
   a The receptionist saw the patient.
   b The receptionist didn't see the patient.
2 When Rodney broke his arm, he grew a beard.
   a He broke his arm with a beard.
   b He broke his arm without a beard.
3 Just before the plane had landed I began to feel ill.
   a I began to feel ill while flying.
   b I began to feel ill on the ground.
4 By the time we got to the cinema, I had got a headache.
   a My headache started before we arrived at the cinema.
   b My headache started after we arrived at the cinema.
5 I stopped eating cake when I got a stomachache.
   a My stomachache started while I was eating the cake.
   b My stomachache started after eating the cake.
6 Ida sat down when she started to feel dizzy.
   a Ida sat down before she started to feel dizzy.
   b Ida sat down after she started to feel dizzy.

3 **Complete the second sentence so that it means the same as the first. Use the Past Perfect and the Past Simple in each sentence.**

1 I wasn't worried about the mystery illness. The doctors found a cure for it before.
   The doctors _____ so _____ .
2 The patient was released from hospital. Then a new problem was found.
   When the new problem _____ .
3 The ambulance arrived. Before then, the police officer saved the woman's life.
   The police officer _____ before _____ .
4 I couldn't pay for my medicine. I left my wallet at home.
   I _____ because _____ .
5 Michael couldn't concentrate on the lecture. He began to feel ill.
   Because Michael _____ .
6 My thumb hurt. I answered all of my text messages.
   By the time _____ .

4 **Choose the correct option.**

1 By the time the ambulance *had arrived / arrived*, the woman *stopped / had stopped* bleeding.
2 My sore throat *went / had gone* by the time I *found / had found* a chemist's that was open.
3 My back *hurt / had hurt* because I *fell / had fallen* down the stairs.
4 I *had / had had* a pain in my right leg before I *ran / had run* the marathon.
5 Hannah's temperature *dropped / had dropped* after she *took / had taken* the medicine.
6 By the time we *got / had got* to Calais on the ferry, I *started / had started* to feel seasick.

8.5 Reported Speech

To report what other people said, we can quote their actual words (Direct Speech) or use Reported Speech.

We do not change the quoted words in Direct Speech:
'We **are playing** on a new basketball court.' → They said: 'We **are playing** on a new basketball court.'

In Reported Speech we often use say (that) and tell sb (that). That may be omitted. We also use indirect objects (me, us, etc.)
'The match is great.' → She **told me/said (that)** the match was great.
'I felt dizzy.' → He told me (that) he **had felt** dizzy.

Tenses change in Reported Speech:

Direct Speech	→	Reported Speech
Present Simple Sam: 'I work.' 'Sue doesn't work.'	→	**Past Simple** Sam said (that) he worked. Sam said (that) Sue didn't work.
Present Continuous Sam: 'I'm working.' 'Sue isn't working.'	→	**Past Continuous** Sam said (that) he was working. Sam said (that) Sue wasn't working.
Present Perfect Sam: 'I've worked.' 'Sue hasn't worked.'	→	**Past Perfect** Sam said (that) he had worked. Sam said (that) Sue hadn't worked.
Past Simple Sam: 'I worked.' 'Sue didn't work.'	→	**Past Perfect** Sam said (that) he had worked. Sam said (that) Sue hadn't worked.
can Sam: 'I can work.' 'Sue can't work.'	→	**could** Sam said (that) he could work. Sam said (that) Sue couldn't work.

Pronouns and possesive adjectives also change:
'**My** brother has bought a new tennis racket.' → She said that **her** brother had bought a new tennis racket.

1 Match the sentence halves.

1 Jason said he wasn't ☐
2 Tracy told me she didn't ☐
3 Daisy said she had ☐
4 Liam told me he ☐

a have a dentist's appointment.
b was checking his pulse.
c feeling dizzy.
d made bad choices.

2 Complete the second sentence so that it means the same as the first.

1 'You are allergic to cats,' said the doctor.
   The doctor told me _____ .
2 'I came out in spots after using that cream,' said Daisy.
   Daisy told us _____ .
3 'I can't work out how to open the bottle of medicine,' said John.
   John said _____ .
4 'You've lost a lot of weight,' Dr Lund said to Magda.
   Dr Lund told Magda _____ .
5 'I practise meditation to reduce stress,' Morris told me.
   Morris told me _____ .
6 'I don't work out enough,' Tracy said to me.
   Tracy told me _____ .
7 'I'm not taking up tennis,' Richard said.
   Richard said _____ .
8 'I've got a runny nose,' said Phil.
   Phil told us _____ .

3 Rewrite the sentences in Direct Speech.

1 Arthur said that the ice rink had been destroyed in the storm.
   Arthur said: 'The ice rink _____ in the storm.'
2 Joe told me he kept fit by jogging every day.
   Joe said: 'I _____ every day.'
3 Harriet said she didn't feel dizzy.
   Harriet said: 'I _____ dizzy.'
4 Judson told me that he was getting over the flu.
   Judson said: 'I _____ the flu.'
5 Maria told me she couldn't make difficult decisions.
   Maria said: 'I _____ difficult decisions.'
6 Alan said he had lost his appetite.
   Alan said: 'I _____ appetite.'

4 Choose the correct option.

1 I *said / told* you that I was allergic to mushrooms.
2 Have I *said / told* I'm feeling a little stressed at the moment?
3 Tammy *said / told* me you'd made a complaint.
4 Luther *said / told* the doctor he had a pain in his chest.
5 Mark and Jill both *said / told* they had to go to the dentist's today.

5 Correct the mistakes.

1 Oli said me that he had passed out at the concert the day before, but he was feeling better now.
2 Ewa told us didn't keep track of her diet, so she didn't know how much weight she'd lost.
3 Hugh said he has broken his hand on the volleyball court last week.
4 Rachel said she sick this morning, so decided to stay at home.
5 Jack said he works all day today so he couldn't join us for lunch.
6 I asked Olga about her favourite sport and she told she did yoga every day.

8.6 Phrasal verbs

Phrasal verbs are formed by a main verb and preposition or adverb, e.g. *look* (main verb) + *for* (preposition) = *look for*

Types of phrasal verbs:

- without an object: *join in, work out, fit in, pass out:*
  *How often do you **work out** in the gym?*
  *Yesterday was very hot and a few people **passed out** because of that.*
- with an object after the phrasal verb or between the main verb and preposition. We only use pronouns (him, them, it) between the main verb and preposition:
  *I **took up** handball and rugby at the same time.*
  *I **took** handball and rugby **up** at the same time.*
  *I **took** them **up** at the same time.*
  ~~*I **took up** them at the same time.*~~
- with an object (both noun and pronoun):
  *Every spring my brother **suffers from** an allergy.*
  *Every spring my brother **suffers from** it.*

Phrasal verbs may also be made of three parts and followed by an object (noun or pronoun), e.g.
look forward to sth (main verb + adverb + preposition + object):
*We **look forward to** playing basketball in our new court.*

1 Match the sentence halves.

1 You should cut ☐
2 It's mean to put ☐
3 My grandfather suffers ☐
4 It isn't easy to cope ☐
5 I really need to catch ☐

a from a sore back.
b sugar out of your diet.
c up on my sleep.
d people down like that.
e with school and work.

2 Correct the mistakes.

1 Patrick is new to the motor racing team, but I'm sure he will fit himself in.
2 David has taken on running and he's so fit now!
3 It's important for team members to get on each other if they are to perform well.
4 If you think there's a problem, remember that you can talk over it with me.
5 If you want to join our rugby match in, just ask.
6 I nearly passed it out when I saw all the blood.

3 Complete each sentence with the correct form of a verb and a preposition in the box.

> behind fall figure give go in join
> out over sign up up

1 You need to _____ at the sports club if you want to be on the handball team.
2 Michael Jordan said you should never _____ your dreams if you want to be successful.
3 I can't _____ how this app works and I need your help, I'm afraid.
4 I've _____ these instructions five times and I still don't understand them.
5 Claire _____ with her schoolwork because she was busy with the volleyball team.
6 Sophie _____ the football match and scored two goals. She's great!

4 UNIT REVIEW Choose the correct answer, A, B, or C, to complete both sentences.

1 You need to ___ out a couple of times a week to stay fit.
  Do you always ___ such long hours in the greengrocer's?
  A take   B work   C keep
2 Don't come too close to me because I've ___ a sore throat.
  I was sad when we lost the match but I quickly ___ over it.
  A got   B had   C suffered
3 You should never ___ somebody down if you want to motivate them.
  Why don't you ___ this face mask on if you're having trouble breathing?
  A get   B put   C keep
4 How do you keep ___ of your heart rate?
  They're building a running ___ next to the school.
  A check   B court   C track
5 I'm ___ forward to the final of the Champion's League.
  Who is ___ after your pets while you're on holiday?
  A going   B looking   C taking
6 It wasn't easy for Jake to ___ in with the boys in the team.
  I can't wear these football boots because they don't ___ .
  A fit   B join   C suit
7 The manager told me ___ he was looking for you.
  He's the chef ___ cooks excellent vegetarian food.
  A who   B that   C why
8 She ___ the decision to leave the volleyball team.
  If you ___ an effort, you would lose more weight.
  A took   B did   C made

PREPOSITIONS

PREPOSITIONS IN PHRASES

AT
at all (2.4): *The place hasn't changed at all.*
at first (2.8): *At first he seemed strict, but now I really like him.*
at the age of (5.4): *Jamie won his first tournament at the age of fifteen.*
at the beginning (4.7): *At the beginning of each lesson there is usually a revision exercise.*
at the door (2.2): *There is someone at the front door; can you answer it, please?*
at the end (5.1): *Rob's moving to Maine at the end of May.*
at the weekend (4.6) (Br.E.)/**on the weekend** (Am.E.): *I like to play golf at the weekend.*

BY
by credit card (7.8): *It's more convenient for me to pay by credit card.*

FOR
for a while (2.8): *At last, he could relax for a while.*
for ages (7.1): *I haven't seen Lorna for ages.*
for instance (6.3): *She's totally unreliable – for instance, she often leaves the children alone in the house.*
for your information (6.7): *For your information, I've worked as a journalist for six years.*

FROM
from time to time (5.3): *We see each other from time to time.*

IN
in common (1.8): *I found I had a lot in common with Mary.*
in fact (1.1): *I know her really well; in fact I had dinner with her last week.*
in favour of (5.2): *Are you in favour of the death penalty?*
in my opinion (3.8): *In my opinion, he made the right decision.*
in need (7.5): *We must care for those in need.*
in the background (3.8): *In the background you can see the school.*
in the corner (4.3): *Jo was sitting in the corner of the room.*
in the end (2.8): *In the end, we decided to go to Florida.*
in the foreground (3.8): *There were three figures in the foreground.*
in the middle (3.8): *Why's your car parked in the middle of the road?*
in the world (3.2): *You're the best dad in the world.*

ON
on a website (6.7): *Responses will be posted on the website.*
on a train/plane (4.2): *There were a lot of tourists on the train.*
on foot (4.7): *We set out on foot to explore the city.*
on special offer (7.1): *I got a really nice cashmere pullover – it was on special offer.*
on my/your etc. own (2.8): *Did you make that all on your own?*
on the one hand ... on the other hand ... (8.7): *On the one hand, they work slowly, but on the other hand they always finish the job.*
on the phone (1.4): *Turn the TV down – I'm on the phone!*
on time (5.1): *In Japan the trains are always on time.*

PREPOSITIONS AFTER NOUNS
attitude to/towards (1.5): *He has a very old-fashioned attitude to women.*
candidate for (6.7): *Sara seems to be a good candidate for the job.*
opinion about/on (1.5): *Can I ask your opinion about something?*
reason for (7.7): *Did he give any reason for leaving?*
solution to (7.8): *The solution to the puzzle is on p. 14.*

PREPOSITIONS AFTER ADJECTIVES
allergic to (8.1): *If you are allergic to nuts, you should tell everybody.*
annoyed with (2.5): *Are you annoyed with me just because I'm a bit late?*
bad at (1.7): *I'm not bad at volleyball.*
capable of (7.3): *Do you think he's capable of murder?*
connected with (5.5): *Police think the killings may be connected with each other in some way.*
crazy about (1.7): *Lee's crazy about cats.*
different from (2.6): *New York and Chicago are very different from each other.*
disappointed with (1.7): *Local residents were disappointed with the decision.*
excited about (1.7): *The kids are getting really excited about our trip to California.*
famous for (4.7): *France is famous for its wine.*
good at (1.4): *Andrea is very good at languages.*
interested in (1.7): *All she's interested in is boys!*
involved in (1.7): *How many people are involved in the decision-making process?*
keen on (1.7): *I'm not very keen on their music.*
mad about (1.7): *I'm mad about shopping, I spend lots of money on clothes.*
obsessed with (1.7): *William is obsessed with making money.*
passionate about (1.2): *I've always been passionate about football.*
proud of (3.4): *Her parents are very proud of her.*
responsible for (6.1): *She's responsible for the day-to-day running of the department.*
sensitive to (1.3): *Good teachers are sensitive to their students' needs.*
serious about (1.7): *I'm serious about politics.*
similar to (3.4): *Your shoes are similar to mine.*
sorry about/for (1.7): *I'm so sorry about your father.*
useless at (1.7): *I'm useless at sport and I'm very unfit.*
worried about (1.8): *I'm worried about the world.*

PREPOSITIONS AFTER VERBS
adapt to (1.3): *Old people find it hard to adapt to life in a foreign country.*
agree on (8.7): *We're still trying to agree on a date for the wedding.*
(dis)agree with (2.2): *I agree with Karen. It's much too expensive.*
apply for (2.4): *Kevin's applied for a job in Atlanta.*
apply to (5.3): *You can apply to five different universities.*
ask for (5.7): *Some people don't like to ask for help.*
care about (1.4): *He doesn't care about anybody but himself.*
communicate with (8.7): *They communicated with each other using sign language.*
compare with/to (3.5): *Compared to our small flat, Bill's house seems like a palace.*
compete against/with (5.5): *We've had to cut our prices in order to compete with the big supermarkets.*
complain about (7.7): *She often complains about not feeling appreciated at work.*
exchange for (7.7): *Can I exchange this shirt for a smaller one?*
focus on (1.4): *In his speech he focused on the economy.*
graduate from (2.6): *Ruth has just graduated from Princeton.*
help with (1.6): *Dad, can you help me with my homework?*
invite to (4.3): *Who should we invite to the party?*
judge by (7.1): *You should never judge people by their looks.*
learn from (1.3): *The student will learn from experience about the importance of planning.*
listen to (1.3): *Have you listened to these tapes yet?*
pay for (5.7): *How much did you pay for that watch?*
recover from (8.1): *It always takes me a while to recover from a cold.*
revise for (5.1): *She's revising for her history exam.*
separate from (4.7): *Separate the egg yolk from the white.*
share with (4.3): *I shared a room with her at college.*
spend on (1.4): *I spent £40 on these shoes.*
start with (1.7): *The festivities started with a huge fireworks display.*
thank for (1.7): *We'd like to thank everybody for all the wedding presents.*

Use a dictionary to translate the phrasal verbs into your language.

believe in (1.4) – _____ : *Do you believe in ghosts?*

belong to (2.4) – _____ : *Antarctica doesn't belong to any nation.*

break up (5.1) – _____ : *We break up in December for our winter holiday.*

breathe in (8.8) – _____ : *The doctor made me breathe in while he listened to my chest.*

breathe out (8.8) – _____ : *Jim breathed out deeply.*

care for (6.2) – _____ : *Angie stopped working to care for her mother.*

catch up on (8.6) – _____ : *You need some time to catch up on your work.*

cheer up (7.3) – _____ : *He bought her some flowers to cheer her up.*

chill out (5.5) – _____ : *We spent most of the holiday chilling out on the beach.*

come back (2.7) – _____ : *When is your sister coming back from Europe?*

come on (5.8) – _____ : *Oh, come on, don't lie to me!*

come out (3.4) – _____ : *When a new superhero movie comes out, it dominates the box office for weeks.*

come out in a rash (8.1) – _____ : *If I eat eggs, I come out in a rash.*

come round (4.3) – _____ : *Paul is coming round to my house for tea.*

come up with (6.1) – _____ : *They still haven't come up with a name for the baby.*

cut out (8.1) – _____ : *Make healthy food choices and cut out things that are bad for you.*

deal with 1. (1.4) – _____ : *They had to deal with big changes in technology.* 2. (7.4) – _____: *Who's dealing with the new account?*

depend on (1.4) – _____ : *The length of time spent exercising depends on the sport you are training for.*

fall behind (8.6) – _____ : *After her time in hospital, Jenny's parents are afraid she has fallen behind educationally.*

figure out (8.6) – _____ : *Detectives are still trying to figure out what happened.*

find out (3.4) – _____ : *We never found out her name.*

fit in (8.6) – _____ : *I never really fitted in at school.*

get away (4.3) – _____ : *The two men got away in a red car.*

get into (5.1) – _____ : *You'll have to work harder if you want to get into college.*

get on (with) 1. (5.1) – _____ : *She doesn't get on with her mother at all.* 2. (8.6) – _____ : *Stop talking and get on with your work.*

get up (1.4) – _____ : *Even when they go out until late, they still get up for work.*

give out (2.5) – _____ : *Give out the leaflets as they're leaving the club.*

get over (8.1) – _____ : *It's taken me ages to get over the flu.*

get through (8.6) – _____ : *Don't worry – I'll get through this.*

give up (5.6) – _____ : *Vlad has given up trying to teach me Russian.*

go out (1.4) – _____ : *Are you going out tonight?*

go over (8.6) – _____ : *I just want to go over some lessons from last week.*

grow up (1.4) – _____ : *I grew up in Glasgow and went to school there.*

hand in (5.1) – _____ : *Some students didn't hand in their homework on time.*

hang out (with) (8.6) – _____ : *I don't have anyone to hang out with at break time.*

hear from (1.7) – _____ : *Have you heard from Jane?*

invest in (7.2) – _____ : *I think it's time to invest in a new pair of jeans.*

join in (8.6) – _____ : *Everyone joined in the conversation.*

keep out (5.5) – _____ : *My coat is really warm and it keeps the rain out.*

let in (4.3) – _____ : *Don't let them in.*

look after (1.1) – _____ : *We look after Rodney's kids after school.*

look for (6.6) – _____ : *He's looked for the file but hasn't found it.*

look forward to (doing sth) (1.1) – _____ : *I'm really looking forward to going to Japan.*

look up (2.5) – _____ : *If you don't know the word, look it up in the dictionary.*

move up (5.1) – _____ : *The kids learn fast, and can't wait to move up to the junior team.*

pass out (8.1) – _____ : *Get an app that tells you to drink water before you pass out.*

put down (8.6) – _____ : *Stop putting yourself down!*

put on (2.8) – _____ : *Let's put some music on.*

put up with (6.1) – _____ : *I don't know how you put up with all this noise.*

put sb/sth off (7.4) – _____ : *The accident put him off helicopters.*

rely on (6.4) – _____ : *If you have a problem, who can you rely on?*

relate to (3.4) – _____ : *They have human experiences that we can relate to.*

return to (2.4) – _____ : *Does Kate plan to return to work after the baby is born?*

sell out (7.8) – _____ : *The tickets are all sold out.*

set off (5.1) – _____ : *I set off for school very early because my lessons start at 7 a.m.*

set up (7.2) – _____ : *In 1976 he set up his own import-export business.*

show around (4.3) – _____ : *Kim will show you around the museum.*

sign up (8.6) – _____ : *Have you tried signing up for some after school activities?*

suffer from (8.1) – _____ : *More and more people suffer from asthma.*

stand up (2.6) – _____ : *All the pupils stood up when the head teacher came in.*

stand up for (3.4) – _____ : *Why didn't you stand up for me?*

stay in (4.3) – _____ : *Let's stay in and watch TV.*

stay up (4.6) – _____ : *We stayed up to watch the late-night movie.*

stress out (8.1) – _____ : *Are those exams stressing you out?*

switch off (8.7) – _____ : *Don't forget to switch off the TV when you go to bed.*

take off (5.1) – _____ : *If you don't want to go, I can take your name off the list.*

take on 1. (3.4) – _____ : *A-list actors are keen to take on superhero roles.* 2. (6.1) – _____ : *The team has taken on a new coach.*

take up (8.1) – _____ : *If you prefer to do your exercise outdoors, take up cycling.*

talk over (8.6) – _____ : *Okay, but it's good to talk things over.*

try on (7.8) – _____ : *Would you like to try this top on?*

turn down (2.5) – _____ : *Can you turn your radio down? I'm trying to work.*

turn up (6.1) – _____ : *She always turns up late when we meet.*

wake up (2.2) – _____ : *I woke up at 5 a.m. this morning.*

work on (1.2) – _____ : *Dad's working on the car.*

work out (8.1) – _____ : *Sue works out in the gym twice a week.*

Answer key

Unit 5, page 60, Exercise 2: 1 Finland, 2 Japan, 3 Brazil

PRONOUNS & NUMERALS

PERSONAL PRONOUNS AND POSSESSIVE PRONOUNS

Personal pronoun as a subject	Personal pronoun as an object	Possessive pronoun (+noun)	Possessive pronoun (no noun)
I'm a student.	Come with **me**.	It's **my** house.	It's **mine**.
Have **you** got a cat?	I like **you**.	It's **your** bike.	It's **yours**.
He works at home.	Can you help **him**?	It's **his** book.	It's **his**.
She's been to Prague.	Listen to **her**.	It's **her** room.	It's **hers**.
Is **it** a famous city?	I can't find **it**.	Oxford (= it) is famous for **its** university.	—
We live in Poland.	Wait for **us**.	It's **our** tablet.	It's **ours**.
You can't sit here.	Can I talk to **you**?	It's **your** car.	It's **yours**.
Are **they** working?	Do you know **them**?	It's **their** money.	It's **theirs**.

DEMONSTRATIVE PRONOUNS, INTERROGATIVE PRONOUNS, RELATIVE PRONOUNS

Demonstrative		Interrogative	Relative
Singular	**Plural**	What? Who? Whose? Which? Where? When? Why? How? (How often? How long? How far? How much? How many?)	who which that whose when where
this that	these those		

NUMERALS

Numbers: 1 – 100

Cardinal numbers	Ordinal numbers	Cardinal numbers	Ordinal numbers
1 – one	first (1st)	20 – twenty	twentieth (20th)
2 – two	second (2nd)	21 – twenty-one	twenty-first (21st)
3 – three	third (3rd)	22 – twenty-two	twenty-second (22nd)
4 – four	fourth (4th)	23 – twenty-three	twenty-third (23rd)
5 – five	fifth (5th)	24 – twenty-four	twenty-fourth (24th)
6 – six	sixth (6th)	25 – twenty-five	twenty-fifth (25th)
7 – seven	seventh (7th)	26 – twenty-six	twenty-sixth (26th)
8 – eight	eighth (8th)	27 – twenty-seven	twenty-seventh (27th)
9 – nine	ninth (9th)	28 – twenty-eight	twenty-eighth (28th)
10 – ten	tenth (10th)	29 – twenty-nine	twenty-ninth (29th)
11 – eleven	eleventh (11th)	30 – thirty	thirtieth (30th)
12 – twelve	twelfth (12th)	40 – forty	fortieth (40th)
13 – thirteen	thirteenth (13th)	50 – fifty	fiftieth (50th)
14 – fourteen	fourteenth (14th)	60 – sixty	sixtieth (60th)
15 – fifteen	fifteenth (15th)	70 – seventy	seventieth (70th)
16 – sixteen	sixteenth (16th)	80 – eighty	eightieth (80th)
17 – seventeen	seventeenth (17th)	90 – ninety	ninetieth (90th)
18 – eighteen	eighteenth (18th)	100 – one/a hundred	hundredth (100th)
19 – nineteen	nineteenth (19th)	101 – one/a hundred and one	hundred and first (101st)

Numbers over 100

1,000 – one/a thousand
3,555 – three thousand, five hundred **and** fifty-five
56,223 – fifty-six thousand, two hundred **and** twenty-three
725,000 – seven hundred **and** twenty-five thousand
1,000,000 – one/a million
1,000,000,000 – one/a billion

IRREGULAR VERBS

Infinitive	Past Simple	Past Participle
be [biː]	was/were [wɒz/wɜː]	been [biːn]
become [bɪ'kʌm]	became [bɪ'keɪm]	become [bɪ'kʌm]
begin [bɪ'gɪn]	began [bɪ'gæn]	begun [bɪ'gʌn]
blow [bləʊ]	blew [bluː]	blown [bləʊn]
break [breɪk]	broke [brəʊk]	broken ['brəʊkən]
bring [brɪŋ]	brought [brɔːt]	brought [brɔːt]
build [bɪld]	built [bɪlt]	built [bɪlt]
burn [bɜːn]	burned [bɜːnd]/ burnt [bɜːnt]	burned [bɜːnd]/ burnt [bɜːnt]
buy [baɪ]	bought [bɔːt]	bought [bɔːt]
catch [kætʃ]	caught [kɔːt]	caught [kɔːt]
choose [tʃuːz]	chose [tʃəʊz]	chosen ['tʃəʊzn]
come [kʌm]	came [keɪm]	come [kʌm]
cost [kɒst]	cost [kɒst]	cost [kɒst]
cut [kʌt]	cut [kʌt]	cut [kʌt]
deal [diːl]	dealt [delt]	dealt [delt]
dig [dɪg]	dug [dʌg]	dug [dʌg]
do [duː]	did [dɪd]	done [dʌn]
draw [drɔː]	drew [druː]	drawn [drɔːn]
dream [driːm]	dreamed [driːmd]/ dreamt [dremt]	dreamed [driːmd]/ dreamt [dremt]
drink [drɪnk]	drank [dræŋk]	drunk [drʌŋk]
drive [draɪv]	drove [drəʊv]	driven ['drɪvn]
eat [iːt]	ate [et]	eaten ['iːtn]
fall [fɔːl]	fell [fel]	fallen ['fɔːln]
feed [fiːd]	fed [fed]	fed [fed]
feel [fiːl]	felt [felt]	felt [felt]
fight [faɪt]	fought [fɔːt]	fought [fɔːt]
find [faɪnd]	found [faʊnd]	found [faʊnd]
fly [flaɪ]	flew [fluː]	flown [fləʊn]
forget [fə'get]	forgot [fə'gɒt]	forgotten [fə'gɒtn]
forgive [fə'gɪv]	forgave [fə'geɪv]	forgiven [fə'gɪvn]
freeze [friːz]	froze ['frəʊz]	frozen ['frəʊzən]
get [get]	got [gɒt]	got [gɒt]
give [gɪv]	gave [geɪv]	given ['gɪvn]
go [gəʊ]	went [went]	gone [gɒn]
grow [grəʊ]	grew [gruː]	grown [grəʊn]
have [hæv]	had [hæd]	had [hæd]
hear [hɪə]	heard [hɜːd]	heard [hɜːd]
hide [haɪd]	hid [hɪd]	hidden ['hɪdn]
hit [hɪt]	hit [hɪt]	hit [hɪt]
hold [həʊld]	held [held]	held [held]
hurt [hɜːt]	hurt [hɜːt]	hurt [hɜːt]
keep [kiːp]	kept [kept]	kept [kept]
know [nəʊ]	knew [njuː]	known [nəʊn]
lead [liːd]	led [led]	led [led]
learn [lɜːn]	learned [lɜːnd]/ learnt [lɜːnt]	learned [lɜːnd]/ learnt [lɜːnt]
leave [liːv]	left [left]	left [left]

Infinitive	Past Simple	Past Participle
lend [lend]	lent [lent]	lent [lent]
let [let]	let [let]	let [let]
lie [laɪ]	lay [leɪ]	lain [leɪn]
light [laɪt]	lit [lɪt]	lit [lɪt]
lose [luːz]	lost [lɒst]	lost [lɒst]
make [meɪk]	made [meɪd]	made [meɪd]
mean [miːn]	meant [ment]	meant [ment]
meet [miːt]	met [met]	met [met]
pay [peɪ]	paid [peɪd]	paid [peɪd]
put [pʊt]	put [pʊt]	put [pʊt]
read [riːd]	read [red]	read [red]
ride [raɪd]	rode [rəʊd]	ridden ['rɪdn]
ring [rɪŋ]	rang [ræŋ]	rung [rʌŋ]
rise [raɪz]	rose [rəʊz]	risen ['rɪzən]
run [rʌn]	ran [ræn]	run [rʌn]
say [seɪ]	said [sed]	said [sed]
see [siː]	saw [sɔː]	seen [siːn]
sell [sel]	sold [səʊld]	sold [səʊld]
send [send]	sent [sent]	sent [sent]
set [set]	set [set]	set [set]
shine [ʃaɪn]	shone [ʃɒn]	shone [ʃɒn]
shoot [ʃuːt]	shot [ʃɒt]	shot [ʃɒt]
show [ʃəʊ]	showed [ʃəʊd]	shown [ʃəʊn]
shrink [ʃrɪŋk]	shrank [ʃræŋk]	shrunk [ʃrʌŋk]
shut [ʃʌt]	shut [ʃʌt]	shut [ʃʌt]
sing [sɪŋ]	sang [sæŋ]	sung [sʌŋ]
sit [sɪt]	sat [sæt]	sat [sæt]
sleep [sliːp]	slept [slept]	slept [slept]
smell [smel]	smelled [smeld]/ smelt [smelt]	smelled [smeld]/ smelt [smelt]
speak [spiːk]	spoke [spəʊk]	spoken ['spəʊkən]
spend [spend]	spent [spent]	spent [spent]
spill [spɪl]	spilled [spɪld]/ spilt [spɪlt]	spilled [spɪld]/ spilt [spɪlt]
stand [stænd]	stood [stʊd]	stood [stʊd]
steal [stiːl]	stole [stəʊl]	stolen ['stəʊlən]
swim [swɪm]	swam [swæm]	swum [swʌm]
take [teɪk]	took [tʊk]	taken ['teɪkən]
teach [tiːtʃ]	taught [tɔːt]	taught [tɔːt]
tear [teə]	tore [tɔː]	torn [tɔːn]
tell [tel]	told [təʊld]	told [təʊld]
think [θɪnk]	thought [θɔːt]	thought [θɔːt]
throw [θrəʊ]	threw [θruː]	thrown [θrəʊn]
understand [ˌʌndə'stænd]	understood [ˌʌndə'stʊd]	understood [ˌʌndə'stʊd]
wake [weɪk]	woke [wəʊk]	woken ['wəʊkən]
wear [weə]	wore [wɔː]	worn [wɔːn]
win [wɪn]	won [wʌn]	won [wʌn]
write [raɪt]	wrote [rəʊt]	written ['rɪtn]

Pearson Education Limited
KAO Two
KAO Park
Hockham Way,
Harlow, Essex,
CM17 9SR England
and Associated Companies throughout the world.

english.com/focus

© Pearson Education Limited 2020

Focus 2 Second Edition Student's Book

The right of Sue Kay, Vaughan Jones, Daniel Brayshaw, Marta Inglot, Bartosz Michałowski, Dean Russell and Beata Trapnell to be identified as authors of this Work has been asserted by them in accordance with the Copyright, Designs and Patents Act 1988.

First published 2020
Second impression 2023

ISBN: 978-1-292-39064-2

Set in Avenir LT Pro
Printed and bound by Neografia, Slovakia

Acknowledgements

The publishers and authors would like to thank the following people and institutions for their feedback and comments during the development of the material:

Humberto Santos Duran
Anna Maria Grochowska
Beata Gruszczyńska
Inga Lande
Magdalena Loska
Barbara Madej
Rosa Maria Maldonado
Juliana Queiroz Pereira
Tomasz Siuta
Elżbieta Śliwa
Katarzyna Ślusarczyk
Katarzyna Tobolska
Renata Tomaka-Pasternak
Beata Trapnell
Aleksandra Zakrzewska
Beata Zygadlewicz-Kocuś

Sue Kay and Vaughan Jones's acknowledgements

We would like to thank all the students and teachers we have met and observed during the development of Focus Second Edition. We are also especially grateful to our wonderful editorial team for their expertise, encouragement and dedication.
Finally, a big thank you to our families without whose support and understanding none of this would have been possible.

Texts

Fairtrade Foundation: Fairtrade Foundation 90; **Pearson Education Ltd:** 20

Images

123RF.com: 73, 122, 122, ammentorp 8, Anna Bizon 115, Apichart Surachartmathin 106, Cathy Yeulet 60, 81, 115, Dejan Jovanovic 130, dimaberkut 14, Dmitriy Shironosov 87, dolgachov 14, 17, dzein 56, georgejmclittle 10932-103, Graham Oliver 75, Iakov Kalinin 12, Ian Allenden 4, Katarzyna Bialasiewicz 84, kzenon 129, lexan 53, Lisa Young 5, Mark Bowden 59, Michael Simons 75, Mr_Vector 130, onston 110, 111, primagefactory 125, serezniy 67, Siarhei Lenets 82, Tamas Panczel - Eross 77, texelart 91, theromb 119, Vladimir Yudin 130, 130; **4Corners Images:** AFLO 51; **Alamy Stock Photo:** ajissues 110, Alex Ekins Adventure Photography 31, Alliance 88, Andrew Hasson 34, Astrakan Images 77, Bailey -Cooper Photography 3 63, Ball Miwako 105, Bert Hoferichter 39, Blend Images 56, 70, Buzzshotz 89, CandyBox Images 66, Charles Stirling 39, ClassicStock 24, Cotswolds Photo Library 69, Cultura Creative (RF) 12, 73, Daniel Lamborn 50, David Angel 95, David Grossman 49, David Wall 51, Dennis Hardley 54, Disability Images 77, DOD Photo 6, Don Smith 21, Doug Houghton SCO 53, Eddie Linssen 95, Egor Lyashenko 27, Eye Ubuitous 23, famouspeople 19, Finnbarr Webster 39, Frans Lanting Studio 23, Giuseppe Ramos 89, Graham Hare 26, Gruffydd Thomas 42, Hero Images Inc. 7, 66, 81, Image Source 9, 80, Interfoto 19, Itsik Marom 42, Janine Wiedel Photolibrary 77, John Lellerman 56, Jozef Polc 52, JR / Agence Vu / Roger Bamber 35, Justin Kase z12z 56, Kate Hockenhull 95, Kee Pil Cho 106, Lou Linwei 107, M&N 24, Maria Sward 47, MBI 11, 11, 11, 109, Mint Images Limites 9, Mode Images 49, moodboard 70, Murad RM 77, ONOKY - Photononstop 80, Oramstock 54, Panther Media GmbH 4, PCN Photography 77, PhotoAlto sas 87, Pictorial Press Ltd 18, Piotr Zajac 108, Purestock 67, Rabia Elif Aksoy 127, RGB Ventures / SuperStock 112, Robert Paul van Beets 51, Roberto Herrett 68, Science History Images 18, Shakeyjon 56, Shotshop GmbH 21, Splash News 65, 65, Stas Tolstnev 28, Stefano Cavoretto 89, Stephen Dorey ABIPP 21, Suchota 96, Suprijono Suharjoto 131, Tom Bible 93, Tommaso Altamura 123, Tony Cordoza 91, Tony Watson 56, Tribune Content Agency LLC 64, Wavebreak Media ltd 45, Wavebreakmedia ltd 70, 80, WENN Ltd 104, 104, Westend61 GmbH 23, 77, 88, wonderlandstock 76, Xinhua 23, Zoonar GmbH 84, Zuma Press Inc. 42, Zuma Press, Inc. 6, 106, 107, Zuma Press. Inc. 65; **BBC Worldwide Learning:** 4, 18, 32, 46, 60, 74, 88, 102, 116, 118, 120, 122, 124, 126, 128, 130; **Fairtrade Foundation:** 90; **Fotolia.com:** auremar 77, Brian Jackson 90, Dmitrijs Gerciks 91, Gordana Sermek 91, Maxim Malevich 91; **Getty Images:** Barcroft Media 51, Gareth Cattermole 38, Hero Images Inc. 83, Indeed 60-61, Issouf Sanogo 90, JR / Agence Vu / AFP Photo / Vanderlei Almeida 35, Paul Redmond / WireImage 94, Steve Debenport 77; **JR / Agence Vu:** 35; **London Dungeon:** 56; **Pearson Education Ltd:** 20, 20, Gareth Boden 49, Jon Barlow 48, 48, 48, Silversun Media Group 117, 117, 117, 117, 118, 118, 118, 119, 121, 123, 123, 123, 123, 125, 127, 129, 131, 131, 131, 131, 131; **Photolibrary.com:** Masterfile 62; **Polish Modern Art Foundation:** Bartek Warzecha 47; **Shutterstock.com:** 40, 128, Africa Studio 61, Artography 21, AVS-Images 77, Blend Images 74, Brandon Bourdages 128, Brownstone Prods/Kobal 41, Daniel M Ernst 74, David Fisher 39, East News / REX 46, Edwin Verin 21, Georgios Kollidas 18, Hopper Stone / Levantine / Kobal / REX 25, Ian Duffield 55, Jordan Strauss/Invision/AP 25, K.Miri Photography 128, Kirasolly 19, lucadp 121, Marvel Studios / Kobal / REX 37, Matej Hudovernik 122, Mike Flippo 128, Mopic 92, Nancy Bauer 91, Neamov 91, Nina Malyna 13, Paul Michael Hughes 77, Peter Hermes Furian 23, Pinosub 21, Radu Bercan 95, Rex 37, ronstik 77, rul vale sousa 62, Sergey Andrianov 91, Sony Pictures/Kobal 40, SSokolov 122, Sukpaiboonwat 128, Tomislav Pinter 128, Universal / Marvel / Kobal / REX 36, View Pictures / REX 70, Warner Bros. Pictures / Kobal / REX 37; **Webb Chappell Photography:** Media Lab 20
Cover images: Back: **Shutterstock.com**

Illustrations

Alasdair Bright (NB Illustration) 78-79, 96-97
Nicholas Gremaud (A Goodson Illustration Agency) 10, 32-33, 98
Ewa Olejnik 59

Videos

BBC video footage supplied by BBC Studios Distribution Limited
FOCUS VLOGS and Interactive Speaking Videos supplied by A Silversun Media Group production for Pearson

Every effort has been made to trace the copyright holders and we apologise in advance for any unintentional omissions. We would be pleased to insert the appropriate acknowledgement in any subsequent edition of this publication.

Multiple-choice cloze

1 Read the text below and decide which answer (A, B, C or D) best completes each gap.
   There is one example.

Exchange programmes

Every year lots of students ⁰_____ on exchange programmes and stay with students in other countries. This practice was first inspired ¹_____ volunteers who helped in other countries in war time.

There are special organisations that help schools plan these and it can be a wonderful ²_____ . Students stay with teenagers of the ³_____ age, who are often ⁴_____ in the same things. Sometimes students ⁵_____ a short time in the other country – maybe two or three weeks – but in some countries students go for longer periods. They can go for as long as a year and also ⁶_____ at a school or college in the other country.

Exchange programmes are good ⁷_____ you meet people from different countries and also learn about living in another country. Of course, it's an excellent way to practise and improve a foreign language at the same time as having ⁸_____ !

Before going on an exchange, it's important for the school to choose ⁹_____ right teenager for you to stay with. You ¹⁰_____ to fill in forms about your personality, family, interests and pastimes.

0	**A** do	**B** take	**C** make	**D** go ⃝
1	**A** of	**B** from	**C** by	**D** with
2	**A** example	**B** experience	**C** event	**D** impression
3	**A** common	**B** same	**C** near	**D** exact
4	**A** keen	**B** passionate	**C** serious	**D** interested
5	**A** leave	**B** make	**C** are	**D** spend
6	**A** go	**B** study	**C** pass	**D** stay
7	**A** for	**B** because	**C** and	**D** that
8	**A** fun	**B** joke	**C** laugh	**D** smile
9	**A** a	**B** some	**C** any	**D** the
10	**A** must	**B** should	**C** need	**D** will

Sentence transformation

2 Complete the second sentence so that it has a similar meaning to the first sentence.
   Use no more than three words.

0 Jane lives near Tommy.
   Jane _doesn't live very_ far from Tommy.

1 I sat down to read a magazine and Dylan came in.
   While I _____ a magazine, Dylan came in.

2 There were some photographs of toys from 100 years ago.
   There were some photographs of toys that children _____ play with 100 years ago.

3 Jane tries not to watch Tommy race in competitions because she gets nervous.
   Jane avoids _____ Tommy race in competitions because she gets nervous.

4 Tommy swims so fast – it's amazing!
   Tommy is _____ swimmer – it's amazing!

5 Jane would like to play golf, but she hasn't got enough money to buy all the equipment.
   Jane would like to play golf, but she can't _____ buy all the equipment.

6 Jane took some photos while Tommy was practising.
   Jane took some photos _____ Tommy's practice.

WORD STORE 1A | Personality

POSITIVE	≠ NEGATIVE
1 _caring_	≠ selfish
2 _____	≠ miserable
3 _____	≠ mean
4 _____	≠ lazy
5 _____	≠ shy
6 _____	≠ silly

WORD STORE 1B | un-, in-, im-, ir-, dis-

1 _adventurous_ ≠ unadventurous
2 dependent ≠ _____
3 honest ≠ _____
4 _____ ≠ impolite
5 _____ ≠ unpopular
6 responsible ≠ _____
7 _____ ≠ insensitive
8 _____ ≠ unwise

WORD STORE 1C | Questions with _like_

be + like > personality

What is he/she like?

1 _____ (adjective)

look + like > appearance

What does he look like?

2 _____ (noun phrase)

like as a verb

What do you like?

3 _____ (noun phrase)

WORD STORE 1D | -ive, -ative, -able, -ing

a~~ct~~ adapt communicate imagine inspire protect

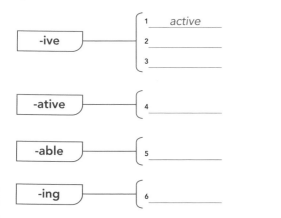

-ive
1 _active_
2 _____
3 _____

-ative
4 _____

-able
5 _____

-ing
6 _____

WORD STORE 1E | Verb + preposition

1 care / _think_ / _____ **about**
2 _____ **in**
3 _____ / focus **on**
4 _____ **to**
5 connect / _____ **with**

MY WORD STORE

My top five words from Unit 1

1 _____
2 _____
3 _____
4 _____
5 _____

WORD STORE GLOSSARY

Words to learn

PARTS OF SPEECH

adjective – e.g. _good, red, shy_
adverb – e.g. _well, badly, often_
article – _a/an, the_
noun – e.g. _table, advice, uniform_
numeral – e.g. _one, two, first, second_
preposition – e.g. _at, in, under_
pronoun – e.g. _it, we, him_
verb – e.g. _teach, learn, remember_

OTHER TERMS

antonym – e.g. _caring ≠ selfish_
collocation – e.g. _go home, find a solution_
compound noun – e.g. _website, text message_
partitive – e.g. _can of cola, box of chocolates_
phrasal verb – e.g. _switch on, find out, give up_
synonym – e.g. _big = large_

WORD BUILDING

prefix – e.g. _unfit, dishonest_
suffix – e.g. _successful, employment_

For questions 1–30, choose the correct answer, A, B or C, to complete the sentences.

1 Tom doesn't care about other people's feelings. He's the most _____ person I know.

  A generous   B emotional   C insensitive

2 I think Sophie is a bit _____ – she never buys birthday presents for her family.

  A shy   B mean   C serious

3 Damien's very _____ . He wants to become someone important and have lots of money.

  A lazy   B honest   C ambitious

4 Zoe loves meeting and talking to people. I'd like to be as _____ as she is.

  A clever   B outgoing   C honest

5 Wow! Adam's really _____ – he writes the most interesting stories I've ever read!

  A protective   B communicative   C imaginative

6 I hate _____ people because I can't stand when somebody lies to me.

  A outgoing   B miserable   C dishonest

7 Paul always expects the worst to happen – he's very _____ .

  A unwise   B protective   C pessimistic

8 I'm not very _____ – I don't like changes or new experiences.

  A generous   B caring   C adventurous

9 I think Jane is perfect to be our leader – she's really intelligent and _____ .

  A sensitive   B sensible   C silly

10 Sarah is really good _____ chess.

  A of   B at   C about

11 When I was younger, I was keen _____ playing tennis.

  A at   B in   C on

12 After twenty years of teaching, Mrs Jones is still _____ it. And her students always enjoy the classes too.

  A worried about

  B disappointed with

  C passionate about

13 I like _____ jeans, but this pair is too tight even for me. I'll try a bigger size.

  A casual   B skinny   C designer

14 I think you should wear a suit and a _____ for a job interview.

  A tie   B hoodie   C uniform

15 We can't afford to spend money _____ things we don't really need.

  A on   B for   C at

16 It took me three months to learn to type on my computer without looking at the _____ .

  A broadband   B keyboard   C printer

17 Take a warm hat and gloves! It's _____ outside!

  A warm   B freezing   C boiling

18 Twenty years ago people used to work on big _____ computers.

  A digital   B desktop   C electronic

19 A lot of people _____ him on Twitter.

  A splash   B follow   C download

20 Does your friend write a _____ about his life?

  A blog   B virus   C menu

21 Did you _____ notes during the Chemistry lesson yesterday? Can I borrow them?

  A do   B take   C invent

22 Do you ever _____ this website? There are a lot of cool articles.

  A go   B visit   C switch

23 This _____ will help you find some useful websites.

  A text message

  B search engine

  C Internet server

24 Can you help me _____ my Facebook profile?

  A spend   B update   C switch on

25 Sorry, my battery _____ while I was calling you.

  A put on

  B went dead

  C gave out

26 Alexander Fleming _____ penicillin – an important antibiotic – in 1928.

  A invented   B discovered   C collected

27 This ecological organisation is trying to _____ the environment and make sure we still have a planet to live on.

  A collect   B observe   C protect

28 He's always wanted to be _____ so he asked for a telescope to observe the sky.

  A an astronomer

  B a mathematician

  C a biologist

29 What dictionary do you use to _____ the meaning of words you don't understand?

  A look up   B check up   C look after

30 Bill Townsend has _____ a computer software company for seven years.

  A made   B gone   C run

WORD STORE 2A | Phones and computers

1 broadband
2 d_esktop_ c_omputer_
3 k_____
4 laptop
5 l_____ p_____
6 password
7 s_____ e_____
8 text message
9 username
10 w_____ b_____

REMEMBER THIS

Compound nouns can be two words (e.g. *text message*) or one word (e.g. *username*).

WORD STORE 2B | Word building

NOUN (subject)	NOUN (person)
1 _astronomy_	astronomer
2 _____	biologist
3 _____	chemist
4 _____	computer scientist
5 _____	mathematician
6 _____	physicist

WORD STORE 2C | Collocations

1 _collect_ specimens (of plants or animals)
2 _____ a theory
3 _____ something (that no one knew about before)
4 _____ an experiment (to learn what happens)
5 _____ research (into a subject)
6 _____ something (that did not exist before)
7 _____ (or watch carefully)
8 _____ measurements (of the size of something)
9 _____ notes (so you can remember information)

WORD STORE 2D | Collocations

data (x3)   the environment   evidence (x2)   hours
a research paper

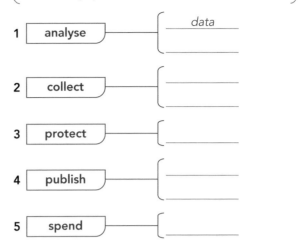

1 analyse — _data_ / _____
2 collect — _____ / _____
3 protect — _____
4 publish — _____ / _____
5 spend — _____

WORD STORE 2E | The temperature

boiling   chilly   cold   freezing   ~~hot~~   warm

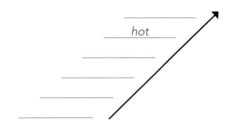

_____
hot
_____
_____
_____
_____

MY WORD STORE

My top five words from Unit 2

1 _____
2 _____
3 _____
4 _____
5 _____

Multiple-choice cloze

1 Read the text below and decide which answer (A, B, C or D) best completes each gap. There is one example.

A frightening experience

One of my ⁰_____ hobbies is acting and I've done a lot of plays with my school and ¹_____ club. When I started acting, I didn't ²_____ to get nervous and I was really confident. I could learn and remember lots of lines with no problems! Then one night I was acting ³_____ a fantastic play called *Shadowlands*. It's about how the ⁴_____ C.S Lewis, who wrote *The Lion, the Witch and the Wardrobe*, fell in love with an American poet called Joy. It's a very ⁵_____ play and Joy dies at the end. I was playing Joy and right in the middle of the second ⁶_____ I forgot my words. It was terrible! Afterwards everyone said that my performance was great, but I was really disappointed ⁷_____ myself.

Now I concentrate much ⁸_____ when I'm on stage, but I've never forgotten that moment. I still enjoy acting, but I don't look ⁹_____ to going on stage as much as I used to. It's more frightening ¹⁰_____ taking an English exam!

0	A nice	B popular	C favourite	D successful
1	A poetry	B drama	C film	D comedy
2	A use	B always	C usually	D find
3	A on	B for	C with	D in
4	A actor	B artist	C writer	D character
5	A relaxing	B moving	C excellent	D funny
6	A act	B chapter	C setting	D album
7	A on	B for	C by	D with
8	A more hard	B harder	C hardly	D hardest
9	A toward	B across	C forward	D over
10	A that	B than	C as	D to

(0 C favourite is circled)

Sentence transformation

2 Complete the second sentence so that it has a similar meaning to the first sentence. Use no more than three words.

0 I had to wait in a long queue to get into the exhibition, but that was OK.
I *didn't mind* waiting in a long queue to get into the exhibition.

1 I arrived back from the concert a few moments ago.
I _____ back from the concert.

2 Hannah and I are going to decide soon what we'll do at the weekend.
We haven't _____ what we'll do at the weekend.

3 The festival last year was more boring than this one.
The festival last year wasn't _____ this one.

4 Justin and I have a meeting tomorrow at 2 o'clock – it's decided.
We are _____ tomorrow at 2 o'clock.

5 The books in the gift shop were too expensive for me to buy.
I didn't _____ money to buy any of the books in the gift shop.

6 Mrs Jing is a quicker reader than Mr Jing.
Mrs Jing reads _____ Mr Jing.

WORD STORE 3A | TV programmes

Factual

1 cooking programmes
2 d<u>ocumentarie</u>s
3 news bulletins
4 travel shows
5 weather forecasts

Light entertainment

1 animation
2 c_____ t s_____ s
3 comedy
4 game shows
5 r_____y TV
6 sitcoms
7 talent shows

Drama

1 crime dramas
2 f_____y
3 horrors
4 musicals
5 period dramas
6 romantic comedies
7 s_____ e f_____ n
8 s_____ p o_____ s
9 thrillers

WORD STORE 3B | Adjectives

1 a<u>ddictive</u> = _____
2 c_____ = _____
3 disappointing = _____
4 em_____g = _____
5 entertaining = _____
6 en_____g = _____
7 e_____t = _____
8 f_____g = _____
9 g_____g = _____
10 i_____e = _____
11 inspiring = _____
12 m_____g = _____

WORD STORE 3C | Elements of a film / TV drama

REMEMBER THIS

British	American
film	movie
go to the cinema	go to the movies

WORD STORE 3D | Art and artists

art   black and white   buildings   public
~~sculptor~~   sculpture

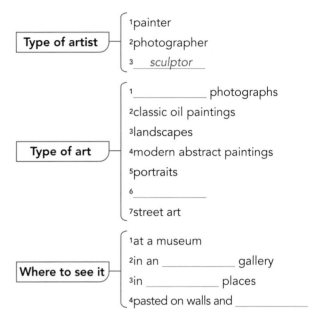

Type of artist
1 painter
2 photographer
3 _sculptor_

Type of art
1 _____ photographs
2 classic oil paintings
3 landscapes
4 modern abstract paintings
5 portraits
6 _____
7 street art

Where to see it
1 at a museum
2 in an _____ gallery
3 in _____ places
4 pasted on walls and _____

WORD STORE 3E | Phrasal verbs

1 _take on_ = accept (some work)
2 _____ = appear (in cinemas)
3 _____ = let sb have sth that was yours
4 _____ = protect
5 _____ = spend time doing sth
6 _____ = understand
7 _____ = deal successfully (with a difficult situation)

MY WORD STORE

My top five words from Unit 3

1 _____
2 _____
3 _____
4 _____
5 _____

For questions 1–30, choose the correct answer, A, B or C, to complete the sentences.

1 Mrs Jennings lives in a tiny _____ with just one room and a small bathroom.

A block of flats

B studio apartment

C detached house

2 Every _____ needs a lot of different brushes and paints.

A painter   B sculptor   C photographer

3 During this course you will learn some basic techniques of oil _____ .

A painting   B sculpture   C photography

4 The main subject of his work is the English countryside – he's a famous ___ painter.

A portrait   B abstract   C landscape

5 Mark enjoys watching _____ shows, where people answer questions and win prizes.

A chat   B game   C talent

6 Where can I buy the _____ of the film? I want to listen to it at home.

A story   B soundtrack   C setting

7 She has already refused to play the _____ of a police officer.

A role   B plot   C dialogue

8 This horror film is really _____ – you never know what will happen next!

A embarrassing

B gripping

C addictive

9 My grandmother is writing her _____ . She wants to tell everyone the story of her life.

A genre   B biography   C autobiography

10 The latest Steven Spielberg's film is a real _____ – it's already made a lot of money.

A blockbuster   B trailer   C genre

11 The events described in this book _____ place in Scotland.

A see   B take   C are

12 How can you watch _____? They've got a hundred thousand episodes!

A science fiction

B soap operas

C weather forecasts

13 I love listening to _____ music – it's so much better than the one on MP3s.

A factual   B life   C live

14 Their new song is number one in the music _____ .

A charts   B awards   C festival

15 I'm going to watch a new _____ of my favourite comedy series tonight.

A article   B sitcom   C episode

16 Mary has got a small _____ in the forest.

A flat

B bungalow

C cottage

17 There are other houses joined on either side of a _____ house.

A terraced   B detached   C semi-detached

18 This apartment must cost a lot. It's right in the _____ , next to the market square.

A suburbs   B city centre   C countryside

19 I don't like working in _____ offices. There are no walls and you can hear everything.

A spacious   B open-plan   C impressive

20 The windows are big, so the house has got lots of natural _____ .

A light   B view   C attraction

21 It's cold inside because the _____ don't work.

A cookers   B fridges   C radiators

22 There's too little space in my _____ – I have no place to put all my dresses and skirts!

A shelves   B cupboard   C wardrobe

23 We need to put a new _____ on the floor in the living room.

A carpet   B ceiling   C cupboard

24 She got to the top of the _____ and looked back at the people below.

A stairs   B ceiling   C floor

25 This conference centre looks very _____ – it's a giant constuction made of metal and glass.

A suitable   B modern   C ancient

26 Will, could you come _____? I'm in the basement and I need your help.

A downstairs   B upstairs   C the stairs

27 Who _____ the ironing in your family?

A has   B does   C makes

28 I'd like to make a _____ about this phone. I bought it here last week, but it doesn't work.

A noise   B decision   C complaint

29 It's difficult to drive here because the streets are very _____ .

A cosy   B narrow   C dense

30 We're planning to visit the _____ of the ancient city of Pompeii.

A pavements   B ruins   C slums

WORD STORE 4A | Describing houses

Type of house

1 a bungalow
2 a cottage
3 a detached house
4 a semi-detached house
5 a terraced house
6 *a block of flats*

Location

1 in the suburbs
2 in a village
3 near the sea
4 in the countryside
5 on a housing estate
6 _____

Location in a building

1 downstairs
2 in the basement
3 on the first floor
4 on the top floor
5 on _____
6 _____

Building materials

1 stone
2 wood
3 b_____
4 c_____
5 m_____
6 g_____

Description

1 traditional
2 m_____
3 s_____
4 o_____
5 c_____
6 h_____

WORD STORE 4B | Inside a house

1 bedside tables = _____
2 bookcases = _____
3 carpets = _____
4 a chest of drawers = _____
5 a cooker = _____
6 cupboards = _____
7 a desk = _____
8 a fridge = _____
9 a front door = _____
10 a kitchen sink = _____
11 a ladder = _____
12 radiators = _____
13 shelves = _____
14 stairs = _____
15 a wardrobe = _____
16 wooden floors = _____

WORD STORE 4C | *make* or *do*

make	*do*
1 your bed	1 your homework
2 a complaint	2 the cooking
3 a decision	3 the housework
4 _____	4 *the washing*
5 _____	5 _____
6 _____	6 _____
	7 _____
	8 _____

WORD STORE 4D | Phrasal verbs

(away   in   out   ~~round~~)

1 come _____*round*_____ = visit sb in their house
2 get _____ from sth = move away from sth
3 keep sb _____ = stop sb entering a place
4 let sb _____ = allow sb to enter
5 stay _____ = stay at home, not go out

WORD STORE 4E | Collocations

(~~ancient~~   dense   hot   lush   nomadic
scorching   volcanic)

1 _____*ancient*_____ city
2 _____ crater
3 _____ rainforest
4 _____ springs
5 _____ temperatures
6 _____ tribe
7 _____ vegetation

MY WORD STORE

My top five words from Unit 4

1 _____
2 _____
3 _____
4 _____
5 _____

Multiple-choice cloze

1 Read the text below and decide which answer (A, B, C or D) best completes each gap.
There is one example.

Where did you grow up?
Read some of our readers' stories.

I have a lot of great memories of the house ⁰_____ I grew up. Now we live ¹_____ the suburbs, but when I was little, my dad got a job in the countryside and we lived in a big old house on the ²_____ of a village. We lived there for ten years and I used to go to the village school. We were ³_____ the sea and my friends and I often explored the beach and the caves in the cliffs. The area is famous ⁴_____ its beaches and white cliffs and it was the ⁵_____ for a popular TV series last year!

I loved that old house. Some people think it's lonely to be in the countryside, but I ⁶_____ being on my ⁷_____ sometimes. If I felt ⁸_____ , I could go up to my bedroom and look out of the window. I had a breathtaking ⁹_____ from there across the fields and to the sea. It was very relaxing and made me feel better. I was really unhappy when we ¹⁰_____ to the town!

0	**A** which	**B** whose	**C** where (circled)	**D** who
1	**A** on	**B** in	**C** by	**D** over
2	**A** side	**B** centre	**C** edge	**D** part
3	**A** at	**B** over	**C** close	**D** near
4	**A** of	**B** on	**C** with	**D** for
5	**A** plot	**B** setting	**C** place	**D** soundtrack
6	**A** wanted	**B** decided	**C** hoped	**D** enjoyed
7	**A** alone	**B** self	**C** own	**D** single
8	**A** miserable	**B** proud	**C** crowded	**D** famous
9	**A** scene	**B** sight	**C** view	**D** picture
10	**A** changed	**B** transported	**C** moved	**D** travelled

Sentence transformation

2 Complete the second sentence so that it has a similar meaning to the first sentence.
Use no more than three words.

0 I've known my classmate Jordan for five years.
I first met my classmate Jordan _five years ago_.

1 Hannah and I learnt French in that classroom.
That's the _____ Hannah and I learnt French.

2 Ms Twinkle won't pass her driving test if she doesn't practise every day.
Ms Twinkle won't pass her driving test _____ she practises every day.

3 It was so embarrassing – my face was completely red!
I was so _____ – my face was completely red!

4 It might rain later, so we'll take the bus home instead of walking.
If _____ later, we'll take the bus home instead of walking.

5 The rule says: 'Always wear trainers in the gym.'
We _____ wear trainers in the gym.

6 I don't know French so I need a dictionary.
If _____ , I wouldn't need a dictionary.

WORD STORE 5A | Education

1 _academic subjects_ = main subjects taught at school
2 _____ = sports and clubs for students after regular lessons
3 _____ = a person from your class
4 _____ = obligatory
5 _____ = academic programme
6 _____ = memorise
7 _____ = with students of different levels
8 _____ = period of the academic year
9 _____ = list of the times of classes
10 _____ = a person with a university degree

WORD STORE 5B | Phrasal verbs

1 _break up_ = stop working at the end of term
2 _____ = manage a difficult situation
3 _____ = get a place (at university)
4 _____ = give a piece of work to a teacher
5 _____ = learn at the same speed as other students
6 _____ = stand in a line
7 _____ = change to the next level, year or school

WORD STORE 5C | Collocations

1 _pay_ attention
2 _____ /get/have a **degree**
3 _____ /pass/fail/revise for **an exam**
4 _____ **tuition fees**
5 _____ /do/hand in/mark **homework**
6 _____ /miss **lessons**
7 _____ /learn from **mistakes**
8 _____ /go to/start/finish/leave **school**
9 _____ /take **a subject**

WORD STORE 5D | *get*

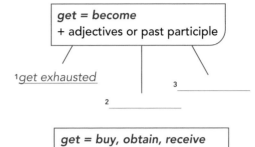

get exhausted   get good grades   get ill
get a job   get into trouble   get nervous
get rid of sth

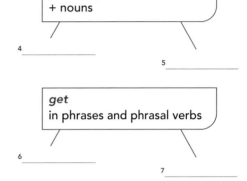

get = become
+ adjectives or past participle

[1]_get exhausted_

2 _____

3 _____

get = buy, obtain, receive
+ nouns

4 _____

5 _____

get
in phrases and phrasal verbs

6 _____

7 _____

REMEMBER THIS

get (to) + noun = arrive
get home
get **to** school
get **to the** station

WORD STORE 5E | *of* and *for*

1 make fun __of__ sb
2 get over a difficulty with the support _____ sb
3 be/become a professor _____ sth
4 have/find a passion _____ sth
5 dream _____ sth
6 make the mistake _____ doing sth

MY WORD STORE

My top five words from Unit 5

1 _____
2 _____
3 _____
4 _____
5 _____

For questions 1–30, choose the correct answer, A, B or C, to complete the sentences.

1 To be a biologist you need to have a university _____ .
   A exam   B subject   C degree

2 As a student of _____ , you should travel to other countries to see the most impressive buildings.
   A Science   B Geography   C Architecture

3 In this country, school education is _____ for children between six and sixteen years old.
   A flexible   B demanding   C compulsory

4 In my opinion, learning new things _____ heart is not the best method.
   A by   B on   C with

5 What's wrong with Ann? Her _____ are very low this term.
   A grades   B abilities   C subjects

6 The school _____ is always full. The food is tasty and quite cheap.
   A gate   B canteen   C curriculum

7 The university has confirmed that _____ will go up next year.
   A gap years   B tuition fees   C entrance exams

8 My brother causes a lot of problems and always gets _____ trouble.
   A into   B with   C out of

9 I got rid _____ all my textbooks when I finished school.
   A at   B of   C with

10 I usually _____ ill when autumn comes.
   A get   B catch   C start

11 This course is very useful. I'm really getting _____ of it.
   A a lot out   B exhausted   C a good job

12 Someone has made a big _____ to the school. We've got enough money now to buy some new computers.
   A solution   B decision   C donation

13 I can't help you this time. You have to do your homework on your _____ .
   A best   B own   C conditions

14 My History teacher's voice is boring. It's hard for me to _____ attention to what he's saying.
   A hold   B keep   C pay

15 On Sundays I usually try to relax and chill _____ in front of the TV.
   A up   B out   C myself

16 Tim is an estate _____ . He sells flats and houses.
   A assistant   B agent   C instructor

17 Our neighbour, Mrs Hill, is now _____ but she's looking for a job.
   A unemployed   B employed   C overtime

18 There's something wrong with the the power cables in our flat. Please, call the _____ .
   A carpenter   B electrician   C interpreter

19 Ann works at a swimming pool. She's a _____ .
   A lifeguard   B carer   C beautician

20 In my opinion, the best _____ for this job is someone who can speak English and French.
   A employer   B candidate   C supervisor

21 It's too late to apply _____ this job.
   A at   B on   C for

22 I can work only twenty hours a week, so I'm looking for a _____ job.
   A manual   B holiday   C part-time

23 I'm afraid Rebecca is too optimistic about her chances of _____ . She has to wait till next year.
   A position   B promotion   C profession

24 My dad wants to _____ when he is sixty-five.
   A retire   B finish   C take off

25 Peter would like to work _____ IT.
   A at   B in   C for

26 We usually have to _____ a lot of overtime in December.
   A do   B get   C make

27 You don't have to come to the office every day. It's OK to work _____ .
   A from home   B indoors   C as part of a team

28 Alison hopes she will be _____-paid in the future.
   A well   B high   C average

29 Your _____ depends on how long you work for a company and how well you do your job.
   A competition   B salary   C retail

30 Did you know that Bill's father got the _____ and is looking for a job?
   A shift   B sack   C fire

WORD STORE 6A | Collocations

Employment

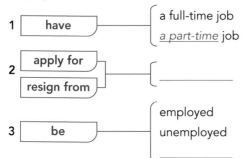

1 have — a full-time job / *a part-time* job

2 apply for / resign from — _____

3 be — employed / unemployed / _____

4 get — fired / _____

Terms and Conditions

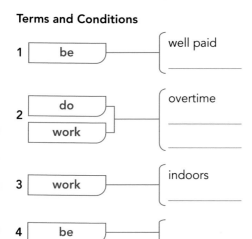

1 be — well paid / _____

2 do / work — overtime / _____ / _____

3 work — indoors / _____

4 be — _____

5 get / have / take — five weeks' paid holiday / _____

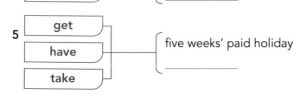

WORD STORE 6B | Describing jobs

1 c*hallenging* = difficult but interesting

2 **creative** = makes you use original ideas

3 **demanding** = difficult and needs a lot of energy

4 r_____e = doing the same thing again and again

5 **rewarding** = gives you satisfaction

6 s_____l = makes you feel nervous

7 **tiring** = makes you feel tired

REMEMBER THIS

you find sth challenging, tiring etc. =
you think that sth is challenging, tiring etc.

WORD STORE 6C | Phrasal verbs

1 ___come___ up with sth = think of or produce sth

2 **put sb off sth** = make sb not want or like sth

3 _____ up with sth/sb = tolerate sth/sb

4 **take sb on** = employ sb

5 _____ up = arrive

WORD STORE 6D | Jobs

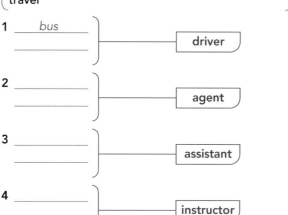

~~bus~~ driving estate office shop skiing taxi travel

1 ___bus___ _____ — driver

2 _____ _____ — agent

3 _____ _____ — assistant

4 _____ _____ — instructor

WORD STORE 6E | Word families

NOUN	VERB	ADJECTIVE
1 charm	charm	*charming*
2 competition	compete	_____
3 peace	–	_____
4 determination	–	_____
5 logic	–	_____
6 reliance	rely (on)	_____

MY WORD STORE

My top five words from Unit 6

1 _____
2 _____
3 _____
4 _____
5 _____

Multiple-choice cloze

1 Read the text below and decide which answer (A, B, C or D) best completes each gap. There is one example.

Making new from old

Read some of our readers' stories.

Last month I was window ⁰_____ and I saw some incredible furniture in a new trendy store. Unfortunately, you can't ¹_____ up a bargain in such expensive shops. If you bought anything there you would be in ²_____ for ages. Instead, you should think about fixing up some old items yourself. I tried and it works! Recently I helped my neighbour clear out her garage. There was ³_____ rubbish in the garage she wanted to get rid of, but because her back ⁴_____ she needed help. During the process, I saw an old table which she said ⁵_____ there for years. The neighbour said I could take ⁶_____ I liked. And I liked the table. It was in bad shape, but I took it home. I searched the Internet trying to ⁷_____ out how to renovate it.

I quickly learnt one thing: most products that are ⁸_____ for refinishing furniture are not safe to use indoors. I ⁹_____ warned about it before, but somehow I forgot. First, I began to feel dizzy, and then I nearly passed ¹⁰_____! I finished the job in the garden. Now I have a beautiful table and there's less rubbish on the planet.

0	A buying	B checking	C shopping	D looking
1	A find	B pick	C take	D find
2	A loan	B lack	C debt	D sale
3	A lot of	B a few	C any	D lots of
4	A pained	B hurt	C felt	D aches
5	A is	B has been	C was	D had been
6	A anything	B somewhere	C someone	D anywhere
7	A learn	B search	C fall	D figure
8	A recommended	B recommend	C recommending	D recommendation
9	A has been	B am	C had been	D have been
10	A out	B down	C over	D by

Sentence transformation

2 Complete the second sentence so that it has a similar meaning to the first sentence. Use no more than three words.

0 I last went to the cinema six months ago.
I *haven't been* to the cinema for six months.

1 Could we meet and discuss it tomorrow?
Could we meet and _____ over tomorrow?

2 They have shown this film in Cannes.
This film _____ in Cannes.

3 We were surprised because there weren't many people in the office.
We were surprised because there were only _____ in the office.

4 'I saw a great programme last Monday', said Tom.
Tom said that _____ a great programme last Monday.

5 In the café, we couldn't find a seat.
In the café, there wasn't _____ to sit.

6 When James came to the meeting, Brenda wasn't there anymore.
When James came to the meeting, Brenda _____ left.

WORD STORE 7A | Shops and services

Clothing and accessories

1 a clothes shop
2 a shoe shop
3 *a charity shop*
4 _____
5 _____

Food

1 a baker's
2 a butcher's
3 a greengrocer's
4 a supermarket

Finance

1 a bank
2 an estate agent's
3 a post office

Health and beauty

1 a chemist's   3 an optician's
2 a hairdresser's   4 a health centre

Other

1 a computer shop   6 a pet shop
2 a department store   7 a sports shop
3 a DIY store   8 a stationer's
4 a florist's   9 a toy shop
5 a newsagent's   10 _____

WORD STORE 7B | Clothes and appearance

I / My clothes look …

1 fashionable
2 good
3 o*riginal*
4 scruffy
5 s_____
6 g_____

I buy / I wear …

1 d_____ clothes
2 good q_____ clothes
3 b_____

Natural materials

1 ca_____
2 co_____
3 denim
4 l_____
5 s_____
6 w_____

Useful phrases

1 It _____ me = it makes me look good
2 It _____ me = it is the right size for me

WORD STORE 7C | Collocations

1 **keep the receipt** = keep the paper you get when you buy something
2 **get a refund** = get your money back
3 **go** *window shopping* = look at things in shop windows
4 **have** _____ = reduce the price on everything
5 **be** _____ = on promotion at a low price
6 **pick up** _____ = buy much cheaper than normal
7 **be** _____ = a good reason to pay the price
8 **last** _____ = be good quality for a long time

REMEMBER THIS

go shopping = shopping for pleasure
do the shopping = buying food and things for the house

WORD STORE 7D | Word families

VERB / VERB PHRASE	NOUN (person)	NOUN
1 be in debt	debtor	*debt*
2 _____	earner	earnings
3 _____	investor	investment
4 _____	payer	payment
5 produce	producer	_____
6 _____	seller	sale
7 trade	trader	_____

WORD STORE 7E | Shopping

1 *shipped* = sent out
2 _____ = for sale
3 _____ = user
4 _____ = an increase
5 _____ = requests for goods
6 _____ = a line of people waiting
7 _____ = place where you pay

MY WORD STORE

My top five words from Unit 7

1 _____
2 _____
3 _____
4 _____
5 _____

For questions 1–30, choose the correct answer, A, B or C, to complete the sentences.

1 The _____ in West Street doesn't have fresh meat on Mondays.

   A baker's   **B** butcher's   **C** greengrocer's

2 Please, go to the _____ and send this letter for me.

   A bookstore   **B** stationer's   **C** post office

3 You can buy a _____ at a jeweller's.

   A doll   **B** ring   **C** scarf

4 How to create _____ at this online bookstore? I want to start buying books.

   A a subscription

   B a delivery

   C an account

5 Use your _____ if you want to listen to music. Dad's sleeping.

   A checkout desk

   B headphones

   C game console

6 You don't need to take any shampoo or toothpaste. There will be some _____ in the hotel room.

   A toiletries   **B** orders   **C** bunches

7 You use a vacuum cleaner to clean _____ .

   A hands   **B** carpets   **C** windows

8 My favourite sports shop is _____ now – I've bought three pairs of trainers cheaply.

   A picking up a bargain

   B on special offer

   C having a sale

9 Oh my! These jeans don't _____! Could I have a bigger pair?

   A suit   **B** last   **C** fit

10 Excuse me, can I ___ these shoes?

   A fit   **B** suit   **C** try on

11 I'm afraid this book is out of _____ , but we'll get more copies next week.

   A size   **B** stock   **C** package

12 I'm sorry, these jackets have _____ . Please ask next week.

   A tried on   **B** sold out   **C** exchanged

13 Excuse me, what's the _____ on this yoghurt? I can't see it.

   A refund   **B** delivery   **C** sell-by date

14 Keep the _____ – you'll need it if you take the shoes back to the shop.

   A purse   **B** receipt   **C** service

15 When Katie _____ her appetite, her mother took her to see the doctor.

   A missed   **B** lost   **C** dropped

16 There are so many _____ projects here that you can't escape from the noise and dust.

   A construction

   B protection

   C purification

17 I love going to the ice _____ to watch ice skaters practise.

   A court   **B** ring   **C** rink

18 Steven came out in a _____ after touching an exotic plant.

   A sore   **B** rash   **C** pain

19 I was surprised when my brother decided to _____ ice hockey – he had never liked skating.

   A take on   **B** get on   **C** take up

20 The exhaust _____ were so thick that it was hard to see across the street.

   A clouds   **B** fumes   **C** masks

21 My grandfather had pains in his _____ and we were worried about his heart.

   A thumb   **B** chest   **C** back

22 After jogging for over an hour, we sat down on a wooden park _____ to rest.

   A bench   **B** track   **C** path

23 If you keep _____ of everything you eat for a week, you can see how healthy your diet is.

   A note   **B** place   **C** track

24 People say that doing yoga can _____ your anxiety and make you feel calmer.

   A remove   **B** delete   **C** reduce

25 A friend invited Sarah to go _____ , but she is afraid of high places so she said no.

   A climbing   **B** riding   **C** racing

26 David loves sweets, so it's difficult for him to _____ out sugar from his diet.

   A take   **B** check   **C** cut

27 Every time you visit the doctor, someone will weigh you and check your heart _____ .

   A speed   **B** rate   **C** pulse

28 On days when the air pollution is very bad, young children and elderly people are most at _____ .

   A danger   **B** sick   **C** risk

29 I have such a _____ throat that it hurts to eat or drink anything!

   A sore   **B** hurt   **C** runny

30 a _____ is a sport where two teams use their hands to hit the ball over a net, not letting it touch the ground.

   A Tennis   **B** Basketball   **C** Volleyball